The story of Captain Scott's first e
him.

Louis Bernacchi's book *Saga of the 'Discovery'* is a comprehensive history of the fascinating ship which was built specifically for Antarctic exploration, and which was used intermittently for such purposes until the early 1930s, when she was given to the Boy Scouts Association. For the next 50 years the Discovery was a training ship for the Sea Scouts and the Royal Naval Reserve, moored on the Embankment in London. Then in 1986 the Discovery returned to Dundee, where she was built, and is now berthed at Discovery Point, where visitors can go on board, and learn the history of the ship in the adjoining museum.

The book covers the ship's building in Dundee, its first – and most famous – expedition as Captain Scott's ship for his first foray to Antarctica, from 1901-1904, and its subsequent history up until retirement. Long after the return of Scott's expedition in 1904 the Discovery continued to serve the cause of Antarctic exploration, most notably when commanded by Sir Douglas Mawson on the B.A.N.Z.A.R.E expedition of 1929-1931.

Bernacchi accompanied Scott on his first expedition. As the physicist, he was responsible for the scientific work, and here recounts the experiences, accomplishments, and setbacks they encountered. Also on that expedition were some of the legendary figures of Antarctic exploration: besides Captain Robert Falcon Scott himself, Dr Edward Wilson and Ernest Shackleton were to experience these harsh conditions for the first time, to be enchanted and enthralled, and enticed back to the continent with, for the first two, fateful results.

Apart from recounting the various expeditions that Discovery accomplished, Bernacchi also provides a useful introduction to the wild life, flora and fauna of the region.

Louis Bernacchi was the only person on Scott's first expedition to have prior Antarctic experience, having been amongst the first party ever to overwinter in Antarctica, from 1898 to 1900.

Saga of the
"Discovery"

§

Louis Bernacchi

Rooster

First published in 1938
Original Rooster Books edition published 2001
This edition revised 2016 to include original pictures and maps

ISBN: 978-1-871510-35-5

British Library Cataloguing in Publication Data.
A catalogue record for this book is available
from the British Library.

Published by Rooster Books Ltd
Royston, Hertfordshire.
www.roosterbooks.co.uk
info@roosterbooks.co.uk

Set in 12 point Minion Pro.

This book is printed on acid free paper.

CONTENTS

Most sincerely yours
L. C. Bernacchi
1906.

J. W. Debenham
BRIGHTON R?
SURBITON.

Preface

IN Scandinavian mythology *Skidbladnir* was the best of ships. To Antarctic explorers Discovery is the modern *Skidbladnir*.

To sailors anxious only to go from port to port, impatient to get under way from one observing station to another, she was slow, cumbersome, and particularly dangerous on a lee shore in a gale of wind, but to us she was, and is, a great exploring ship, endowed with every virtue. She was strong. She was safe. She was defiant of the fiercest storms and of the heaviest ice-floes. She forced her way through hundreds of miles of dense pack-ice beyond all outer chartings, and sailed where none had sailed before. It was a thrill and a wonder to watch her battling in the ice, and it filled us with a deep sense of pride. She visited many strange polar lands, grim and silent. She wintered far south beyond the Southern Cross, at the foot of the great volcano Erebus, amidst scenery of Andean grandeur.

The aggregate distance she sailed during her three famous voyages must be not far short of 150,000 nautical miles, and she discovered and surveyed at least 2500 miles of new lands, ice-barriers and glaciers.

She was a Happy Ship, and at the end of it all we were left with a sense of achievement—a sense of fulfilment.

This is the story of her voyagings—her Saga.

If it gives *Discovery* her proper place and weight in the story of exploration it will have achieved its purpose, for it is an outstanding fact, perhaps not generally understood, that Captain Scott's first expedition was more successful than his subsequent venture.

In telling the story it has been necessary to have recourse to my own diaries, to memories, and the memories of some of my companions. Captain Scott's *Voyage of the"Discovery"*, the best book of any Antarctic expedition—original, accurate, full of fascinating information and written in fine literary style—has been closely consulted.

I express my grateful thanks to the Council of the Royal Geographical Society for permission to reproduce some of the old *Discovery* photographs, taken, chiefly, by Lieutenant (now Vice-Admiral) R. W. Skelton, R.N.; to Sir Douglas Mawson, F.R.S., for supplying information regarding his expedition and for some beautiful photographs taken by J.F. Hurley; to Mr. G. Mackay of the Royal Geographical Society for drawing the map to illustrate the first voyage; to Dr. H. R. Mill and to Dr. R. G. Simmers (meteorologist to Mawson's expedition) for reading through the original manuscript dealing with this particular voyage; to Flight-Lieutenant S. Campbell, Lieutenant W. R. Colbeck, R.N.R., and Captain K. N. MacKenzie for various notes and incidents in connexion therewith; and to John Murray for permission to quote extracts from Scott's *Voyage of the "Discovery"*.

The Discovery Committee, Colonial Office, have supplied me with some information and photographs in connexion with cetacean research, and Dr. N. A. Mackintosh, the present Scientific Director, has kindly read the chapter and suggested various small alterations. Professor A. C. Hardy's papers on the work carried out by *Discovery* on this purely scientific cruise, and his contribution to *The Polar Book* on Marine Biology, have been particularly useful. The diagrams illustrating the seasonal distribution of whales are based on the splendid maps prepared by Johan T. Ruud for the Norwegian Whale Fishery Assurance Company.

Finally, I am particularly indebted to Miss Janet Mackay, Barrister-at-law, for her valuable assistance in compiling the saga. Her knowledge of Antarctic exploration is comprehensive, accurate and quite unprejudiced.

Discovery had outlived her period when late in 1936 a member of the Discovery Committee called at the Headquarters of the Boy Scouts Association with the novel suggestion that the Scouts should take her over as a Training Ship for Sea-Scouts, and as a memorial to Captain Scott and his comrades. The rest is best told in the words of Lord Hampton, Chief Commissioner, Boy Scouts Association:

"The acceptance of this wonderful offer was contingent upon three main factors: firstly, the co-operation of the Government of the Falkland Islands, to whom the ship still belonged; secondly, the raising of a sum of money sufficient to ensure her proper upkeep; and thirdly, the consent of the Port of London Authority to allot her moorings in a spot easily accessible to the boys who were to use her.

"In due course all three of these conditions were fulfilled, and the old *Discovery*, ship-shape and Bristol-fashion once more, was accepted on behalf of the Association by His Royal Highness, the Duke of Kent, Commodore of Sea Scouts, at the hands of Sir Herbert Henniker-Heaton, Governor of the Falkland Islands.

"The ceremony took place in the presence of the Chief Scout, the Colonial Secretary, and a distinguished company, including six members who had sailed on her first voyage. Now she lies at her last berth in the heart of the Empire she has served so well.

"If there is any value in tradition, any inspiration to be gained within the wooden walls which have witnessed so much of what is best in British seamanship and human character, may those who have the care and use of her in the days to come find happy comradeship, and in their turn be inspired to Adventure in the Service of their Fellows."

Louis Bernacchi

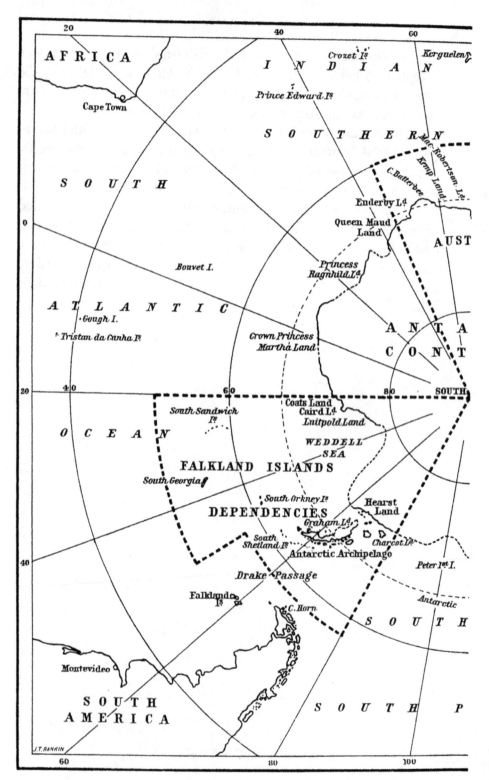

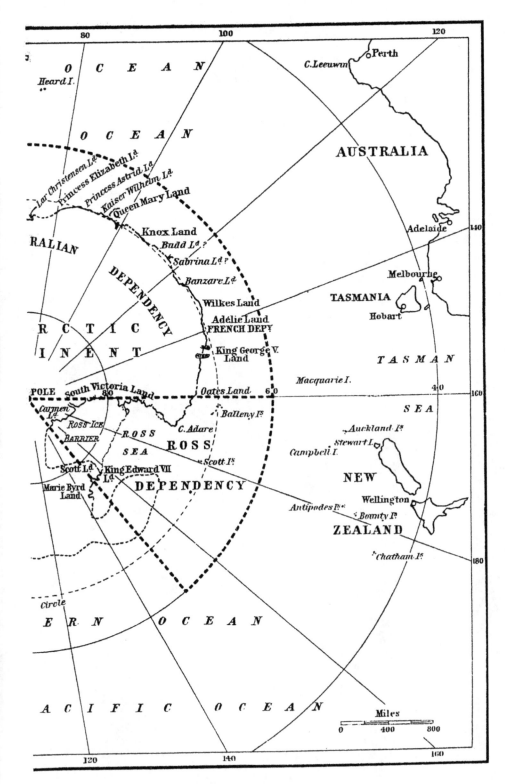

One

"Discovery"

THE long line of explorers of the Southern Seas extends back into Spanish days, and the work was taken up by those large-hearted Elizabethans who did really feel the "frost and cold, the ice and snow, and whales and all that move in the waters did bless the Lord and did magnify Him for ever". The line passes down from sailing ships to steamships until to-day we stand with the aeroplane.

When on 25th July, 1901, I received letters from Commander R. F. Scott, R.N., and the Presidents of the Royal Society and the Royal Geographical Society, offering me the post of Physicist to the National Antarctic Expedition in the *Discovery*, I had been back from my first Antarctic Expedition in the *Southern Cross* less than a year, and was still at work for the Royal Society reducing the magnetic and other physical observations taken at Cape Adare during the first winter spent by man on the Antarctic Continent.

Although the *Southern Cross* work was not quite completed, I accepted at once. I remember at dinner that evening the conversation inevitably drifted round to the *Discovery* preparations, and my father, who was an Antarctic enthusiast, saying, "I bet you would like to be going with her," and when I replied, "I *am* going with her," the complete incredulity of the family.

But there was a great deal to be done.

The physicist who had been appointed some months before had been compelled, at the last moment, to retire owing to unfitness, and, although I had been magnetologist at the Melbourne Observatory for two years, I was unacquainted with the various up-to-date magnetic instruments to be employed. There was also the *Southern Cross* work to complete.

The *Discovery* sailed on 6th August, and soon after I crossed over to the Potsdam Observatory near Berlin, to see and study the workings of our new instruments. These had been designed by Professor Eschenhagen, a brilliant German physicist, and practically nothing was known about them, even in Germany. They had not been seen in England. They were extremely delicate, and doubts were expressed as to whether or not they could be operated under Antarctic conditions. However, they did work, not without trouble and anxiety, and kept a continuous photographic record of the movements of all the magnetic forces in those high latitudes for a period of two years—a most valuable record indeed. There were also new types of pendulums to measure the force of gravity, and a new type of Milne Seismograph (Earthquake Recorder) to be investigated.

I sailed for Australia in the Orient liner *Cuzco*, on 16th September, taking the various new instruments with me, and, ultimately, joined the *Discovery* at Port Lyttleton, New Zealand, when she arrived.

It is appropriate here to tell the story of this ship with so glorious an exploring record: how she was built, and how she came to be built at this particular time.

Scott's *Discovery* was, in fact, the sixth ship of that name to win a place on the explorers' scroll of fame. The first *Discovery* was the tiny ship, no larger than a fishing smack, in which Henry Hudson sailed in 1610, to die in the great Arctic bay which bears his name, the victim of mutinous seamen; in which after two more voyages to the Canadian Arctic, in 1615, William Baffin, the greatest navigator of his time, sailed on the will-o'-the-wisp quest for the NorthWest Passage.

As Hudson and Baffin were the first two captains to take observations for the dip of the magnetic needle, so *Discovery* (I) must have been one of the first ships in which this important work was carried out—inaugurating a tradition in scientific research worthily followed by all her namesakes, and by none with more distinction than Scott's *Discovery*, in which a work of analogous value to seamen was carried out—observations establishing the variation of the magnetic needle in the far Southern seas.

Almost exactly a century later another Discovery (II) sailed on a voyage of exploration into Hudson's Bay. And in 1776, when the Admiralty fitted out two ships to be under the supreme command of Captain James Cook, on his great voyage of exploration, one of them was aptly named *Discovery* (III), and was anchored off the lovely Hawaiian shore in February, 1779, when Captain Cook so tragically met his death.

The next *Discovery* (IV) was Captain George Vancouver's ship, which surveyed and circumnavigated the island on the coast of British Columbia, which now bears his name, and in her he had a share in the early charting of the Australian seaboard.

In 1875 the British Government made its first official effort on either pole, and the *Alert* and *Discovery* (V) under Captain George Nares, R.N., endeavoured to reach the North Pole. Leaving the ship the following summer, a sledge party manhauled boats and supplies northwards over the hummocky ice, characteristic of the frozen Arctic seas, but differing from the Antarctic pack-ice. They travelled 276 miles back and forth in order to make 73 miles northward, when scurvy forced them to abandon the effort.

Scott's *Discovery* (VI) was sent out on what may be called the Learned Societies' Expedition, that is, under the combined efforts of the Royal Society and the Royal Geographical Society, with the blessing of the British Government, to the extent of £45,000, and the very practical cooperation of the Admiralty. Sir Clements Markham, the President of the Royal Geographical Society, was the dominant figure behind the expedition. He was regarded as its "Father". Sir Clements was a man of great personality and determination which, unhappily, sometimes brought him into conflict with others interested in the plans for *Discovery's* work.

A Fellow of the Society, Mr. Llewellyn Longstaff, actually enabled the expedition to start by making a munificent donation of £25,000 to the funds. It was a princely gift, ranking with the patriotic generosity of Felix Booth in the adventurous days of Elizabeth and Oscar Dickson, the Swede who financed the Nordenskiöld expedition in 1883 to discover the North-East Passage, and for which the former had received a baronetcy and the latter a barony.

Longstaff received an expression of thanks from the Learned Societies, and a niche in polar history.

It was the most ambitious scientific expedition which ever sailed from England, an expedition the objects of which included, to quote Dr. John Murray of *Challenger* fame, "the more definite determination of the distribution of the land and water of our planet, the solution of many problems concerning the ice age, the better determination of the internal constitution of the superficial form of the earth, and a more complete knowledge of the laws which govern the motions of the atmosphere and hydrosphere".

More particularly, *Discovery's* voyage was to embrace the following programme:

1. To determine the nature and extent of the Antarctic Continent.
2. To penetrate into the interior.
3. To ascertain the depth and nature of the ice-cap.
4. To observe the character of the underlying rocks and their fossils.
5. To make a magnetic survey in the Southern Regions to the south of the 40th parallel. The greatest importance was attached to the magnetic observations and no pains were to be spared to ensure their accuracy and continuity, since there were to be International Term days as agreed by the German and British Committees.
6. To take meteorological observations every two hours.
7. To observe the depths and temperatures of the ocean.
8. To take pendulum observations for the force of gravity.
9. To sound, trawl and dredge.

For the realization of this extensive programme, *Discovery* (VI) was to be specially built, and so to enjoy the distinction of being the first ship ever designed in England for scientific exploration. It was a matter calling for great deliberation over detail. Should *Discovery* follow the lines of the old English whalers, built to sail the high seas and push forcefully through the pack-ice? Or should she adopt the saucer-like construction of Nansen's *Fram*, which had proved well adapted to passive security in the heavy pack-ice, the lateral pressure of which merely tended to raise her above the surface—so it was said.

While the *Fram* type might live longer in the heavy ice, it was not conspicuously seaworthy, and in the case of an Antarctic expedition, with vast oceans of tempestuous seas to navigate, might never reach the ice. After considering it from every angle, it was decided to adopt the proven whaler lines.

But another difficulty presented itself. In order to withstand the ice *Discovery* must be built of wood, for only wood construction

CAPTAIN ROBERT FALCON SCOTT, C.V.O., R.N.

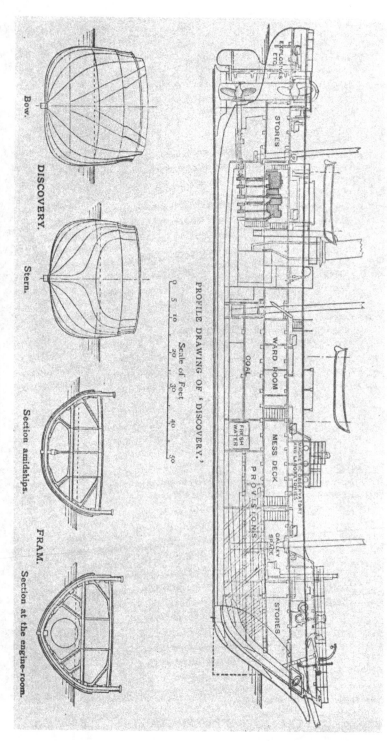

OUTLINE DRAWINGS OF DISCOVERY AND FRAM

has the combined elasticity and strength to oppose successfully the battering of the pack-ice. And already in 1899 England's whaling days had passed, and wood craftsmanship was passing. The adze and plane were giving way to the steel punch and riveter. When tenders were invited for construction of the new wooden ship, there was only one reply from a firm with experience sufficiently recent to promise efficient building. It was therefore in a shipyard on the Tay, which had been known in Dundee's flourishing whaling days as Stevens' Yard, that in March, 1900, the keel of *Discovery* was laid. She was designed by Sir W. E. Smith, late Chief Constructor at the Admiralty, and Lieut. R. W. Skelton, our Chief Engineer, superintended the building throughout.

Three months later her name had been chosen, her massive oak frames already were being raised, and Stevens' Yard was a busy scene of construction.

Frames of solid English oak, eleven inches thick, were lined by solid planking four inches thick, while the outside was covered by two layers of planking, one six inches thick and the other five. In other words, the sides of the new ship were twenty-six inches through, and as the frames were so closely placed, would be composed almost throughout of twenty-six inches of solid wood, as compared with the half-inch steel plates which constituted the usual ship construction, but which quickly would have been pierced in the pack-ice. Oak and pitch pine composed the massive outer layers, while the inside lining, less exposed to damp with its corollary of decay, was of Riga fir, and the whole, inside and out, was covered with a hardwood skin—mahogany and oak within, without, greenheart and English elm.

The whole was stiffened and strengthened by three tiers of beams, running from side to side, with stout transverse bulkheads, and in the lower tiers the beams were eleven inches square and placed at intervals of something less than three feet. Such a ship could resist immeasurable strain; such strain that, when in a heavy Antarctic gale, she crashed head foremost on to a shoal, and for hours was hammered on the shingly bottom, although beams and decks buckled upwards at each blow, and at times the whole ship was visibly distorted in shape, yet when the wind dropped and the tide rose, and she slid safely from the shallows, but for the loss of her false keel she was almost undamaged.

But the strength and stiffness of her sides was nothing to that of her bow, which was built to play its part in battering through the pack-ice. No single tree could have provided the massive stem, which rose from the strong keel, in a network of solid oak girders and struts, scarfed to fit together in one enormous block, which was fastened strongly, piece by piece, with long strengthening bolts running fore and aft, to bind the whole together. Only here was steel employed, in an outside layer of plates upon the wood to protect it from the wearing action of the ice. A bow so strongly built it would be almost impossible to damage, and the knowledge of its stoutness was a comforting thought when the grinding, crushing ice-floes hammered us in months to come with a force that seemed to have behind it the inhuman determination of a whole ocean bent on our destruction.

Strength, however, was not the sole consideration. Shape was equally important, and the overhanging stem of the old English whalers was adopted and increased to an extent never before seen in any polar ship. This enabled the charging vessel to glide upwards on an ice-floe until the bow was two or three feet above the surface. Then the weight of the ship, pressing downward, would crack the floe, and the bow would drop, and *Discovery* would forge ahead to repeat the operation. *Discovery*, in short, was built to act as her own ice-breaker.

Her bow was invincible, and as far back as the mainmast supporting beams and bulkheads maintained her rigidity. But farther aft the boilers and engines necessitated the omission of many of the cross-beams, and the stern with its rudder and screw became, inevitably, what Nansen described as the Achilles' heel of any polar ship.

Screw and rudder were capable of being detached and lifted through the deck to facilitate repair of damage. We lived to be grateful for that feature. Even with the advantage this type of construction afforded, the removal of a broken rudder and the fitting of a new one in place proved to be heroic work. Fortunately we were near the reasonably protected Robertson Bay when it was discovered that our rudder had been completely shattered by some hidden projecting foot of ice. But even in such favourable circumstances work-parties laboured for almost twenty-four hours before the spare rudder was secured in place.

From the very nature of its duty the rudder could not be thoroughly protected, but the builders of *Discovery* introduced for partial protection an entirely new feature—an overhanging stern. Although the whaling community of Dundee, watching the construction with excited interest, predicted all sorts of evils from such an unheard-of innovation, not the least of which was that it would break off entirely, the builders were more than justified. When we reached the ice-floes it formed a buffer which prevented heavier blocks from crashing into the rudder. In a heavy swell, too, it was an advantage, causing us to lift more readily to the waves, and only when the wind had dropped or we were, for any purpose, stationary, did it cause inconvenience. Then, as the rounded under-surface came down with a crash to the sea, the whole ship vibrated with the shock.

Yet with all this *Discovery* leaked, in the tradition of wooden ships, mysteriously and persistently. The leak in time became as much a part of the ship as the ancestral ghost in an old castle, and when, on the anniversary of leaving Cowes, the Dishcover Minstrels gave their famous show in the Royal Terror Theatre, renowned throughout Antarctica, one of the questions which Mistah Johnson asked of Mistah Bones was, "What am de worst vegetable us took from England?" The reply was, "The Dundee Leak."

The "Dundee Leak" gave us many anxious hours, many hours of unnecessary, back-breaking toil, ruined quantities of our supplies, and after our two years in the ice, when disuse had taken its inevitable toll upon the efficiency of our equipment, might have resulted in the loss of the ship—had we not, fortunately, encountered a period of comparative calm.

When we were frozen in, the leak had disappeared, but as soon as we were in open water, it was with us again, and now the pumps were blocked and frozen. The water rose till the engine-room was awash. The rolling of the ship made it necessary to draw the fires, and for a day we tossed helplessly.

When I joined the expedition at Port Chalmers, after her months-long journey, *Discovery* was put in dry-dock and workmen searched for the defect. Her bottom was scraped and thoroughly caulked, and when the leak persisted still, the contractor, for his own satisfaction, undertook, without expense to us, to give her another examination. She was subjected to an inch-by-inch inspection that it seemed no weakness could elude, but when she was floated again, the sea seeped in softly and irresistibly. Nothing more was humanly possible and we submitted to the inevitable.

Two cylindrical boilers and a set of triple-expansion engines gave *Discovery* 500 horse-power. There was a condenser for supplying fresh water, and a small dynamo for electric light, which the engineers, innocent of the velocity of Antarctic winds, planned to replace by a deck windmill when we should finally reach our objective. That scheme was a complete failure, and after the windmill had been demolished twice by the angry polar winds, the idea was abandoned and we were forced to content ourselves with paraffin lamps and candles—until paraffin and candles showed signs of running low and necessity, that most able mother of invention, took a hand. The result was that the last winter in the ice saw us with more efficient lighting than the first. Calcium carbide had been provided with a view to lighting the Magnetic Observatory with acetylene, but that had proved impracticable. Now the engineers built the necessary equipment for acetylene lighting of the ship, installing a generator which functioned perfectly, as the gas formed gave off sufficient heat to prevent the water from freezing.

To return, however, to Dundee—for the ship was not yet launched. One feature of construction that presented tremendous difficulty was the Magnetic Observatory. It was not enough to build a ship which could weather safely the Antarctic storms and overcome the obstacles presented by the polar ice. *Discovery's* voyage was to be primarily a voyage for scientific observation. It was essential that records should be accurate, and the presence of iron or steel in proximity to magnetic instruments would render their findings valueless. It was impossible to exclude iron and steel entirely from the ship, but the stipulation had been made that no magnetic materials should be used within a radius of 30 feet of the observatory: 30 feet fore and aft, 30 feet on either side, 30 feet above, 30 feet below, must be free of any metal which could influence the magnetic instruments. It was a problem of almost insuperable difficulty, and was only solved with immense trouble and expense. Down by the foremast and up to the front of the mainmast, down to the bottom of the ship, and up into her rigging, everything within the stipulated radius must be of copper or other non-magnetic metal.

Parts of the rigging, which in an ordinary sailing ship would have been of wire, in *Discovery* must be made of hemp, and that meant special weaving, for in order to provide the necessary strength, ropes were required of a size rarely, if ever, used in latter-day sailing ships. The fastenings of the hull, and the furnishings of the ship, all had to be of special material. The zoological and biological laboratories on either side of the meteorological observatory were not permitted to contain so much as a bottle brush of steel wire nor an iron tool of any kind. And even when all these elaborate precautions had been taken, down below in the provision rooms were supplies which could not possibly be preserved in brass containers.

The magnetic ordinance had many minor and amusing variations—officers without the charmed circle slept on luxurious spring mattresses, while those within it were forced to content themselves with hard wooden battens. The buttons on some of the cushions were discovered to be made of iron, and had to be stripped off and replaced by lead. And those who were billeted within the circle were even threatened at one time with the necessity of shaving with brass razors!

Each time the navigator took observations, knives and all sorts of instruments were confiscated from their owners, and placed beyond the radius of influence, and there was an awful moment on our return journey from New Zealand, when it was discovered that, during the whole of one set of observations, a parrot had been hanging on the mess-deck in a cage of iron wire.

But although the regulations caused both amusement and annoyance, the result was well worth while, and the records made in *Discovery* during her long voyage more nearly approached perfection than could have been possible otherwise. Those taken at winter quarters were never subject to the variation caused by the proximity of interfering metals. A special asbestos hut was built, so far removed from the *Discovery* that no foreign influence could enter, and for two long years, thereafter, I left the warmth and companionship of the wardroom every few hours, day and night, for the cold passage to the magnetic hut, lucky if I had only to face the cold, and often struggling with the fury of a blizzard; able to find the hut only with the help of guiding ropes.

The wardroom, with the cabins opening from it, was for three years the home of eleven officers, including Captain Scott; a warm, wood-panelled room, 30 feet by 20 feet, with a huge stove at the after end, and a table down the centre. A player-piano provided entertainment for a conspicuously untalented mess, as far as musical accomplishment was concerned. And there a communal life was lived, while for sleep and privacy and work, which could not be carried out in the cheerful din, were the cabins. The crew's quarters were larger and, in one respect at least, more comfortable, for beneath them were the provision rooms and holds, which even in the coldest weather maintained a certain warmth. But below the wardroom was the coal-bunker, and the coal-bunker communicated with the engine-room, and the engine-room with the weather.

The temperature of the coal-bunker was always below freezing-point, and although the deck above us had been well-insulated, that precaution had been overlooked in the deck below, and except for a linoleum, we were unprotected from the draughts.

There were no port-holes in the ship, and light came from the deck-lights, covered with thick glass. The problem of ventilation was even more difficult, and many were the arguments between the exponents of an even temperature and those of fresh air at all costs. Skylights were constantly flying up and down until a compromise was made on the basis that at 7.30 every morning the door of the companionway should be opened, and left open until the air below was thoroughly renewed, and after that it should remain closed, except by common consent and when the temperature rose above sixty degrees.

In an expedition such as *Discovery's* which might be ice-locked in the south for years, the space devoted to supplies was necessarily great, and fuel was the problem of chief concern. Food would be replenished from the animal life we would encounter in Antarctic seas, but there would be no possibility of replacing coal after we had left New Zealand. Three hundred and thirty-five tons of coal in all left England, including a deck cargo of forty-two tons for immediate use, and at Port Chalmers, in New Zealand, the inroads into the supply during the journey out were made good, so that we finally left civilization with a like supply.

Coal was of necessity one of our most treasured possessions, and as our consumption was about 1½ tons a day, even with banked fires, each day under steam made a marked difference in our stock. During our long imprisonment in the ice, boilers were never lighted, and consumption for cooking and warming the ship was reduced to 15 cwt. a week, but even with that minimum, when we were free from the ice at last, we had only 40 tons remaining—not enough to take us to New Zealand. Fortunately the relief ships were able to make good our shortage.

It was chiefly to *Discovery's* canvas that we looked for conservation of our fuel. But the sails were less satisfactory than the hull, and were quite inadequate for producing even reasonable speed, and with one exception, when we flew under bare spars before a terrific gale, the jib and mainsail were the only sails ever dewed up for stormy weather. Rarely, if ever, have top-gallants been carried through such storms as *Discovery* experienced, while in light winds the small spread of canvas made her an extremely sluggish sailer.

The lack of canvas, too, by conducing to slow progress, augmented her tendency to roll, and even before she had entered the notoriously tempestuous regions of the "Roaring Forties", a roll of ninety degrees had been recorded, forty-five degrees to either side. That weakness had attendant disadvantages, for the deck cargo of live sheep, shipped from New Zealand on the journey south, as well as those taken aboard from the Falkland Islands on our homeward voyage, were reduced with horrifying rapidity by loss overboard.

On 21st March, 1901, *Discovery* glided smoothly into the waters of the Tay, splashed with her christening champagne, broken on her bow by Lady Markham. She was ready for her masts and engines, and the journey to the Thames for the rest of her equipment—a gallant vessel, rigged as a barque with fore, main and mizzen masts, drawing 16 feet, her displacement 1620 tons, her registered tonnage 485, length over-all 198 feet, and at the water-line, 172 feet, breadth 34 feet, and depth amidships 18 feet; and with accommodation, equal in all respects to that of a man-of-war of similar size, for forty-four souls.

The great canvas awning, like a huge tent, that was to be fitted over her when in Winter Quarters, to keep out the Antarctic weather, had been made at Dundee. Her boats were ready, a sailing cutter—which was not taken south—and five 26-foot whaleboats and two Norwegian prams. And in the shortest possible time she sailed for her berth in the Thames, her house-flag, also made at Dundee, flying—the cross of St. George at the hoist, the fly swallow-tailed, party per fesse, argent and azure (for ice and sea), and bearing the globe of the Royal Geographical Society. Bordure argent and azure.

Her construction had proceeded well to time, and everything promised speedy departure, when one of those disputes almost inevitable under committee management threatened to wreck the whole expedition. The representatives of the Royal Society demanded that the leader of the scientific staff, Professor J. W. Gregory, F.R.S., a well-known geologist, should reign supreme, at least on land. The Royal Geographical Society insisted that the naval leader, Captain Scott, should be supreme on land as well as sea, and must not be called upon to entrust the safety of his naval ratings, on whom the safety of the ship depended, to a civilian. Deadlock resulted, and the crisis only passed with the resignation of Professor Gregory, when Captain Scott became the recognized leader of the expedition.

The work of fitting out proceeded. Zoological, geological and meteorological equipment were assembled, and supplies were stowed.

On 1st August, *Discovery* anchored at Spithead to carry out that most important requirement, swinging the ship—that is, the ship was turned slowly round, whilst errors in her compass at each point were determined. Although so much care had been taken in her construction, yet it had been impossible to eliminate all magnetic interference, and it was most necessary to note, before she sailed, exactly what the influence would be upon the compass, as well as on the magnetic observatory.

Within four days that work was done, and on 5th August, *Discovery* tied up to a buoy in Cowes Harbour, her black, solid hull, her short masts and heavy rigging forming a striking antithesis to the delicate beauty of the yachts gathered for the famous Cowes Week.

Just before midday King Edward and Queen Alexandra came on board to offer their best wishes for the expedition's welfare.

The King said: "Captain Scott, officers and crew of the *Discovery*, it has often been my lot to bid good-bye to an expedition going away on warlike service. It gives me great pleasure to wish good-bye and good luck to an expedition going away on service from which the whole world will benefit. I wish you good-bye, good luck—and God speed."

For one member of the crew, at least, adventure already had started, for Queen Alexandra's pet Pekinese, more courageous than discreet, embarked on investigations of its own which precipitated it into Cowes Bay, and was only saved from drowning by the quick action of the seaman who dived overboard to the rescue.

After the departure of the royal visitors—and the over-enterprising and damp Pekinese—the ship was thrown open to the public for the afternoon. But, with the extensive and serious business in hand, there was little time for hospitality, and at noon on 6th August, 1901, less than eighteen months after her keel was laid, the staunch little polar explorer slipped from moorings, bound on her great adventure.

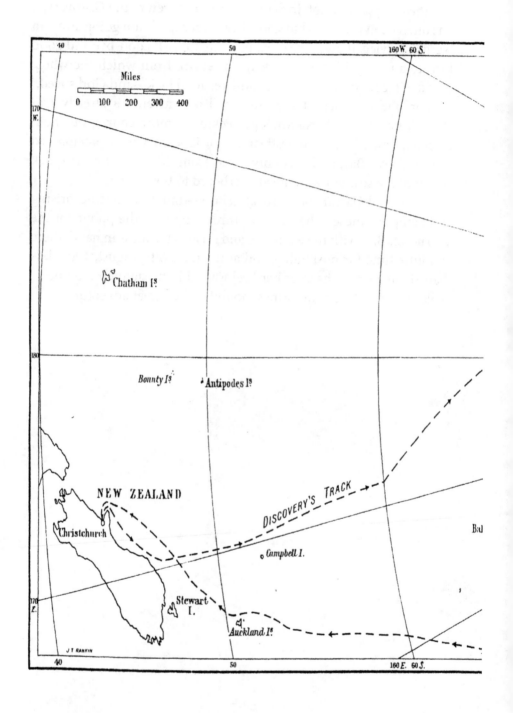

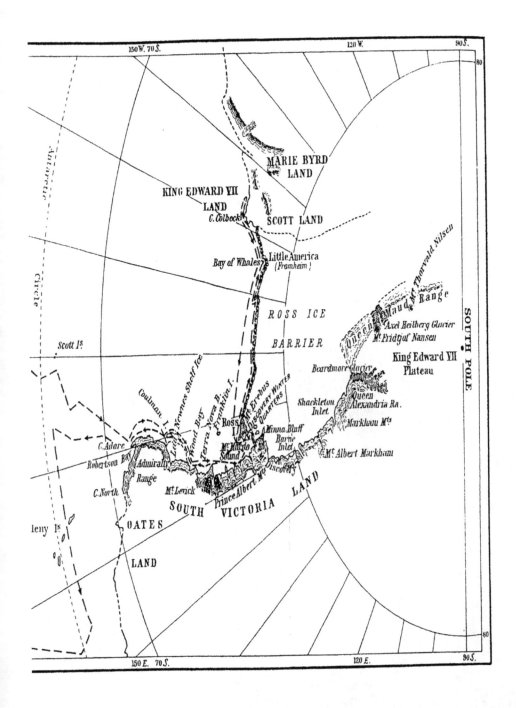

Two

Vast Wonderland

DISCOVERY was a sluggish sailer, and it was not until 29th November that she was reported off Lyttleton Heads. I had arrived at Lyttleton about a week before, and was waiting on the quay when she berthed next day. Twenty-five sledge dogs that had come from England in a cargo boat in charge of Seaman Weller were waiting too.

But if she had proved slow, she had proved also staunch in a succession of heavy gales in the "Roaring Forties and Fifties", and already she had made a start on her scientific work. When no farther on her voyage than South Trinidad, an unknown petrel had been discovered and named *Æstrelata Wilsoni*, in honour of the zoologist, Dr. Edward Wilson. Already, too, she had had her baptism of ice, when after encountering an interesting magnetic area in Lat. 51° S Long. 131° E., Scott had decided to steer south to explore more effectively, and had continued until he crossed the 60th parallel.

She had provided also that terrifying experience which is a constant menace to wooden ships—the cry of "Ship afire!" Half-clad figures tumbled from their berths to discover, fortunately, that the outbreak was not serious, but caused by some oilskins left too near a lamp and set alight in the heavy rolling of the ship, and not discovered until the adjacent woodwork was ablaze. Astounding stories of her wonderful ability to roll were told, stories which I was able to verify only too often when during stormy weather, at each end of the periphery of the semicircle her masts described, they dipped deep into the ocean. On one occasion a roll of fifty-two degrees to port and forty-eight degrees to starboard was recorded.

I had met already some of the men who were to be my daily companions for the next three years, but I knew little of them, and I was unknown beyond the fact that I was the only one on board who, previously, had been to the Antarctic. It was only in New Zealand that we began to be acquainted. Captain Scott, with his striking personality and charm of manner, his courage, his enthusiasm for science, had the ability to inspire loyalty and devotion. He had understanding and knowledge and never failed to stand up for what he considered right: an ideal leader for such an expedition—although he had his weaknesses too, for he was very human. Dr. Edward Wilson, not yet quite recovered from the malady which had kept him long a patient at Davos, but which the pure air of Antarctica completely cured, was a deeply religious man, but also intrinsically good; good in the sense in which that word is seldom used, in which St. Paul employed it when he wrote: "Scarcely for a righteous man will one die: yet peradventure for a good man some would even dare to die." The second in command, Lieut. A. B. Armitage, R.N.R., the navigator, and Dr. R. Koettlitz the botanist and bacteriologist were both experienced in Arctic exploration. And there were Charles Royds, Reginald Skelton and Michael Barne, all R.N. lieutenants; Lieut. Ernest Shackleton, R.N.R., Hodgson the biologist, and Ferrar the geologist.

Owing to damage to the provisions caused during the journey out by the famous Dundee leak, the holds were cleared for re-stowing, and *Discovery* went into dry-dock to undergo an unsuccessful attempt to discover the defect, while her full complement of officers and men found billets ashore. Additional supplies were bought, including New Zealand butter to replace the tinned Danish variety, and when the search for the persistent leak at last was abandoned, restowing began. Every hole and corner of the ship was utilized for something, and even the private cabins found space for packages and crates, until the Plimsoll line had sunk so deep it was forgotten. And when the holds were filled the decks received their share and soon became almost impassable with their cargo of coal, live sheep and howling sledge dogs.

From this most un-ship-shape confusion, on 24th December, 1901, we watched the blue outline of friendly New Zealand fade into the twilight of the north.

Notwithstanding the confusion on deck, my first impression of *Discovery* at sea was one of perfect delight, compared with the small, rather unseaworthy *Southern Cross*, scarcely more than half her size, in which I had previously sailed south.

I was soon comfortably installed in the cabin next to Captain Scott, which had become the "show cabin" whilst in New Zealand, where

OFFICERS AND MEMBERS OF THE SCIENTIFIC STAFF ON BOARD DISCOVERY, 1901

Left to right:— Wilson, Shackleton, Armitage, Barne, Koettlitz, Skelton, Scott, Royds, Bernacchi, Ferrar, Hodgson

PETTY OFFICERS AND SEAMEN ON BOARD DISCOVERY, 1901

the ladies had nicknamed us "The Babes in the Wood" because of our wooden ship and our youthfulness. The average age of the forty-four souls on board was only twenty-five, and few were married. Scott himself, then a bachelor, was only thirty-three and in the prime of his physical and mental powers.

Discovery throughout the whole of her three years' commission was what is known as "A Happy Ship". One cannot recall a serious quarrel either amongst the officers or the men. She was a "floating abode of harmony and peace". We were lucky, too.

On the afternoon of 2nd January we sighted our first iceberg, outlying sentinel of the approaching pack. On the 3rd we crossed the Antarctic circle—earning the sailor's traditional right to drink a toast with both feet on the table. Ice-blink was visible on the horizon, that white reflection of the ice-fields announcing the presence of the pack hours before the ice itself is seen.

During the night we encountered the first scattered fragments of sea-ice, feeling mild shocks even in this light formation, as the bow forced its way through the honeycombed floes. When morning came ice was all around, and we were forcing our way through the grinding floes, twisting and turning to take advantage of the open pools and lanes. It was a magical sight, and one never to be effaced from memory. The alabaster whiteness of the floes was intensified by the exquisite green colouring of the cracks and cavities, and the dark pools of open water. Here and there were bright yellow patches of plankton life, which biologists have discovered to be formed by myriads of tiny organisms.

Animal life was everywhere. The albatrosses had vanished, but in their place were the denizens of the ice—the slaty southern fulmar, the Antarctic petrel with its white breast and brown-barred head and wings, the voracious skua gull, and the lovely snow petrel. The squawk of penguins filled the air, as they discussed with never-satisfied curiosity the strange phenomenon *Discovery* presented. Seals slept on the larger floes, waking to gaze on man with wide-eyed incomprehension of their possible danger.

We were already making our collection, and when a penguin-hunting party left the ship the penguins, too, set out at the same time to investigate the strange animals who had invaded their habitat—

utterly fearless, for in their experience the only danger was in the sea where the killer whale and sea-leopard made banquets of unwary birds. Over the floes they waddled, raising and lowering their flippers in the most ludicrous fashion, until they reached the hunting party, which they encircled slowly, making a critical examination from every angle. They did not know that hidden ferocity existed in the strange beings they surrounded.

Whenever seals were sighted the ship's course was altered until she was sufficiently close for the rifle to do its work. The decks became a gory scene, for while the zoologist and his assistants skinned seals and penguins, both for food and scientific research, our sheep too—or such of them as had not been swept overboard in *Discovery's* rolling—were prepared for the larder. There was no danger now in carrying mutton instead of sheep, the equable Antarctic ice-box temperature took care of that, and the rigging was soon laden with frozen carcasses that promised future feasts.

It was not so easy to dispose of the scientific specimens. The preservation of a seal weighing ten hundredweight is no simple task. When the skin is taken off with the thick layer of blubber which surrounds the body, it must be placed in brine for preservation—and the lurking persistence of the smell of blubber is not the most pleasant company.

There was no knowing how long *Discovery* might be in the pack-ice—*Southern Cross* had taken forty-three days to work through to open water—and Captain Scott decided that we should keep our belated Christmas on 5th January. After the morning service and a special Christmas dinner, we tied up to an ice-floe for an afternoon of "winter sports" and to try our efficiency on ski, new to nearly all the ship's company. I had served my novitiate at Cape Adare. But even with the disadvantage of complete inexperience we closed the afternoon with races, and officers and men on their unaccustomed footing dashed about in all directions, with constant collisions and falls. In the evening, as we pushed onward, a sing-song was held below, to the accompaniment of ice-floes grinding along our sides.

During our passage through the pack the scientific officers were put on duty as additional watch-keepers on the bridge. Those long, calm, Antarctic "nights" under the midnight sun were very beautiful with the skies a blazing colour and all nature pleasing and restful. But even there sleep is inexorable. So when, on one occasion, Shackleton came on duty to relieve me at four in the morning, full of verses and warmth-giving navy cocoa, I lacked enthusiasm. Shackleton was a poet and that morning poetically very wide awake, and in his wheedling Irish manner he kept me from my waiting bunk reciting endless verses in the voice and manner of an old-time tragedian—"One moment, old son," he wheedled, as I edged towards the gangway, "have you heard this?" and he would quote Browning, his favourite poet—obscure lines that neither Browning nor Shackleton understood, much less a cold and yawning physicist. That was the signal to throw politeness to the ice-floes and dive down to my watch below.

The pack-ice of the Antarctic is a phenomenon peculiar to the far Southern seas. The Northern extremity of the world is one vast ice-covered ocean; that of the South, an ice-bound continent. In the long winter months the Antarctic sea freezes northward for hundreds of miles from land, and to a depth of from three to seven feet. But with the coming of the long summer days in these latitudes, under the constant sunlight and comparatively warm temperature, the ice breaks up. By the beginning of November the land stands out again, distinct from the ocean, and the currents and prevailing southerly winds combine to bear the ice constantly northward until it meets contrary winds and currents, which prevent its going farther. Since there is land to the south the supply of sea-ice becomes exhausted, and the pack remains more or less stationary, grinding and crashing into smaller and smaller fragments, until it forms a vast belt of broken, melting blocks that girdle the whole Antarctic continent.

In some places, as our unfortunate experience in *Southern Cross* had proved, the ice belt extends almost to the land. Again, as we found in *Discovery*, confirming the experience of other explorers, it narrows to such proportions that it can be traversed in a few days. The important factor is that once the pack-ice is passed, an open sea is reached. Although the pack varies so in density and width, yet the variation appears to be constant, and the narrow section of the belt always has been found by those sailing on a certain meridian southward of Australia. Explorers who have chosen other routes have suffered varying degrees of difficulty, culminating with that of the

Belgica expedition in 1897—9, which was caught for twelve months in the pack.

We had yet to learn, however, how short our own struggle was to be. We hoped for the best, but prepared for something less than the best, and when on 6th January the ice became so close that we could make no headway under the power of a single engine, whilst waiting for steam in the second boiler, we took the opportunity of replenishing our supply of water. Although we had condensers, and could have used sea-water, yet it would have necessitated an expenditure of coal, and contrary to the belief of the old explorers that sea-ice is salt ice, the salt is always forced to the surface, and below the upper stratum of some eighteen inches the ice is clean and sweet. By far the most economical plan of obtaining water, therefore, is by melting this ice.

We chose a floe, ran the ship alongside, planted ice anchors, and the watering party, with picks, shovels and boxes, swarmed over the side. In order to speed up the work officers and men laboured together, and while some dug with picks, others carried the filled boxes or larger blocks across the floe, and still others stood ready to take them over the side. The ice heaped up on the deck was reduced as fast as the tanks could be fed, but the digging proceeded so vigorously that the supply soon exceeded the demand. The order, "Hold, enough," brought all trooping on board again, the ice anchors were uprooted, the engines revolved, and *Discovery* pushed once more through the pack.

Early on the morning of 8th January a strong "water sky" was seen, for just as the presence of the pack is heralded by a white reflection upon the horizon, so the open sea casts its darker shadow. The ice-floes, though closely packed, were becoming very small, and rose and fell on the slow sea swell. Then suddenly we were in the open sea, with only long, loose ice-streamers to remind us of the past five days. The thick pall of leaden clouds which had been over us during the whole journey through the pack suddenly lifted, and the sun shone in a pale clear sky.

We celebrated by "splicing the main brace" and at our dinner in the wardroom drank to the future in champagne, so that when we heard the cry "Land ho!" about 10.30 that evening, we were already

DISCOVERY HEADING THROUGH PACK ICE

A TYPICAL ANTARCTIC ICEBERG
Photo by L.C.B. in 1898.

in a joyful frame of mind. All gathered on deck for their first sight of the Antarctic continent, where far away the glorious peaks of South Victoria Land glittered under the midnight sun. The water was a mass of quivering, shifting colour, and a phalanx of deepest purple clouds marshalled in the path of the sun gave an unearthly radiance to all around. It was a scene of fantastic and unimagined beauty, and we remained on deck till morning.

Discovery now headed for Robertson Bay, formed by the long peninsula of Cape Adare, where the *Southern Cross* expedition had wintered, and to me it was like an exciting home-coming to see the familiar outline of the grim plateau, which makes the spot more inaccessible from the land than from the sea. Here loose streams of pack-ice again appeared, so that it was necessary once more to keep a look-out in the barrel called the crow's nest, to "con" the ship through. Early the following morning a party went ashore to take magnetic observations, and we all visited the hut, which stood exactly as it had been left—with a note pinned to one of the bunks addressed to the commander of any future expedition, and a quantity of provisions in a perfect state of preservation.

Carstens Borchgrevink of the *Southern Cross* was a Norwegian who had spent some years in Australia as a schoolmaster, and had been permitted to sign on, temporarily, as a seaman on board a small Norwegian whaler making a summer cruise to Antarctic seas. The ship had reached Cape Adare, and he had been the first to leap ashore, thus being the first man to place foot on the Antarctic continent. On his return, fired with enthusiasm for Antarctic exploration, he at last, after many unsuccessful efforts, persuaded the well-known publisher, Sir George Newnes, to fit out an expedition to sail in the *Southern Cross*—an old Norwegian whaler.

Borchgrevink, in many respects, was not a good leader, but the expedition was as well equipped in regard to foods, dogs and sledges, polar gear and scientific instruments as most modern expeditions. What he did, he did alone, with no help from official bodies or committees, but his plans cut into those already being formed by Sir Clements Markham for the great *Discovery* expedition. Markham was ruffled and annoyed. It follows that Borchgrevink was not a "White-headed Boy" of the Royal Geographical Society. As a small pioneering expedition without influence or backing, beyond the very liberal finance of Sir George Newnes, that of the *Southern Cross* stands unchallenged. The results were of pre-eminent importance. We had passed the first winter ever spent on Antarctic land within the Circle, and the first complete series of magnetic and meteorological observations were scientifically taken, and later published by the Royal Society.

These observations proved how disturbed were magnetic forces in Antarctica and gave the near position, at that time, of the South Magnetic Pole. The nature of the Antarctic winter on shore was shown for the first time, and important data collected in regard to atmospheric circulation. Until then no one had heard of the fierce Antarctic cyclones, known as blizzards, that blow over the great continent. Cape Adare was nearly in the centre of the world's lowest barometric area.

Many biological specimens, entirely new to science, had been discovered (later to be fully described by the Natural History Museum authorities), and geological specimens collected of the unknown continental rocks. The habits of penguins and seals were studied, and the first photographs of Antarctic lands, ice formations, and fauna were taken, which, even to-day, compare favourably with those of modern expeditions.

Unfortunately, and notwithstanding the splendid sledging gear and over seventy suitable dogs, the grim and lofty Admiralty Range made the interior inaccessible from the pebbly beach at the foot of Cape Adare, which had been the winter quarters.

Later, on the return of the *Southern Cross*, landings had been made for the first time on Coulman Island, Franklin Island and in Wood Bay. The large and well-sheltered Lady Newnes Bay had been discovered, and finally, Ross's Great Ice Barrier landed upon for the first time, in the extensive bight later to become well known as the Bay of Whales, the highest southern latitude so far attained.

Recognition came to Borchgrevink thirty years later, when, in 1930, he received the Patron's Gold Medal from the Royal Geographical Society. He died soon after.

The *Discovery* expedition saw thousands of Adélie penguins sitting on the little heaps of pebbles which take the place of warmer, softer nests in less arduous climates. The young birds were already half grown, for the summer was well advanced, and we watched the antics of these fascinating inhabitants with absorbed interest. It was easy to understand the error of the half-blind old priest in Anatole France's *L'Ile des Pingouins*, as the little black figures in their white shirt fronts toddled forward on short fat legs to welcome us, and as we saw the ordered communism of their lives. This was the great holiday time, before the winter cold separated the penguin colonies, and squads of young birds were being put through their paces, tobogganing on their breasts over the snow, diving and swimming. Their discipline must be seen to be believed—a company forms at the nests, a squawk of command starts it shuffling to the water; another squawk and it turns, all together, right turn, left turn, and even right about turn. But like civilized society, penguin-land has its outsiders: low fellows, dirty and unkempt, who live by themselves at some distance from the respectable law-abiding citizens, always brawling, thieving, and indulging in a general lack of respect for established authority—and always being punished for it.

Even in their social intercourse, penguins show a strange similarity of habits with human beings. There are comparatively few favourable nesting spots on the Antarctic shore, and twenty miles separated the Cape Adare community from its nearest neighbour. Yet I have seen, late in the season when the young chicks are sufficiently grown to stand the journey, but the sea-ice has not completely disappeared, little parties set out in the direction of the next colony. And half-way there parties from the neighbouring colony would meet them, and after a merry visit and much chattering, they would separate, each group returning home. This was not coincidence, but happened repeatedly, and never did the parties miss each other. How did they signal to arrange the visit? How did they so exactly find their way across the miles of ice?

Magnetic observations were carried out in the midst of the curious chattering penguins, while the naturalists of the party wandered farther afield, and were rewarded by finding a Wilson Petrel nesting in the high rocks. And later in the evening, with a party, I went ashore again to leave in the hut a cylinder containing information regarding our voyage, and to visit the lonely grave of Nicolai Hanson, the

Southern Cross zoologist, then the only human grave on the Antarctic continent.

At 3 a.m. we sailed from Cape Adare, working southward through the land pack, as close as possible to shore. And on that glorious clear morning of still beauty, *Discovery* came nearer to disaster than ever she had been before. The pack suddenly became heavier than anything we had, so far, experienced, and twist and turn as she would she could make little progress. Finally, before one monster floe she was brought to a standstill for half an hour, and the strong tide which was running seemed determined to carry her upon a mass of bergs. She struggled desperately and gradually the tide stream slackened, and by 8.30 she had won through to safety.

On 12th January we sighted Coulman Island, and as the glass was falling, Captain Scott made for an open-water shelter under the lee of the high cliffs of the island. The wind rose to a full gale at sea but, thanks to our position, only reached us in occasional gusts, and we were able to make good use of our time with the trawl-net, which brought joy to the heart of Hodgson, our biologist, in the wealth of strange fish, crustacean and polyzoa which it brought aboard. But trawl-net weather was fleeting. The storm grew worse, and by the 14th our anemometer measured a ninety-mile gale, squalls now sweeping down from the cliffs with such terrific force that we could not keep the ship in place. As evening approached we were driven upon a line of pack-ice and small bergs, and all through the night that followed *Discovery* struggled through the blinding spray and drift, menaced again and again by bergs which drove upon her from the darkness. Morning, however, brought a clear sky and safety once more, and after leaving at Cape Wadworth another record of our voyage, we steamed for Lady Newnes Bay, and the first sight for most of the ship's company of so-called barrier ice.

From this point the journey increased in interest. Wood Bay, which we had known on the *Southern Cross* expedition, I had hoped might provide our winter quarters, for it is well protected and free from pressure. But Wood Bay was not yet free of ice and Captain Scott feared to waste valuable time if he waited for it to clear. And so, perhaps, was lost an opportunity for reaching the South Pole years before it finally was accomplished, for Wood Bay leads immediately and easily to the Polar Plateau, reached in later years at a much less accessible spot. The mileage would have been greater, but the travelling easier, and at least we could have reached without difficulty the South Magnetic Pole, at that time only about one hundred and fifty miles from the bay.

It was one of those "might-have-beens" which change the course of polar history. We turned south to pass around the headland called Cape Washington and towards the frozen desert of the Great Ice Barrier.

The weather had cleared, the sea was free of ice, and the atmosphere so rare that we could see at the same time the peaks of Coulman Island and the smoky crest of Erebus, two hundred and forty miles apart.

Nowhere in the world is there so rarefied an atmosphere as in Antarctica, and nowhere in the world does it play such tricks on travellers and explorers, with its refraction and mirage. In its strange light mountains become molehills and molehills mountains, whole ranges, higher than the Alps, are transported in vision hundreds of miles from their true position.

So it was that Sir James Clark Ross charted his Parry Mountains, seen in the distance from the sea, as in a position directly south of Mount Erebus, and Captain Scott, finding no mountains there, decided that Ross's discovery was a myth, and named the selfsame mountains, situated in reality about one hundred miles westward of Erebus, the Royal Society Range. It has been shown that both these great explorers were deceived—Ross, seeing them thrown forward in mirage, was deceived in their position; Scott, coming on them from the north, found them in their proper place, and was deceived into thinking he had discovered a new range.

A similar and even more spectacular deception was experienced by Sir Douglas Mawson, for Mawson in his first *Discovery* expedition sailed over a sea which had been charted in 1840 as Wilkes Land, and miles farther south charted his own Mac-Robertson Land. But when he returned on his second *Discovery* expedition, he had the unique experience of disproving his own discovery, and for a distance of some three hundred miles sailed over his own Mac-Robertson Land to chart a still more southerly coast-line.

Sailing southward in *Discovery* we landed first at a sheltered spot called Granite Harbour, then at Cape Crozier, and later at the foot of the mighty, active volcano Erebus, 13,000 feet high, where we were destined to spend two years imprisonment in the ice. Each time we landed we took magnetic observations, and each time the other members of the expedition made their own contributions to science.

It was at Granite Harbour that Shackleton found the first signs of vegetable life which *Discovery* had encountered in Antarctica, though *Southern Cross* had made similar discoveries. At Cape Crozier, in the midst of another penguin colony, we left the third record of our voyage, in a cylinder attached to a post sunk in the moraine-drift.

At Cape Crozier Captain Scott in company with Wilson and Royds climbed a volcanic cone which gave them their first sight of the Great Ice Barrier. And the mystery of the ice plain, nearly as large as the whole of France, exercised its irresistible attraction. On 21st January we passed the base of Erebus and began to skirt the Barrier.

We had now reached one of the then unsolved mysteries of Antarctica—the ice-sheet which extends eastward from Erebus for over 500 miles. I had formed the opinion from examination when with *Southern Cross* that the Barrier was the gigantic tongue of a gigantic glacier, or the combined tongues of many gigantic glaciers, pushing ever outward from the mountains, which at the time were thought to continue due south and not curve round gradually to the east as later was found to be the case. But the theory was not yet proved, and among the problems which *Discovery* hoped to solve was whether in fact it was glacial or sea-ice built up with snow deposits. We sailed along its borders, mile on mile. From the comparatively moderate height of seventy feet, it rose so gradually that the variation seemed rather to be a nearer view than a perpendicular increase. It was only by measurement that we learned that the ice cliffs rose in rare places to the astonishing height of two hundred and eighty feet. But even these heights were less than those recorded by Ross, just as the Barrier itself proved not to extend so far north as Ross had found it. In the short space of sixty years the ice had receded something like fifty miles. Did this mean that the ice age in Antarctica was drawing towards it close?

For days we steamed along the white ice cliffs, whiter than the cliffs of Dover, but every hour they varied in outline and height, so

CAPE ADARE

LANDING AT CAPE ADARE

that there could be no monotony. Gradually the height decreased. On 24th January it rapidly fell to 80 feet. On the 25th it was only 30 feet. Then it rose again to 80 feet, and as suddenly dropped to 15 feet. And so the gradual decrease continued—120 feet, 20 feet, 90 feet, 8 feet. From time to time great masses calved off to float away as icebergs. Here was the great mother of the Antarctic bergs which floated northward in majestic silence, often as much as ten miles in length. Fine weather gave place to fog, and we groped along with only a veiled view of the ice which was becoming tortured and broken on its surface, indicating the proximity of land. And on 30th January, just as the bell sounded for dinner, the officer of the watch reported black patches on the horizon, which looked like clouds. Dinner waited as we watched. The black patches assumed more definite shape. Soon there was no doubt that they were rock out-croppings. We had discovered Edward VII Land. This new land was first seen by Shackleton, who was the officer of the watch, and the first entry in the deck log is made by him.

For two days more we continued along the ice cliffs. The fog lifted, but the weather became colder and new ice was forming on the sea. Again and again we tried to work in a north-easterly direction through to the supposed coast, but although we entered several promising channels, all ended in solid ice, with no view from the crow's nest but the endless ice-field. There was still a chance that, with patience, we might be able to push farther towards the land, but always there was the consideration of the coal supply, and Captain Scott decided that the wise course was to return.

Working backward on our course, late on 3rd February, we reached the great bight in the Barrier which was named later by Shackleton the Bay of Whales, but which had been located by the *Southern Cross*, and there *Discovery* tied up alongside the low barrier.

I saw at once that it resembled the most southerly anchorage of *Southern Cross* reached on 17th February, 1900, and when observations were taken we found that in fact *Discovery* lay only about one mile south of *Southern Cross's* position.

In 1900 I had been one of a sledging party to trek southward on the Barrier to 78° 45' S., the farthest south—at that time. Now again I had the good fortune to be one of another sledging party which Captain Scott permitted to make a preliminary Barrier journey. While those remaining with the ship prepared for the ascent of the captive balloon which the War Office had provided for reconnaissance purposes, Armitage and I, with four seamen, a small tent and a theodolite, and one day's provisions packed upon a sledge, left the ship at 5.15 p.m., pushing onward until 9 p.m., when we decided to halt for the night.

Unfortunately, the tent was built to accommodate three men, and we were six, and two—Armitage and Petty Officer Cross, each weighed almost fourteen stone. To sleep in such close formation called for more endurance than at least one polar explorer possessed. After about an hour of more or less silent suffering I left the over-populated area for the great open spaces of the Barrier ice. I was well clothed, and in the warmth of the sun, still shining through the night, with the temperature hovering around zero, I fell asleep, curled up in a snowbank. I was turned out about 6 a.m. when, after a quick breakfast, Armitage, Cross and I set out to go as far southward as we could before the necessity of reaching the ship at noon compelled us to return. We reached Lat. 79° 3' S.—some eighteen miles farther than the sledgers of *Southern Cross* had made.

The balloon observations meantime had not provided anything like the practical information which our short sledging expedition had gained, regarding the surface of the Barrier, and when in the evening *Discovery* put to sea again, it was with the conviction that such apparatus was not worth the space it occupied.

Our return along the Barrier was marked by much lower temperatures than we had experienced on our outward journey, and all things pointed to the advisability of an early settlement in winter quarters. Captain Scott had decided already that McMurdo Sound would afford the greatest opportunity for sledging exploration, when the next season's sunlight permitted that activity, and at ten o'clock on the night of 8th February, with the aid of ice anchors, *Discovery* was secured to an ice foot off Mount Erebus.

It had not been intended originally that *Discovery* should winter in the ice, but that a small party should be landed, and the ship retire northwards before the season closed. Having found so sheltered an anchorage, however, Captain Scott decided to remain. Alas, it was

THE GREAT ICE BARRIER, ICEBERG AND PACK ICE

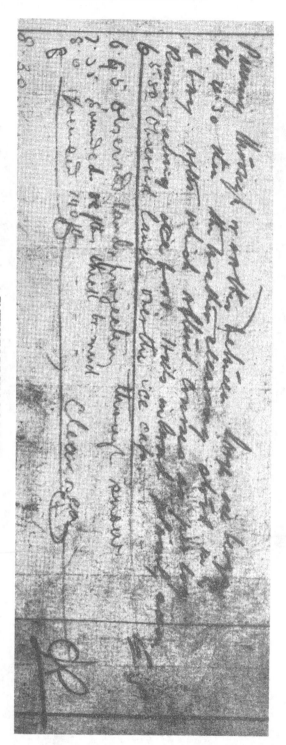

ENTRY IN DECK LOG BOOK

so sheltered that it was more than two years before the ice broke up again!

The sectional hut, which we called Gregory Lodge, and which was to have housed the landing party, was now erected as a storehouse, and a shelter for exploration parties if the ship should be so unfortunate as to be driven from her moorings. It was most unsuitable and its chief function later was to provide us with the Royal Terror Theatre. But one of the first tasks was to find a site for it—not a simple matter on a small plateau of volcanic rubble, frozen solid to within some inches of the surface, and many weary hours were passed with pick and shovel before the foundations could be fixed and Dailey, our carpenter, proceed with his work on the frame.

Meanwhile, there were all the hundred and one preoccupations of preparing for the long night. The asbestos huts, though they proved also unsuitable, must be erected, well removed from the magnetic metals of the ship, and food, above all things food, must be provided in sufficient quantities to vary the fare, mostly in tins, which *Discovery* carried.

Fresh food is the chief preventive of scurvy, and as there was no vegetable life, our only safety was in fresh meat. The ice became a shambles as penguins and seals marched unsuspecting to the sacrifice. All was now a scene of indescribable activity. The butchers worked on the ice, the carpenters on the hut and the kennels for the dogs— though that was wasted time, for the dogs despised them and preferred to curl up in the snow. Reconnoitring sledge parties, ski parties and ordinary tramping parties went out in all directions to form some estimate of the obstacles which might lie in wait for future spring exploration.

At intervals, by way of questionable rest, football games took place on the ice. There was, too, the all-important task of naming landmarks in the vicinity—and Cape Armitage, Observation Hill, Castle Rock, Crater Heights, The Gap, and Arrival Bay soon added their quota to world geography.

The days were now growing shorter. Sunset still seemed almost to mingle with sunrise, but there began to be a distinguishable period when it was night—a strange luminous night, that beggared description in the rich colouring of its sky, but indubitably night. The lazy ascending smoke of Erebus assumed, when the sun sank, a fiery glow. The eerie beauty of the long Antarctic night was taking its hold upon a continent.

And now, before the winter had begun, in the strange twilight of the gods which had begun to settle, tragedy came to us. On 4th March a sledging party comprised of Royds, Koettlitz, Skelton and Barne and eight men set off in an attempt to reach Cape Crozier. For a week the weather continued fine, but on the 11th we awoke to find a strong wind blowing and the air filled with driving snow. At half-past eight that evening our tranquillity within the ship was rudely shaken by the report that four men were to be seen approaching. Four men returning, when eleven had set out!—that could spell only disaster.

When they reached the ship they proved to be four of the seamen, Wild, Weller, Heald and Plumley. They had been sent back, they reported, in charge of Mr. Barne, and there had been with them besides, four other seamen, Quartley, Evans, Hare and Vince. A blizzard caught them on an icy slope somewhere beyond Castle Rock. Hare disappeared, and Barne with Evans and Quartley had turned back to look for him. They had not returned, and after waiting until it seemed madness to wait longer the five seamen had set out towards the ship, and finding themselves on an ice slope above a high cliff that fell to the sea, suddenly Vince had slipped, shot past them and disappeared over the edge. Vince, definitely, was lost. They feared the others also were gone.

The hours which followed can only be imagined. Armitage set out with a land search party, of which I was one, while Shackleton with a picked crew of six took out the whaleboat. Those who were left could only strain their eyes hopefully through the driving snow and wait. Three hours passed, and through the drift Ferrar appeared—with Barne, Evans and Quartley. He had been sent by Armitage to guide them back while the search continued for Vince and Hare. An hour later the main search party returned, unsuccessful, and soon after the whaler, with her exhausted crew. There was slight chance of seeing either Hare or Vince again. Meanwhile, the survivors, suffering from frostbite, required all our attention, and when the ship's company settled down to a few hours' rest, the shadow of calamity was over us.

Another search party went out on the 12th and found the

abandoned sledges and two of the dogs. But of Vince and Hare there was no trace. On the 13th it was still blowing and the temperature was six degrees below zero, when about 10 a.m. a lone figure was seen crawling down a hillside. The men working at the hut were the first to realize that it was one of the lost sledgers, and rushed out to assist him, and five minutes later Hare was aboard—hungry and exhausted, but in full possession of his faculties, and entirely free of frostbite! His was one of the strangest adventures that ever befell an Antarctic adventurer. Finding himself separated from his companions and unable to locate them in the blizzard, he had pushed on in what he thought to be the direction of the ship, until he fell exhausted. He remembered nothing more until he had awakened in a snowy grave some thirty-six hours later; pushing aside his blanket of snow he had recognized Castle Rock, and started for the ship. Poor Vince was not so fortunate, and when we saw the slope on which he fell, we knew that nothing could have saved him. His grave was in the icy sea.

The days were now shortening perceptibly. There was a distinct difference between day and night. It was becoming colder, and on 30th March—it seemed appropriate that it was Easter Sunday—there were ice-flowers on the newly frozen sea, waxen white formations, with radiant prismatic colours where the low-hung sun's rays touched them. Autumn was at an end. Sledging had been a failure. Food, clothing—everything was wrong. There would be much to think about, and much to rearrange during the long winter night. On 23rd April the sun made its final, brief appearance, leaving as a substitute only "trailing clouds of glory", that faded from day to day. Soon, only the smoke and vapour of Erebus, floating high above the crater, reminded us by their midday radiance that somewhere the sun lived on. Then that reminder, too, was gone. It was winter and it was night.

Three

Hibernation

IN 1902 the isolation of the Antarctic was an isolation difficult to appreciate to-day. There were no aeroplanes and no radios. There was no possibility of communication with the outside world, and no news of the world could reach us—no assistance, either, if disaster came. We must make ourselves a self-sustaining unit, and provide against all the evils which might befall us. Just how numerous those evils might be was already evidenced by the death of seaman Vince, so sudden and unexpected, the disablement of Captain Scott, by a severe knee sprain sustained in a fall, and the broken leg of Chief Steward Ford, also the result of a fall on a rough snow slope near the hut.

There was, too, the uncertainty of the long Antarctic night, of which I had experience at Cape Adare, in a tiny hut, fifteen feet square, lashed down by cables to the rocky shore. The night there had been shorter than we would now experience, as we had been farther north, but officers and men, living together in so restricted a space, ten of us in all, had found tempers wearing thin long before it passed. To those who had not yet experienced the polar darkness, anticipation was probably worse than realization, and some feared the results of nervous irritation before the winter passed. That was an experience, however, from which *Discovery* saved us. A winter in "Gregory Lodge" might have been little better than a repetition of the boredom and irritation engendered at Cape Adare. With *Discovery* our home, each officer had his own sanctum, and the men in their quarters could enjoy their leisure in their own way. The friction of conflicting tastes was eliminated from the beginning.

The organization of our work, so that each had his own task and was left to do it without interference, was another long step towards harmonious living. Singly or in little groups we carried on, seldom seeing the other members of the mess during the day, except at meals. And the comparative formality of meals, and more especially dinner, helped to preserve an atmosphere of civilized tolerance such as has been seldom found in polar exploration. The traditions of the naval service, which in some things might have proved a disadvantage, in the trivialities of day to day living, were of infinite benefit.

It was a wardroom regulation that each member took his turn as President of the mess. Installed at the head of the table, and invested with a little wooden mallet, he was charged with the duty of keeping order between the grace—"Thank God"—with which our dinner started, and the drinking of the King's health. No betting was allowed, nor any suggestion of even a mild oath, and if anyone offended the gavel fell, and the President pronounced his sentence, usually a fine on the guilty one, in the form of port all round. Transgressors were few, but there were some incurable delinquents, and I remember on one occasion fining Shackleton five times during one meal, for offering to bet that someone was wrong. Payment for many rounds of port made opinion open to modification.

The first step in settling down to winter life was to establish our routine. There were certain things which must be done daily, certain things which must be done almost every hour. The scientific staff was as closely tied to scheduled hours of work as the marine stewards and the cook. The meteorological records were one of the important objects of the expedition, and every two hours the instruments must be visited, the barometer and thermometer readings registered, the anemometer examined and wind direction and velocity observed. That was Royds' work, and every two hours from 10 a.m. to 10 p.m. he made his rounds. For the balance of the twenty-four hours the wardroom took turns in relieving him of his duties, so that each officer spent every eleventh night on duty.

The magnetic observations were my personal responsibility, and as no one else understood the adjustments of the delicate instruments employed, there was no relief. For the ordinary routine work there were self-recording instruments which required to be visited once or twice a day, but on the 1st and 15th of every month, the international term days, I had to visit the magnetic hut every two hours of the twenty-four, to change the photographic recording sheets.

Barne and Hodgson spent their days in the open air. Hodgson with pick and shovel and lines and net, fishing for specimens of marine life, and Barne on his interminable and uninteresting task of taking sea temperatures. Both worked alone from preference, though seaman Weller in his spare time haunted Hodgson's fishing-holes, and it was to Weller that the honour went of catching the largest fish ever landed in Antarctica. It was minus its head, for a seal had bitten off that necessary appendage just as Weller flung his harpoon—in fact the harpoon had struck the attacking seal, missing the fish—but both seal and fish were landed, the headless body measuring some three feet six inches, and weighing something like forty pounds.

Wilson and Koettlitz, less bound by hours than any of us, could carry on at night as well as during the day, for most of their work was done within the ship. When Wilson's supply of zoological specimens ran out, he filled in time perfecting his now famous water colours, and when a fortunate encounter brought a supply exceeding the demand, the surplus was frozen to await his convenience, brought to the wardroom as required, to be thawed out—usually upon the beams that crossed the skylight above the table—and left there until they began to "talk", as the smell of their thawed-out condition was described. The all-pervading odours of biological jars and taxidermy were soon so familiar to us that we could tell the moment we entered the wardroom who had been hardest at work. Koettlitz was utilizing to the full a set of bacteriological instruments presented to him by Guy's Hospital before he sailed, examining the interiors of seals, penguins and skua gulls, and everyone was eager to peer through his microscope at the fearful and wonderful bacteria he sometimes found, Alas, most of us were so unable to appreciate his enthusiasm that he instituted the "Order of the Ass"—of which I became a member—fourth class!

Each day began for the men with the collection of ice for the water supply, and in the wardroom with the thorough airing which the addicts of fresh air demanded. At 8.30 the men had their breakfast, and from 9 to 10 the wardroom engaged in the same rite, the disciples of warmth-at-anyprice often appearing completely dressed, even to fur-lined gloves, to emphasize their point. At 9.15, after prayers, the men were told off for the work of the day. By this time the hammocks on the mess-deck were lashed up and stowed away—and in their sleeping arrangements, it might be noted, as well as in the warmth of their quarters, the mess-deck had the advantage. The slung hammocks could be kept dry and comfortable, the more pretentious accommodation of the officers, with their bunks built against the ship, were soon distressingly damp from the condensation of the interior moisture on the extremely cold cabin sides.

Breakfast for both officers and men consisted of porridge, bread and butter, marmalade and jam. During the active life we lived when daylight was still with us there had been also hash or stew or seal liver. Now in more sedentary days only seal liver tempted us to extend the meal. Soup, seal or tinned meat, and jam or fruit tart was the routine dinner, varied on feast days by frozen mutton, and in all meals wardroom and mess-deck fared alike. The only difference was in the time at which the meals were taken, the men having dinner at noon, the officers at six in the evening. The single standard in food had been a wise precaution against possible mess-deck grievances, for at times there was more than a little ground for complaint. Our cook, shipped at the last moment from New Zealand, to replace a trained cook who had become "too big for his boots", proved both inefficient and dirty, and although the ward-room made the best of it, for cooks cannot be replaced in Antarctica, the mess-deck was not so easily satisfied. Our cook was stronger in talks than in cookery; when, later, he left in the *Morning* it was calculated that his thrilling experiences in many other parts of the world extended over a period of 590 years!

There was one who found himself in serious trouble for his epicurean tastes, a merchant seaman who must have signed on in a moment of mental aberration. He was not made for polar exploration. He did not like the Antarctic or anything to do with it, and had been heard, during one of the very cold autumn sledging journeys, to sit up in his sleeping-bag and with chattering teeth apostrophize the night—"Fancy *me* from bloody Poplar, on the bloody Ice Barrier, in a bloody sleeping-bag, gorblimey!"

No doubt on the mess-deck he applied the same adjective to the cake which caused the trouble, though when the ship's company was paraded in strict naval style, so that he might make his complaint with due ceremony, he only demanded mildly of the Captain, as he fished an offensive lump of something from his pocket—"Do you call this caike?"

Scott had no sense of humour when discipline was infringed upon, and discipline demanded surely that a man who approached his

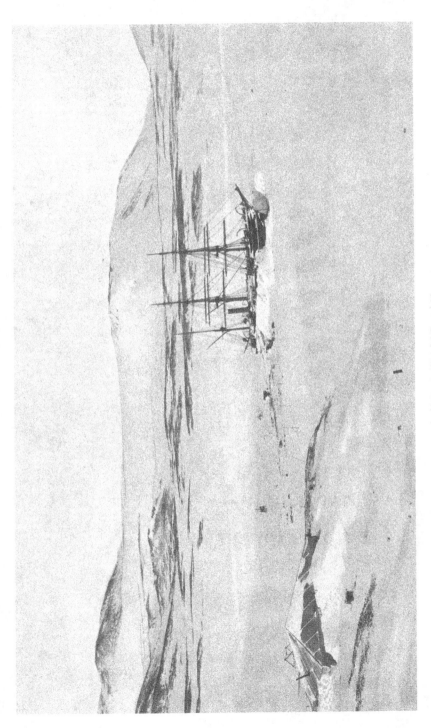

WINTER HARBOUR, 1902

MIDWINTER DAY ON MESS DECK

commanding officer in such a way, be ordered to instant execution. In the circumstances he was severely punished.

If he could be a stern disciplinarian, Scott was also anxious to give as much personal liberty as possible. Smoking on the mess-deck was allowed at all times, and when during the darkest winter days work was slack, the men had their evenings free and often their afternoons. While "Shove ha'penny" seemed to be their favourite sport, and books like *Fights for the Flag* and *Deeds that won the Empire* their favourite reading matter, yet it was chiefly from the mess-deck that the Royal Terror Theatre recruited its performers. We in the wardroom were engaged in weightier matters, preparing debates, for example, on such subjects as "Women's Rights" and other long-dead problems, which occupied the mind of man at the beginning of the century. On these occasions the less one spoke the more one said. There was even one memorable evening when the rival merits of Browning and Tennyson came up for judgment. Shackleton backed Browning while I, more sentimental then, argued for the moving depths of beauty to be found in the verses of the Poet Laureate. Whether by my masterly exposition or because the wardroom generally shared my preference, Tennyson won—although only by one vote.

The concert programme of 1st May is typical of the artistic standard of our entertainment.

Lantern slides showing the building, launching and sailing of *Discovery.*

Song	The Old Flag, ...Mr. A. Pillbeam
Song	Annie Laurie, ...Mr. Allan
Song	Where Grows the Sweetest Flower,	Mr. Duncan
Song	The Cobbler, ... Mr. Page
Song	Old and New, ...Mr. Bernacchi
Song	Vicar of Bray, ...Mr. Wild
Song	McPherson's Feud, ...Mr. Clarke

GOD SAVE THE KING

What we lacked in artistic merit, we made up in enthusiasm.

The *South Polar Times*, a monthly journal, was another wardroom effort, though many fine and red-blooded contributions came from the lower deck. Ernest Shackleton showed an especial aptitude for Kipling-esque verse. Under the modest nom-de-plume of "Nemo" he gave us rolling sonorous rhythms. One of his contributions was "To the Great Barrier":

Mother of mighty icebergs, these Kings of the Southern Seas,
Mystery, yet unfathomed, though we've paid in full our fees,
Eyes strained by ceaseless watching, when the low grey fog doth screen
Your walls from our aching vision, and the great grim giants you wean
Away from your broad white bosom, where for aeons untold is laid
Each yearly tribute of fallen snows, that this wonderful plain has
    made.
We have felt, more than seen, the danger close ahead of our long jib
    boom,
But a turn of the icy wheel has made for us more sea room.
We have sailed from your farthest West, that is bounded by fire and
    snow,
We have pierced to your farthest East, till stopped by the hard-set floe,
We have steamed by your wave-worn caverns; dim, blue, mysterious
    halls.
We have risen above your surface, we have sounded along your walls.
And above that rolling surface we have strained our eyes to see,
But league upon league of whiteness was all that there seemed to be.
Ah, what is the secret you're keeping, to the Southward beyond our
    ken?
This year shall your icy fastness resound with the voices of men?
Shall we learn that you come from the mountains? Shall we call you
    a frozen sea?
Shall we sail to the Northward and leave you, still a Secret forever to
    be?

The screen of anonymity encouraged versifying, and another contributor calling himself "Fitz-Clarence"—in private life Lieutenant Michael Barne—heralded returning day:

There steals upon us day by day a change;
Stealthily creeping o'er the Antarctic world,

Three months of night in seeming endless range
Into a realm of twilight have unfurled.

Night's shadowy form, yet bending darkly o'er,
Her wings, erstwhile outspread, begins to fold,
And wakening Day proclaims his reign once more
Casting before him beam on beam of gold.

Now fades the silver crescent to the view,
Isis, the goddess of our night is spurned;
Her beauty faded into opal hue,
Her glory overcome, to dullness turned.

Yon distant Western mountains' roseate sheen
Seems touched with brush of painter, great, unknown
Above them Venus hangs, pale beauty's queen,
As though in rapture drawn to Earthly throne.

Another less poetic outburst by the same author dealt with the eternal round of meteorological and magnetic observations:

"An Observation! what is that?" I think I hear you say,
"A scientific function that is practised every day?"
Not only every day, I fear, far oftener than that,
A useless entertainment, and it fairly knocks me flat.
To ascertain the object of this idiotic game
Of taking observations, is my everlasting aim.

To be aroused from slumber at the deadest of the night,
To take an observation, gives us all a morbid blight;
How in the name of all that's blank, can temperatures down
    here
Concern those scientific men at home, from year to year?
To us alone they matter, for it's cold enough, alas!
To freeze the tail and fingers off a monkey made of brass.

We even had a sports page, and our correspondent on the lower deck reported the exciting progress of sporting events there in the style of a professional cricket observer:

The first of what has proved an interesting contest of skill occurred on the evening of 8th May, when Mr. H. Blissett met Mr. W. Peters in an exciting game of Shove 'Apenny. The final score was three to nil in favour of Mr. Blissett. Mr. Peters, however, contested every game closely and it was not until the final point was scored that the result was at all certain.

On Friday Mr. Heald played Mr. Wild, and by some phenomenal play in the first game, managed to score amid loud and ringing applause. Here, however, his effort ceased to gain the required chalks, and Mr. Wild, whose play had been very steady, soon forged ahead and playing a strong finish, won handily; score, three games to one.

The games had to be postponed on account of darkness. . . . On Monday, the moon came out early and the play was resumed. . .

There were coloured caricatures of the officers on the lines of the then famous "Spy" depicting all the eccentric and peculiar traits of the victim, extremely popular with all—excepting the victim; coats-of-arms, too, were assigned to each, combining the fertile ideas of the wardroom but artistically drawn by Wilson.

But the *South Polar Times* was designed to be instructive as well as amusing, and articles by the scientific staff dealt lengthily with such subjects as Polar Plant Life, Antarctic Seals, Geology of the Antarctic, Terrestrial Magnetism, The Mariner's Compass. One copy only was published, typed out by Chief Steward Ford, with spaces left on almost every page for Wilson's illustrations. On the day of publication it was ceremoniously handed to Captain Scott, and after making the rounds of the wardroom passed on to the mess-deck, and was read and re-read until it was almost worn out.

Entertainment, however, sometimes became almost a "Roman holiday", and when Royds was operated upon for a cyst on his cheek, the general reaction was one of pleasurable interest rather than sympathy for the unfortunate victim. Dr. Koettlitz, nothing loath to perform the first operation in Antarctica, gladly prepared for the event. The wardroom table became the operating table. I volunteered as nurse, and rolled up my sleeves to play the part convincingly, while Koettlitz brought from their hiding-places a formidable array of knives, pincers, scissors, lint, gauze and bandages, explaining ghoulishly the exact function of each. Armitage took charge of the phial of patent freezing mixture, and the rest of the wardroom gathered round. The effort at first was not a success, for the freezing mixture functioned so thoroughly that the knife would not penetrate the skin, and while we waited for it to thaw a little, all joined in terrifyingly reassuring remarks to the patient. Again the knife was applied, and this time, to our intense satisfaction, blood flowed. Our questions as to whether it hurt or not brought a most emphatic "Yes". But the cyst was removed and the cheek stitched up, and Royds was distinguished for the rest of his life by a diminutive scar, a record of the first surgical operation performed in Antarctica.

Another of the duties of the doctor ranked also as entertainment— the monthly examination of the whole ship's company, including weighing, measuring and taking blood samples to ascertain the consistency of the red corpuscles. On the first day of each month the wardroom paraded in pyjamas, everyone was weighed, chest measured and expansions noted; waist, calf, forearm and upper arm measurements recorded, and strength of grip. Then with a special needle and a small test-tube the blood samples were taken—to be tested at leisure. The next night the mess-deck went through a similar performance. Afterwards results were posted, and although no one knew what they might mean, we took great satisfaction from the fact that there was no general falling off in weight, only slight fluctuations in strength, and that in most cases the blood gradually grew richer.

Weather was a constant topic of conversation, and we discussed the weather, not in the accepted fashion, merely for something to say, but because it was of all-absorbing interest. Our only information of the conditions we might expect was based on the experience of continuous cyclonic winds suffered by the *Southern Cross* party at Cape Adare, and *Discovery* was frozen up some five hundred miles farther south. No one could guess what might be in store for us, yet on that depended, more than all else, our success or failure.

Would the sea-ice hold?

Already the strait had been cleared of ice on more than one

occasion by the terrific winds. If the ice of our little bay broke up, we might be in a precarious position, for boilers and engines had been dismantled. Would the spring weather permit the southern sledging journey Scott was planning? If not the success of our efforts would be severely curtailed.

Would the dogs stand the winter? Nature in her inexorable course had taken no account of the fact that they were now at the opposite end of the earth, and they had begun to lose their heavy coats just at a time when winter was closing down, which would have been for them the spring in the land from which they came.

Would our own health stand the rigours of the sunless night? We found that, in fact, the night was in one sense less rigorous than we had anticipated, for while hurricane followed hurricane, when the wind and storm most fiercely enveloped us the temperature invariably rose. It was on the days of still beauty, when the wind fell and the snow lay like a velvet pall, that the mercury dropped until it no longered registered. It was not the cold we had to fear, but wind and blizzard, blowing relentlessly from the south, blinding and deafening, day after day, so that within a few yards of the ship one might be forever lost.

It was just as winter was ending that I had an experience of the bewildering effect of blizzard which might have ended fatally. With Skelton's help I had been taking pendulum observations, which had kept us busy for several hours at the Observational Hut. When we had left the ship the weather had been reasonably fine, and we had not put on our wind clothes. Now that observations were completed and we were ready to return, we found a blizzard raging. It was impossible to see three feet ahead. We followed the guide ropes until we reached the shore, but there they disappeared, having become drifted over. The distance from shore to ship, however, was only some 120 yards, and we struck out across the open space, only to realize after about ten minutes' struggle with the storm that we must have mistaken our direction.

We decided to work back to shore and start again, and keeping the wind on our left, as our guide, finally we found the ragged edges of shore ice. But we could not locate the rope. Was it to right or left of us? We could only guess, and turning right, we groped along on hands and knees, clinging to the shore by thrusting our hands into the tide crack.

From time to time we stood up and shouted with all our strength, but nothing happened. All around blackness, and the biting wind which drove snow into our boots and trousers, while drifting snow turned into ice pads in our eye-sockets. For nearly two hours we continued our search. We had either missed the rope or turned in the wrong direction, and we knew that unless we found shelter soon, in our light clothing we would be frozen. In a final united effort we shouted for help, and this time we were heard. Some of the men had been rehearsing with Royds in the hut for the minstrel show that was to be produced on the anniversary of our leaving England. They, too, had lost the rope, but there were twenty of them, and they had formed a living chain that was able to span the breach. It was a lucky escape for us, and a most unpleasant experience. We found next morning that we had been within touching distance of the ship.

The week's work ended on Friday. Saturday was devoted to "clean ship", and in the morning living spaces and lockers were turned out and scrubbed, while at the same time holds were cleared, ice in the fore-peak chipped out, and upper deck "squared up" and a fresh layer of clean snow sprinkled over the soiled surface. On Sunday we put on different clothes—not always newer or cleaner, but at least a change. And at 9.30 came Sunday inspection, when the men fell in on the awning deck, and by the light of a lantern carried by the boatswain, Captain Scott and the executive officers passed in solemn procession. Then came the only military order of the week—"Front rank, one pace forward, march"; the men were inspected and dismissed. Church followed, and to the tolling of the ship's bell the congregation assembled. The Captain read the service, Koettlitz the lessons, and Royds played the organ—and he played it extremely well. Reponses were chanted and hymns sung heartily. Seals, no doubt, popped their heads out of their water-holes to listen, and if the curious penguin colonies had not long since left our shores, they must have had much to discuss as the volume of sound echoed over the ice. Service over, all looked forward to the feast of New Zealand mutton which distinguished our Sunday dinner, and to make sure of an adequate appetite to do justice to such an occasion, most of the ship's company took an extra long walk.

Our great winter festival was on midwinter day, and like old-time pagans we celebrated with feasting and music the commencement of the return journey of the sun. It was two months since its red disc had disappeared below the northern horizon, and never was pagan jubilation in honour of the returning life-giver more heartfelt than ours.

The long night had not lacked interest. It had brought none of the horrors which might have been feared. But the age-old worship persisted deep in the consciousness of each of us. The mess-deck was particularly gorgeous, with chains and ropes of coloured paper, japanese lanterns and gaily decorated tables, each with a fanciful ice centrepiece, lighted from within. And the stokers' mess surpassed all in imaginative design, with a finely carved ice head of Neptune. It was the stokers, too, who displayed the most originality in their selection of a special culinary treat, the last thing in the world one would have thought of in such a land, and when the officers made their rounds, they were regaled with dishes of ice-cream. Then came the distribution of gifts provided by Royds' mother, and an extra tot of rum, before we returned to the wardroom and our own dinner, which ended in an evening of song. Even the dogs caught the infection, and joined with a chorus of wild barking, and the fun continued until the early morning hours, when we all went out into the calm, clear moonlight, to shout a final pæan to the returning day.

Those clear, bright moonlight nights were always a time of solemn ritual among the dogs. From a white silence, with the animals coiled in placid sleep, suddenly one would raise its head and from the depths of its throat would come a prolonged dismal howl. As the note died away, another would take it up, and then another, till even the soundest sleeper in the ship was roused. There was no snapping or snarling, only an ordered baying to the moon, weird and hair-raising, with every suggestion of some savage, sacred ritual.

Slowly the sun rose, and soon at midday, unless the blizzard hid it, great streaks of crimson light slashed the northern sky. Plans for the summer's work began to take definite form. All through the winter Captain Scott had been engaged in interminable calculations

IN WINTER QUARTERS: BOW OF DISCOVERY

OBSERVATIONAL HUT AND THE PHYSICIST

DIGGING OUT THE BOATS

regarding sledging equipment—food, clothes, sledge-weights, methods of packing, methods of hauling. All had been thought out with exhaustive care so as to avoid the weaknesses only too evident in the short trial journeys of the autumn. And unfortunately, although *Discovery* possessed a library of several thousand books, and among them a number on Arctic exploration, by some oversight those which would have been of most assistance had not been included. We could gain no advantage from the experience of the more recent explorers, Nordenskjöld, Nansen and Peary.

The workshop, the particular sanctum of Skelton and his engine-room staff, was now a scene of animation, and on the mess-deck the ship's sewing-machine hummed unceasingly, as weird garments for spring sledging journeys took shape. Strangely enough, the only sewing machine on board was a Singer, the private property of Petty Officer Cross. One of the problems with which everyone was struggling was the discovery of some method of protecting nose and cheeks from frostbite. I do not know why we had overlooked that excellent specific which had proved so valuable to the *Southern Cross* winter party, a coat of glycerine. All sorts of masks were tried, each as unsatisfactory as the last, for there was no way of overcoming the quick congealing of the moisture of one's breath upon anything with which it came in contact. The thick fringe of wolf-skin which the Esquimo wears around his face was obviously a logical protection, breaking the force of the wind, and confining the warmth of the face, tempering, too, the light of the sun reflected from the snow, which was to prove a hardship in causing snow-blindness. But we had no wolf-skins, and we invented a sort of windbreak of felt, which we wore around our faces.

Down below in the store-room sledging provisions were being weighed and packed, and, out upon the ice, a large complement already was commencing the Herculean task of freeing the ship's boats from the sea-ice, a task which was not finished until more than six months had passed, and which then provided still another stretch of weary work for Dailey, our very efficient carpenter, that of making them sea-worthy.

As winter closed down and the canvas deck-covering was being fixed over *Discovery*, it had been found that the boats interfered with its fitting, and Captain Scott had ordered their removal to the sea-ice. It was then that I had my one and only experience with what seemed an unreasonable side of his nature. I had been through a winter before, and had seen the effect of the unbelievable weight of snow which accumulated upon the ice, pressing it down into the sea so that the water displaced flowed over it, making a top layer of slush, until that, too, froze. When I saw *Discovery's* boats spread out upon the ice, I had indicated this possible danger. The result was an experience I did not care to repeat, for I was told, in no uncertain terms, to attend to my own speciality. Now the worst fears were realized. The driving winter blizzards had filled the boats and covered them, the weight of the snow upon the vast surface of bay ice had pressed it beneath the water. It had frozen, and the boats were embedded in the solid floe. Digging was completely unsuccessful, and finally it was determined to saw them out. As the ice at that point was some fourteen feet thick, the colossal nature of the task can be imagined.

At first an island of ice containing all the boats was sawed free, but that refused to rise, and it was necessary to saw each one out separately. The wonder is not that it took more than six months to accomplish, but that it ever was done at all. Finally the ice was chipped away from each embedded boat, unfortunately taking with it, in every case, large portions of the sides. And then repair work started.

On 21st August the sun was due to show itself above the northern horizon, but driving wind and drift prevented our seeing it until the next day. Mighty shadows appeared above the southern horizon which remained mysterious for a long time, and many awe-inspiring speculations were made until it was discovered they were thrown in the sky by the mighty volcano behind. Pups now appeared in our dog colony, real products of Antarctica which, when at last they sailed to a milder climate, had to be taught to drink! Accustomed to *eating* water in the form of snow, they suffered thirst for days before they learned the function of a pan of water placed before them.

Winter was over. The return of the sun marked the last issue of the *South Polar Times*. There would be no more concert parties or minstrel shows, no more debates or Shove Ha'penny matches. There was work to be done, and no excess of time in which to do it. Sledging journeys were to be made in every direction, short journeys, long journeys, journeys to the east, journeys to the west and journeys to the south. Depôts of food were to be laid down well to the south, to replenish the supplies of the returning southern sledging party, to be led by Captain Scott himself, but which would not start until early in November.

Snapping dog-teams, untrained and during the whole winter unaccusomed to the feel of harness, went off more or less unwillingly under the guidance of unpractised drivers. Weird inventions in wearing apparel were tried out, weird methods of transport—teams of dogs only, dog-and-man teams, and men alone, harnessed to heavily laden sledges, disappeared into the white wastes.

On 2nd September, Captain Scott set out on a preliminary journey, to test the efficiency of his equipment and to discipline his dogs before the great southward effort. A few days later another party left under Lieutenant Armitage, and finally Royds and I were left alone, unable to leave for more than a few hours our magnetic and meteorological instruments. On 3rd October, Scott's party returned. Armitage and his contingent were already back, but back with trouble, for scurvy had appeared amongst them. We had thought that by our care in matters of cleanliness and food we should have avoided it. Although we had all looked pale in the returned daylight, we had felt no impairment of vitality. Yet Armitage returned with three members of his party suffering severely from the dread disease— Ferrar the geologist, Petty Officer Cross, and Heald a seaman, all with discoloured, swollen limbs and spongy gums. A careful examination of the whole ship's company was made immediately and revealed in almost every one some slight indication of infection. Scurvy, it is said, is due to the absence of a comparatively simple substance in the diet, viz. Vitamin C, the chemical formula of which is $C_6H_8O_6$. It is present in oranges, lemons, blackcurrants, green leaves and potatoes.

At once our food regime was changed. Tinned meat became taboo, and fresh seal meat and an increased allowance of bottled fruit a compulsory part of our diet. The cook, too, was taken to task, for the general distaste for seal meat was largely due to his careless culinary methods. A marked improvement in meals resulted, and within a fortnight all ate the despised seal with relish. Soon the effect on general health was obvious, and when on 9th October a seal-hunting expedition went out to replenish our supplies, Cross already was well enough to accompany it.

Koettlitz had taken advantage of the returned daylight to grow a fresh supply of mustard and cress in his boxes of Antarctic soil, scraped up in spoonfuls here and there, and providing a much more satisfactory crop than he had been able to produce on flannel with the aid of chemicals. The garden under the wardroom skylight was all too small, but it gave one good green feed all round. By the beginning of November symptoms of the disease had almost completely disappeared, and on 2nd November, Scott set out according to schedule, on his long-planned southern journey, with Shackleton and Wilson as his companions.

Four

Pully-Hauley

THE autumn sledging had been a failure, and Captain Scott had spent most of the long winter planning for better success with the return of day. The trial journeys proved to some extent the soundness of his calculations. The badly packed, top-heavy sledges with "everything on top and nothing handy" as the seamen expressed it, had been replaced by compact, shipshape, well-balanced loads. The haphazard collections of provisions had given place to canvas bags, each packed with one week's allowance for three men, each, in turn, in its smaller linen bag. Men and dogs had become acclimatized. But there were still unplumbed depths of inexperience. We did not know how to put up a tent in a blizzard, nor how to secure it in place when it was up. We did not know how to manage the cookers effectively, nor even how to put on our sledging clothes properly. Possibly competitions in making camp, including all the multifarious duties to be performed in a tiny tent before toggling down for the night, might advantageously have taken the place of moonlight football matches during the comparative idleness of the winter, and competitions in dog driving would have taken the keen edge off our ignorance of that most important accomplishment. Possibly the appointment of two or three men to specialize in dog driving would have lessened our transport inefficiency. We knew not and we knew not that we knew not—and, as the Arab proverb says, such men are—not exactly wise.

The weakness in land transport plans, however, went back to the days of organization of the expedition. Once we were in Antarctica with our inadequate equipment, there was nothing to be done— except perhaps to learn to use it with the greatest possible efficiency. It is an interesting and surprising feature of the organization of the expedition that Sir Clements Markham, the "father" of the venture, while appreciating to the full the desirability of having a ship specially built to cope with the stormy, ice-laden Antarctic seas, yet apparently had little idea that to cope with Antarctic land conditions successfully would require equally careful preparation. It was here that our shortcomings were most sadly evident. We recognized the forces to be met with in the struggle with the sea. But to travel on land—one just travelled.

Even in 1902 man-hauling of sledges was an out-moded idea. The efficiency of dog transport had long been proved. Yet although the expedition had been planning for many years, there was no reliable information available regarding dog transport. There was in the minds of all English explorers, perhaps, the unacknowledged thought that a dog was a pet. True—in Siberia, Alaska and Canada dog teams were in everyday use for winter travel. They had been successfully utilized by the Scandinavians in Arctic exploration. But that did not alter the idea that the dog was primarily a pet. It was as if the futility of putting a pet pony to haul a heavily laden van were to condemn the whole idea of horse transport.

Sir Clements Markham was inexorably opposed to using dogs as beasts of burden. He found nothing incongruous in letting man take on that rôle. In 1850 he had been with the largest of the many Franklin Search Expeditions, sailing in one of the ships of a squadron, the *Assistance*, under Captain Erasmus Ommanney. Sledges were then man-hauled, and he considered it the only thinkable method.

A comparison of *Discovery's* land transport methods with those of some other expeditions is illuminating to the point of heartbreak. Leaving out of consideration air travel, for that was scarcely dreamed of in 1902, leaving out motor tractors, for the motor-car was still an unreliable adolescent—which even in its maturity is far from satisfactory in below zero temperatures, and impossible on crevassed glacial surfaces—there remained only dogs as an alternative to man-hauling—though Shackleton, after the fiasco of *Discovery's* dog transport efforts, did conceive what J. Gordon Hayes, in his *Antarctica* calls the "whimsical notion of using ponies". They were a pathetic failure, and Shackleton on his second Antarctic venture turned unreservedly to dogs.

There were arguments for man-hauling, of course. Except for the *Southern Cross* expedition, polar ex-ship journeys had been confined to the Arctic, and Arctic ice, being sea-ice, broken and jammed and refrozen, presents the worst possible surface for dog haulage. On one of Peary's Arctic journeys over ice-jams in a temperature of sixty degrees below zero, sledges and loads had to be carried on the backs of men over the almost impassable surface. Many similar incidents occurred on Arctic ice.

But Antarctic ice is continental ice, and presents entirely different conditions. While torn and crevassed and piled in fantastic heaps where it borders the land, due to the pressure of the slowly moving glacier ice, yet once away from the shore the surface of the Great Ice Barrier took on the nature of, say, the great Canadian prairies in winter, over which howling blizzards blow, just as in Antarctica—and at similar temperatures. Much was unknown regarding Antarctica, but that at least was common knowledge. And even in crevassed areas, the comparatively light weight of dogs, the distribution of that weight, and the speed with which they can cross snow-bridges, were strong arguments in their favour. Travelling conditions in Antarctica, in fact, proved much more analogous to those which the hunters and trappers of the Canadian plains experienced than those which Arctic explorers had met. The only intelligent transport was by dogs.

There is another advantage, too, in the use of dogs. If the worst comes to the worst a dog may be eaten. The tragic death of Lieut. Ninnis, on Sir Douglas Mawson's *Aurora* expedition, would have meant the death of Mawson and Dr. Mertz as well, but for dogs.

Ninnis was driving a sledge on which practically all the food had been packed, and the collapse of a snow-bridge precipitated him, with dog-team and all supplies, into an unfathomable crevasse. One dog-team remained, and Mawson's return journey is one of the epics of Antarctica. Mertz died on the way, and Mawson thought the dog-meat diet was the cause, but Mawson himself struggled on, and after ninety-one days of indescribable suffering and privation at last reached safety. Shackleton, too, after the loss of *Endeavour* in the ice, was reduced to eating dog. He found it "surprisingly good and tasty". However that may be, and whatever the prejudice against it, the fact remains that when travelling in regions where no food exists, it may spell the difference between life and death.

There must have been some suspicion in the minds of the organizers of the *Discovery* expedition that there was something to be said for dog-haulage. Though Scott had written Sir Clements

Markham that "conquest is more nobly and splendidly won by man's unaided effort than by forcing dogs to suffer," yet possibly Scott did not accept fully the idea that they need be made to suffer. He states the true fact plainly in his *Voyage of the Discovery*—"the real cruelty to a dog lies in over-working or under-feeding it". Whatever may have been the reasons leading to the decision, it was eventually determined that *Discovery* should take a complement of dogs. But it was a half-hearted concession, for only twenty-three were purchased, and although it was known that Eastern Siberian dogs were larger and stronger than Western, and that Canadian dogs were better than either, yet Western Siberian dogs were chosen— "because it would save time". Allowing for accident and the weeding out of the less suitable animals, even in the most favourable circumstances, not more than one efficient team could be expected.

Even the little *Southern Cross* expedition had carried seventy-five dogs, and incidentally brought most of them back to civilization fit and well—one, given to me by Borchgrevink, to return with *Discovery*, died on Scott's southern journey. Amundsen, a few years later, took one hundred and fourteen, and with teams of twelve dogs, drawing lightly loaded sledges—some 770 lb., as compared with weights up to 2100 lb. on *Discovery's* sledge journeys—made his spectacular dash to the South Pole, keeping his animals so fit that on one day of the return journey as much as sixty-two miles were covered. On the outward journey he had permitted no such exertion, and carefully husbanding their strength had limited their daily effort to from seventeen to twenty-five miles. Miraculous speed, even that, when compared with our southern party, on which the best day's run was just over eleven miles. The average was five miles a day.

Our dogs were handicapped by loads beyond their power, even had they been well fed, which they were not. The very conditions which Captain Scott envisaged as being the only form of cruelty—overwork and under-feeding—were the conditions under which they served. "A whip and a hard heart", to quote Scott again, urged them on until they dropped in their tracks exhausted. Their sledging ration, reduced to a minimum, turned out to be tainted, so that within a few days they were all suffering from poisoning, and it is a tragic commentary on the general ignorance that the sledging ration on which they were to make their supreme effort should have been dried stockfish which had become tainted in the tropics, while piled up on the shore at winter quarters were considerable supplies of Spratt's cod-liver oil cakes. They were discovered some sixteen years later by a depôt-laying party from Shackleton's *Aurora*, still in perfect condition, and were used with striking effect in reconditioning their travel-worn and starving dog-teams. It is also interesting to know that descendants of those very dogs of Shackleton's that went with Admiral Byrd's expedition were kept fit and strong on American "dog-chow" cakes, composed of molasses, soya bean oil, meat, meal, whole meal, dried milk, corn— and *cod-liver oil*.

Amundsen fed his dogs on seal meat and on dog. He had no sentimental qualms about killing a dog which showed signs of failing, yet he never allowed his dogs to pull more than they were able, nor longer than they were able, and however fit and willing they appeared, at fixed intervals he rested them for two days and fed them to repletion, knowing the time well spent. But it was only his almost unlimited supply of dogs which had enabled him to take enough food either to spare that time or indulge in feasting.

Of *Discovery's* twenty-three dogs—or rather twenty-four, for my dog Joe was added to the quota in New Zealand—four had been killed in fights during the winter. Some of those remaining obviously were unfit for any sustained effort. Shortage of dogs meant shortage of food. Hard-worked dogs in cold weather require as much as 5 to 6 lb. per day each. It was impossible to carry enough to feed adequately either men or animals over the long periods of absence from the ship which our slow transport made necessary. It was a vicious circle, which could not be overcome. Slow transport meant inadequate feeding, and inadequate feeding caused slow transport. Nor was the suffering confined to the dogs. Unfortunately, concentrated so-called foods were in the first flush of popularity, and added their burden of debility, dysentery, and scurvy to men already tried to the limit.

As I have already said, the autumn sledging had been a conspicuous failure, not only as regards attainment of objectives, but one life had been lost. With the coming of spring fresh attempts were made with the wisdom gleaned from autumn experience, but an experience all too limited to give warning of the contingencies that might arise. A fair idea of our sorry ignorance may be gathered from the spring journeys of Captain Scott himself. On 2nd September a party of six officers and men started on a reconnaissance journey to the north, "mainly in order to test the various forms of harness which we had on trial and to find out whether the dogs pulled best in large or small teams". That first day they made eight miles. Four sledges were taken, with four dogs harnessed to each. On 5th September they returned to the ship, having learned that dog-teams should not be divided into such small units. That was one step in the right direction, but strangely enough the knowledge was not based on pulling power of the animals but on the rivalry between the teams. It had seemed to be a point of honour with dogs of any one team to fight at sight the dogs of any other team.

On the 17th Captain Scott set out again, this time with only two companions, Shackleton and Barne, who already had been chosen to accompany him to make his southern journey. It was a day of bright clear sunshine and very low temperature, and the party made 12½ miles, camping at 5.30 in the afternoon, with the thermometer at forty-eight degrees below zero, and a keen wind from the south-east. They had supper and settled down in sleeping-bags, to be awakened some time later in a world of lashing snow, with the tent conspicuously absent. A violent gale was raging and the air was filled with blinding snow. The wildly flapping tent was still clinging to the bamboo poles on the windward side, but it was evident that it would not remain there long unless something was done.

With freezing fingers the three companions pulled the tent back into place, half sitting on the skirting to keep it down, half grasping it to hold it against the tearing force of the wind. Hour after hour they crouched clinging to their shelter. The skirt of the tent would gradually pull from under them, fly up, and getting a fresh hold they would pull it down again and lever themselves over it once more. Sleeping-bags became filled with snow until they were lying in masses of chilling slush; mitts were in the same condition, and the slippery canvas pulling through their grasp, it became necessary to use bare fingers to haul it in again.

Taking advantage of lulls in the wind, gradually a sledge was unloaded, and the tent skirting weighed down with biscuit and petrol tins. All day the struggle with the wind was waged, and it was not until

CAPTAIN SCOTT IN FULL COLD WEATHER SLEDGING KIT

A PULLY-HAULEY SLEDGING PARTY

six o'clock in the evening that the tent was secure—at the cost of such frost-bitten hands that Barne, who suffered worst, did not recover in time to take his place with the southern party. With the tent at last secure, they were able to spare time for food, and lying in their wet sleeping-bags ate some cold pemmican and chocolate. They had not had a moment to think of the dogs, but they, good Arctic animals, curled up nose to tail and covered by the drifting snow, had uttered not a sound, waiting in the manner of their tribe for the blizzard to blow over.

By the next morning that had occurred, but clothing and sleeping-bags were all so wet that there was nothing for it but to return to the ship and dry out equipment. One more item of sledging wisdom acquired by cruel experience—"It will certainly be a very long time before I go to sleep again in a tent that is not properly secured," Scott wrote of that adventure.

On the 24th Captain Scott again led out a little party, but Barne's badly frozen hands eliminated him from further effort for some time to come and Boatswain Feather was taken in his place. As loads had been left at what Scott called their "desolation camp", and the party travelled light until they were picked up, that day they made twenty-three miles. The weather was now fine, and by the 27th they approached the Bluff, a landmark near which it was proposed to leave a depôt of supplies to be picked up by the southern party on its return. But Antarctica still had surprises in store, and nearing the Bluff the party came on a crevassed region of torn and twisted ice. By the 29th they were winding amongst deep, blue crevasses, crossing on snow-bridges where possible, skirting them when no bridge presented.

Suddenly, Scott, who was breaking trail, heard a shout, and turning round saw that Feather had disappeared. Hurrying back he found the boatswain dangling on a single trace in the depths of a formidable crevass. The sharp ice-edge had cut through one strand of his harness, as it tautened to his fall, and he had had a very narrow escape from death. Feather rescued, the party pushed on, the dog-teams joined now, but half an hour later another shout announced yet another accident. This time it was a sledge which had disappeared, and was hanging vertically in a cold blue chasm. The supplies were on it, intact. It was too heavy to be pulled up and had to be unloaded where it hung. Feather volunteered for that unpleasant task, and was let down on a length of Alpine rope while other lines were used to pull up the various packages.

Experience had taught one more lesson. Henceforth crevasses were to be treated with respect. The party was roped together, Scott continued to lead, Feather led the dogs, and Shackleton followed in the rear to keep an eye upon things in general.

There was more wisdom than those ladies of New Zealand had imagined in their nickname given to *Discovery's* complement. We were, indeed, "babes in the wood". However, all went well, and on 3rd October Scott with his party returned to the ship—to find the problem of scurvy to be faced.

A complete change of diet seemed to have eradicated all trace of that evil before 2nd November, when a start was made on the long-planned southern journey. But the cure was, for the sledgers at least, only temporary, for scurvy is a food deficiency disease and cannot be avoided where deficiency exists. At winter quarters the fresh meat diet had its satisfactory effect, but the southern travellers, condemned to live on concentrated foods, were denied that safeguard.

The importance of food was not in those days realized. Vitamins had hardly been heard of. With a view to reducing the weight of loads, food supplies were reduced to a minimum, and that minimum was chosen not for nutritive value but for lightness and ease in handling. The starvation diets on which English Antarctic sledgers work can only be described as fantastic. Seven and a half ounces of pemmican were allowed for one man for one day. That was a maximum. If travelling fell behind schedule even that was reduced. And strange concoctions, the contents of which nobody knew, were hopefully thrown into a cooker, with a few inches of melted snow, and with a ship's biscuit, or half a biscuit, or in unlucky periods a quarter of a biscuit, were supposed to make up a meal. As a result hunger was the predominating feeling in everyone.

Even in those conditions splendid work was done. But what might not have been accomplished by well-fed men? Unwashed, unshaven, hungry, wet and cold, dog-tired from unremitting beast-of-burden labours, there was no energy left for imaginative effort. One day was like another day, except for changing weather and light and surface conditions, a period of hungry straining misery to be followed by a night of hungry shivering misery, until with the thawing out and gradual warming of sleeping-bags from the body's heat, troubled sleep came—haunted by dreams of repasts that were always snatched away before the dreamer fed. Food and still more food was the theme of everyone's imagination, and strange imaginary messes were sometimes evolved. I remember on one occasion that Petty Officer Cross asked me, "What would you think of this, sir? Take some sardines and wrap them in sausage meat, with streaky bacon outside that, and cook it in a nice puff pastry—" We cut short his ramblings before his imaginary meal had completely ruined our digestions. On that particular sledge journey it was our greatest gustatory thrill.

The southern journey expedition, which had started out with every hope of reaching a really high latitude, was soon suffering severest disappointment. Dr. Wilson had been chosen to take the place of Lieut. Barne, who was incapacitated by his frozen hands. The dogs had started off with such a will that for several miles two men rode on the sledges to increase the load and hold them back. When the supporting party, which had been sent out three days earlier with supplies for an additional depôt, was overtaken, the dogs' load was increased to 2100 lb.—something over 100 lb. per dog. Even with that they pulled with a will and eleven miles were covered. On the 12th the depôt laying party started back, to report to us in the ship the high hopes of the southern travellers. But already the bad food combined with the terrific weight that they were hauling had begun to affect the dogs. The next two days showed only fifteen miles gained, and the animals were completely exhausted when camp was made. The cheerful yapping and excitement with which they had greeted the morning harnessing gave way to dull acquiescence. On the 15th hard pulling until five o'clock in the afternoon covered only three miles, and the next morning the animals had so much difficulty in even starting the load that it was decided to divide it and resort to relay work. Thereafter the southing averaged about five miles for the next ten days. To make that, fifteen miles back and forth had to be travelled, and although the weight of the load was halved, on the 18th it was eleven o'clock at night before even that was done.

One more lesson had been learned from sad experience, and on the 19th Scott wrote in his diary: "The lesson to future travellers in the South is obvious in that they should safeguard their dogs as securely as they do their men. But now it was too late to profit by the hard-gained knowledge. There was nothing for it but to push on, and a " hard heart and a whip" were the daily routine, with one man— they took it in turns—harnessed with the dogs to the heavy sledge. Now one led, one drove the dogs and used the whip, and one pulled with the dogs.

The party had already reached a farther south position than man had ever attained, and but for the worry regarding the possible complete breakdown of transport, in spite of all the routine hardships, they must have been filled with happiness and exhilaration. On the morning of 21st November they awoke to bright sunshine and a new coastline at their right, appearing very near but receding as they strove towards it, as all mirage recedes. The surface was becoming smoother and the snow surface thicker, offering splendid ski-ing facilities, but the snow caked on the runners of the sledges. Skis were tried out and discarded as unsatisfactory and caked sledge runners adding to the burden of the already heavy loads accepted as inevitable.

For three days they travelled towards the new-found coastline, which still seemed as distant as when they saw it first. But on 24th November Captain Scott took a meridian altitude, and found to his delight that they had reached Lat. 80° 1′ South. All charts of the Antarctic regions at that time showed a blank white circle beyond the 8oth parallel. Even the most imaginative cartographer had not dared to pass that limit. Whatever the troubles and trials they suffered, that space upon the map would be no longer blank, and conscious of achievement they spurred on to greater effort.

On the 26th a blizzard blew up suddenly, giving a compulsory day's rest to both men and animals, but on the 27th, although the men had benefited, the dogs curled up under the snow blanket could scarcely be dragged to their feet, and some were so cramped that it was several minutes before they could stand. A hopeful start was made with the full load, but it was impossible to move it, and the old relay work was again decided on, with this change—that it was determined to leave a depôt as soon as they could reach some outstanding landmark, which would enable them to find it on their return journey. But nine hours

PULLY-HAULEY PARTIES

HARNESSING THE DOGS

of supreme effort made only four miles. Day after day, heartbreaking labour continued, and it became more and more difficult to make even that distance. Several of the dogs already had reached the stage when they could scarcely walk, much less pull any weight in the traces.

On 9th December the first dog died, and on the 10th only two miles were travelled, and for the next four days the most strenuous exertion could not improve upon that distance. By the 14th a spot had been reached where it was considered safe to leave a depôt, and thus lighten the burden of hauling. In thirty-one days of nightmare effort little more than half a degree of latitude had been gained, or slightly more than one mile a day. Yet over 330 miles had been covered, in relay work.

The Great Barrier was, however, revealing its secrets. In addition to the discovery of land, atmospheric phenomena, never before recorded, made their appearance. At times clouds of ice-crystals thinly veiled the sun as in a glittering tenuous garment, reflecting its rays so that the whole arch of the heavens was traced with circles and lines of brilliant prismatic or white light. The coloured circles of a bright double sun-halo touched or intersected a line paralleling the horizon, above which a glorious, prismatic ring encircled the zenith. Away from the sun appeared a bright fog-bow, with a mock sun at each intersection of the horizon circle. Scenes of brilliant, bewildering beauty were presented, in which all the known polar atmospheric phenomena combined in concentrated splendour, scenes which for a moment brought forgetfulness even of failing transport.

With lightened loads the little party pushed on. But new difficulties had arisen. Subsiding snow-crusts, broken by the weight of the sledge, at first filled both men and dogs with sudden fear, when with a crack, as of a pistol shot, followed by a long-drawn sigh, the snow sank. Even a subsidence of two or three inches brought a momentary suggestion of insecurity. Thus one more discovery was made, for Shackleton digging down to investigate found layers of hard crust each separated by a foot or so of soft snow crystals, formed by repeated blizzards followed by warm sunshine, which had melted the surface. When this froze again, it made a solid crust imprisoning a certain amount of air. It was the crust which broke with the report of a gun, and the sigh that followed was escaping air. This, then, was one of the peculiarities of the Great Barrier's formation. This accounted for the stratified layers which appeared in the towering cliffs above the sea.

The fruits of the southern journey already were worth while, but "we are gradually passing from the hungry to the ravenous", Scott wrote, "we cannot drag our thoughts from food, and we talk of little else". So they pushed onward in the fine, bright weather, past a varying coastline of rocky eminences and rounded hills, that rose to great peaks 10,000 to 15,000 feet high, in the valleys of which gigantic glaciers made their slow way towards the Barrier ice that stretched away far as the eye could see.

Snowblindness was becoming almost a chronic ailment, with its accompaniment of headaches and stinging pain, and Wilson was the worst sufferer, for though while travelling the whole party wore snow goggles, whenever they paused for rest or meals, Wilson filled in the time with sketching, and for that work removed his goggles. Dog after dog had failed, and by 20th December only fourteen remained, and they were in so emaciated a condition that the next day all three men joined the team in pulling. There was no escaping the fact that none of the team could continue southward much farther, and Shackleton had developed swollen, inflamed gums, which are the first warning of scurvy. The already meagre rations were reduced by the elimination of bacon, for it was decided that at the rate at which food was going, the biscuits would not last, and that allowance must be reduced. The small supply of seal-meat that had been brought had been reduced by one of the dogs, which gnawed through his tether in the night, and had consumed a whole weeks allowance before it was discovered. The maximum amount of food which now could be allowed was only 1½ lb. per man per day. Breakfast consisted of tea and a small portion of pemmican and biscuit; lunch was a small piece of seal-meat, half a biscuit and eight to ten lumps of sugar; while supper was something less than a pannikin of pemmican "hoosh"—warmed up in melted snow—and a pannikin of cocoa. Food nightmares made up the daily breakfast conversation—one dreamed of sitting at a well-spread table, with arms tied; one grasping a steaming dish, which slipped from his hands; or one lifted a juicy piece of—beefsteak, perhaps—to his mouth, and at that moment fell over a precipice. In his consciousness of greedy hunger, each man insisted on taking what he thought was the smaller portion—for his conscience sake, until the resulting arguments brought about a new régime, suggested by Shackleton. The food was divided as equally as possible by one, another turned away and shut his eyes, the divider pointing to a portion would say, "Whose?" and he of the shut eyes would name the owner.

On 24th December, Dr. Wilson made a physical examination of the whole party, and reported to Scott that Shackleton's gums were worse. But the weather was fine, bearings showed they had reached Lat. 81½° S., the possibilities that lay ahead were too tempting to be disregarded, and Scott determined to push on. At least the dogs did not seem to have grown much worse during the past few days—and to-morrow would be Christmas. For a week the thought of Christmas had filled all minds. It had been decided to celebrate the day by having enough to eat, and by using enough oil to warm it properly. For that one day, at least, there would be no lunching on a piece of seal-meat, carried all morning in one's pocket to thaw it out.

Following is Scott's description of the day—"When we awoke to wish each other a 'Merry Christmas' the sun was shining warmly through our green canvas roof. We were outside in a twinkling, to find the sky gloriously clear and bright, and not a single cloud in its vast arch. Away to the westward stretched a long line of gleaming coastline; the sunlight danced and sparkled in the snow beneath our feet, and not a breath of wind disturbed the serenity of the scene. It was a glorious morning, but we did not stay to contemplate it, for we had even more interesting facts to occupy us, and were soon inside the tent sniffing at the savoury steam of the cooking pot. Then breakfast was ready, and before each of us lay a whole pannikin-full of biscuit and seal-liver fried in bacon and pemmican fat. It was gone in no time, but this and a large spoonful of jam to follow left a sense of comfort which we had not experienced for weeks and we started to pack up in a frame of mind that was wholly joyful.

"After this we started on the march, and felt at once the improvement of the surface that came to us last night; so great was it that we found we three alone could drag the sledges, and for once the driver was silent and the whip but rarely applied. The dogs merely walked along with slack traces, and we did not attempt to get more out of them.

No doubt an outsider would have thought our procession funereal enough, but to us the relief was inexpressible; and so we trudged on from 11.30 to 4 p.m., when we thoroughly enjoyed our lunch, which consisted of hot cocoa, plasmon, with a whole biscuit and another spoonful of jam. We were off again at 5.30 and marched on till 8.30, when we camped in warmth and comfort and with the additional satisfaction of having covered nearly eleven miles, the longest march we have made for a long time.

"Then we laid ourselves out for supper, reckless of consequences, having first had a Christmas wash and brush-up. Redolent of soap we sat around the cooking-pot whilst into its boiling contents was poured a double "whack" of everything. In the hoosh that followed, one could stand one's spoon with ease, and still the Primus hissed on, as once again our cocoa was brought to the boiling-point. Meanwhile, I had observed Shackleton ferreting about in his bundle, out of which he presently produced a spare sock, and stowed away in the toe of that sock was a small round object about the size of a cricket ball which, when brought to light, proved to be a noble plum-pudding. Another dive into his lucky-bag and out came a crumpled piece of artificial holly. Heated in the cocoa, our plum-pudding was soon steaming hot, and stood on the cooker-lid crowned with its decoration. For once we divided food without 'shut-eye'.

"I am writing over my second pipe. The sun is still slowly circling our small tent in a cloudless sky, the air is warm and quiet, all is pleasant without, and within we have a sense of comfort we have not known for many a day; we shall sleep well to-night—no dreams, no tightening of the belt."

The effect of even one good feed convinced Scott of the false economy of stinted rations. He knew now that "the additional weight of a proper allowance of food would have amply repaid us by the maintenance of our full vigour". But starvation rations were again the rule, as the southward journey continued. The glorious, panorama of mountain ranges which opened up with every mile tempted onward, but by 30th December, with only a fortnight's food left to take them back to their nearest food depôt, it was madness to go farther. Observations showed that they had reached between Lat. 82° 16′ S. and 82° 17′ S. One more effort was made to reach the land, but again, as they approached the shore, impassable ice-chasms barred their way, and reluctantly they turned northward.

Daily the dogs were dropping now, never to rise again. The men too were weaker, and as a result, even the light load that remained made heavy pulling. Twelve days passed. Would they reach the depôt and on 12th January, Scott wrote: "The depôt is a very small spot on a very big ocean of snow; with luck one might see it at a mile and a half to two miles, and fortune may direct our course within this radius." Fortune smiled, and at midnight on the 13th the sun broke through the clouds which had obscured it during the homeward march. Scott tumbled out of his sleeping-bag to get a meridian altitude—the trying duty of the navigator on all barrier journeys—and sweeping the horizon with his telescope, made out a black speck in the distance that was undoubtedly the depôt. But although the luck had held, a medical examination the next morning showed Shackleton now in a serious condition, and symptoms of the debilitating disease had appeared in the whole party.

Shackleton was so seriously ill that all speed for the ship must be made if his life was to be saved. Two dogs still remained, but they were in such a weak condition that their assistance could not offset the additional weight of their food, so they were sacrificed. Loads were rearranged, and the sledges repacked, with everything eliminated that was not absolutely necessary. The weather thickened, and, in the dull grey of sky and snow, inequalities in the surface could not be seen, so that falls were frequent and progress painfully slow. Already Scott was considering what was to be done if Shackleton collapsed completely, which seemed more and more probable. The seal-meat at the depôt, by which alone their scurvy could be kept in check, would last for fifteen days. They could only hope for the best. Days of "blind" hauling, when no landmark was visible and the overcast grey sky merged in the grey ice, were followed by days when the sun shone brightly.

On 25th January the Bluff came into view and behind it rose the comforting smoke of Erebus—though still more than one hundred miles away. Two days later the peak itself raised its head behind the dark outline of the Bluff, and on the 28th the last depôt was reached. There was food in plenty now, but Shackleton was so ill that he could not move, and both Scott and Wilson had reached the stage of swollen limbs and gums. A blizzard kept them two days encamped, and on the 30th, when the weather cleared, Shackleton was able to stagger along beside the sledge. Four days more of painful effort, and the whole party was safe on board by a dangerously narrow margin.

Five

A Letter from High Altitudes

WINTER HARBOUR, Lat. 77° 51′ S.,
February, 1904.

My DEAR FATHER AND MOTHER,

The two Relief Ships, *Morning* and *Terra Nova* entered McMurdo Strait on 5th January, and pushed to within seventeen geographical miles of our Winter Quarters, but were prevented from getting closer by the frozen unbroken surface—communication was immediately established, and twenty-fours hours later the mails were on board the old *Discovery*. We were surprised to see the *Terra Nova*, and to hear that the Government had undertaken our relief, and that some friction had taken place between the Royal Geographical Society and the heads of the Ministry. The whole business is most deplorable and unwarranted. There was absolutely no necessity for a second ship, and it is a needless waste of public money. As a matter of fact, she has been quite useless to us, and even if we had had to abandon the *Discovery*, and, as Sir Clements Markham has expressed it, "leave her in the ice as a monument of a great achievement", the *Morning* had ample space to take us all back as far as New Zealand. However, now that the *Discovery* has got out, and without any assistance from the *Terra Nova*, I suppose those who are responsible for this action will not feel so mightily pleased with themselves.

Although the last year of our imprisonment had been monotonous and long—in my case rather so, for it is my third winter and fifth summer in these desolate latitudes— it has been a most successful one. The best of relations still prevail on board, and there is not the slightest indication of any discord. There has been no accident of any kind among the officers and men, nor have any more symptoms of scurvy appeared, due, without a doubt, to our having strictly tabooed all tinned meats, and confined ourselves entirely to seal-meat and skua-gulls. The sledging, if not quite so sensational as last year's, has been better carried out and more extensive. The scientific work, too, is an improvement on last year. But I am proceeding a little too fast. I must tell you something of our second spell of 120 days of darkness.

After the departure of the *Morning* on 2nd March, 1903, and when we had fully realized that there was but small hope of our release, we immediately settled down to our old humdrum life and made preparations for the forthcoming winter. Numbers of seals and skua gulls were killed and buried in the snow for consumption. The winter awning was spread again over the ship, sides banked up with snow, and everything made as snug as could be. Our supply of oil and candles was very scanty, and in our cabins we were only allowed two candles per week, which were barely sufficient for dressing purposes. We had a fairly large supply of carbide for making acetylene gas which, so far, had not been used. This was now utilized, and burnt in the wardroom and on the mess-deck from 9 a.m. to 11 p.m. for about five months. It gave a brilliant illumination and was entirely satisfactory.

Towards the end of March we had quite given up hope of getting out, the temperature already had fallen very low, and as early as 8th April it had reached -50° F. The early winter months were intensely cold, colder than the corresponding months in 1902, but less windy, and the heavy blizzards, so frequent in 1902, were comparatively few. On 16th May we registered the lowest temperature ever observed within the Antarctic regions, namely -67.7° F. On that day I went out with the Captain and Koettlitz to the thermometer in the Strait, and, although the temperature was so low, it was not at all inconvenient. However, the slightest wind at this temperature causes exposed parts of the face immediately to become frostbitten. During the winter the scientific work was continued as before—magnetic records with the variometers, seismograph, pendulum observations, atmospheric electricity, aurora observations. The second year's work confirmed the results of the first, and from this point of view are valuable. The *South Polar Times* was again instituted, and I was elected its Editor. Three numbers were issued—one in April on the day the sun sank below the horizon, the second on MidWinter's Day, the third in August, when the sun reappeared. All three numbers are larger than any of last year's, and I trust the standard is as good.

At last the long winter months came to an end, and preparations for the spring sledge journeys pushed forward. During the winter I had requested permission from the Captain to undertake an extensive sledge journey across the surface of the Great Ice Barrier south-east from the ship, for the purpose of examining this ice-sheet over an extensive area, and to run out a line of magnetic observations. He at once approved the plan, but, as the naval officers were here for that purpose, he would have to send one of them (Lieut. Royds) in charge. I had no objection to this, provided I had a free hand to do what work I wanted. So it was arranged we should start in November on a thirty-five-days' journey. This was to be one of the principal journeys. Another party under Barne was to try to penetrate south-west, and the third and most important one, under the Captain, to penetrate due west as far as possible into the interior.

In September food depôts were laid out to the southwest and west, and these depôt journeys of a little more than a week's duration were extremely trying ones, for the temperature only too frequently was below -50° F., and, occasionally, below -60° F. One of the September journeys was to Cape Crozier, where Wilson collected something like fifteen Emperor Penguin eggs, and a number of young birds apparently born some time in August, but still quite small and in the feathery pouch of the mother.

The Captain's party started in October, and was away over seventy days, and did some splendid geographical work. The inland ice was reached at an altitude of something like 9000 feet, thence they proceeded straight inland and penetrated to about 270 geographical miles, or 310 ordinary statute miles, as you are acquainted with. The journey was an arduous one—food was reduced to a minimum on account of the weight—the temperature, while on the inland ice, was very low, -20° F. to -40° F. even in December, and there were some narrow escapes from crevasses.

The inland ice is simply a plain of snow something like the surface of the Great Ice Barrier, and perhaps something like the interior of Greenland. Here and there small undulations of the surface were noticed, but nothing else was seen. This extensive journey certainly goes to show the existence of a considerable continental area.

I am sending you a copy of my daily diary kept on our barrier journey. It is just as it was written in the rough after a heavy day's march, and, therefore, rather crude, but it will give you an idea of the kind of existence and work such a journey entails. We left the ship on 10th November, and continued on a due south-east course for 155 geographical miles, or 178 statute miles, reaching Lat. 79° 32′ S. and Long. 175° 55′ E. The total number of miles out and back was 356, which we did in 31 days, or an average of a little over 10 miles a day, the best average done here without dogs. We had about180 lb. each to drag. This dragging was very heavy on account of the bad surface, and as the temperature was generally below zero, with a strong wind and drifting snow from the south-west, the trip was not altogether enjoyable. We averaged something like nine hours actual pulling a day. I had observations for latitude and longitude to take (for we had to find our position each day, having no landmarks at all to guide us) and one and a half hours magnetic work to do at the end of every third day's march. These magnetic observations will, I think, prove of considerable value.

Unfortunately, our food supply was most inadequate, and we suffered badly from hunger. I have never before suffered from real want of food. We, of course, saw no new land, nothing but the barren, level surface of the barrier, with few undulations to break the monotony.

The journey was considered a most successful one.

As soon as the sledging parties had returned (15th December), with the exception of Captain Scott's, the whole of the ship's company proceeded to a spot ten miles to the north of the *Discovery*, pitched a large camp on the sea-ice, and commenced sawing operations. From the very first this was obviously a futile task. The ice was seven feet in thickness, the rate of sawing a channel made good was about 120 feet a day, and we had no means of getting rid of the ice—so it froze up again almost as soon as sawn.

The Captain returned on New Year's Day, and at once stopped our foolish operations.

A few days after the relief ships arrived, but they could get only within seventeen miles of the *Discovery*, and day after day passed without getting much closer. Captain Scott's orders from the Admiralty were very definite. If the *Discovery* could not be freed by the end of February, she was to be abandoned in the ice, and all scientific work, instruments and personal property removed to the relief ships, with officers and crew, and the ships were to proceed at once to New Zealand where arrangements would be made to convey us home.

You can, of course, imagine our reluctance to leave our good old ship behind, and as the days went by and hope grew less and less, faces became very long indeed. In the meantime all scientific records and instruments were conveyed to the *Terra Nova* by sledges, and at last nothing remained but our private property and ourselves.

On 12th February the relief ships were still five miles away. All hands were now employed blowing up the icefloe with gun-cotton, and hundreds of pounds were thus expended. No doubt it did some good and weakened the ice, but I do not think to any considerable extent. On the 14th there was a sudden break up of the ice in McMurdo Strait due, principally, to a northerly swell. While we were at dinner in the evening a message was sent down to the wardroom that the two relief ships were within half a mile of our Winter Quarters. Little time was lost in finishing dinner and making our way to Hut Point, from which point of vantage we could see the ships just below us ramming at the two years' solid ice separating us. At 11 p.m., amid ringing cheers from three ships' crews, they broke through the belt of ice into an open pool off Hut Point, and made fast within a few hundred yards of our bows.

Later, at Sea.

Still we were not yet free. The ice in the small cove held us in a firm grip, for here its thickness was fourteen feet. However, on the 16th we exploded two huge charges of gun-cotton close to the bows and aft of the ship, which shook us from stern to stern, and lifted the ice in the cove, cracking it in all directions. In a few minutes we were free, and the old *Discovery* swung easily around at her anchorage. You can imagine how deeply thankful we were. Steam was at once raised, the anchor heaved up, which had been down for two years, and in the morning of the 17th we slowly moved out of our Winter Harbour. From this moment until the day we reached Auckland Islands our so far amazingly lucky ship was pursued by ill-luck, and had accident after accident, until we thought we would never get back to New Zealand after all.

As we headed out of Winter Harbour with steam in one boiler only, there was a strong wind blowing from the north, which, possibly, caught our bows, being so light and high out of the water, and blew us round. At any rate I do not know quite how it happened, but the next moment we were ashore off Hut Point. For a short time no one thought it to be anything serious, and the engines were kept going ahead, but as she did not move our yards were braced and sails set, but still without success. Matters now looked rather grave. The wind increased, to a gale, bringing with it a heavy sea, which caused the ship to bump heavily on the bottom. The position became graver, the seas commenced to break right over us and against the perpendicular ice cliff from which we were only about fifty feet distant, and large pieces of timber, apparently from the keel, floated up and drifted away. Down below one could scarcely hear another speak for the crashing noise of the timbers, and the decks, when she bumped, bent like whalebone and broke some of the thick glass deck-lights.

Some *Terra Nova* whalers who were on board, and who should know something of this type of ship, expressed the opinion that she would soon "break her back" and "go to pieces" if this wind and sea continued. Judging by the quantity of timber being torn off her bottom, the bending of the decks and beams, I thought so too.

If she had gone to pieces we may have had some difficulty in getting ashore, for we were just out of reach of the ice cliff. Between the ship and the cliff the sea was a boiling mass of foam, and the launching of a boat on the windward side was almost impossible.

Fortunately the wind abated, the sea moderated, and the bumping became less violent. There was no sign of either relief ship; both were somewhere out in the middle of the strait hidden by the drifting snow. At 6 p.m. it was reported by the officer of the watch that the ship appeared to be moving astern. There was a rush at once for the deck. The stern had swung round. Full speed astern was put on the engines, all hands commenced to roll the ship by running all together from one side to the other, and at last, to our intense relief, she slowly commenced to slide off the bottom and in fifteen minutes we were again in deep water. We had been aground exactly eight hours; perhaps the most anxious eight hours in the history of the *Discovery*.

The next day we lay alongside a tongue of land ice, forming a natural quay, and took in coal and provisions from the *Terra Nova* and *Morning*, and in the afternoon all three ships left McMurdo Strait for good and headed northwards. *Terra Nova* was to keep with us, if possible, but *Morning* was to go on to the Auckland Islands, where all ships were to rendezvous in Port Ross.

We tried to get into Wood Bay for purposes of magnetic observations, but could not on account of heavy pack-ice.

Between Wood Bay and Coulman Island we encountered a long deep swell from the south-east with no wind. Something went wrong with our pumps; water gained rapidly, for *Discovery* was rolling her sides under water, where, after two years' exposure to the rigours of the Antarctic climate, the seams were open. For some hours we were in a sinking condition. At last, after much trouble, steam was raised in a small auxiliary engine on deck and the pumps were working again: not a moment too soon, for the sea water had reached the furnaces and the fires had to be drawn.

Between Coulman Island and Cape Adare we discovered that our rudder was shattered by encounter with some projecting ice and required immediate attention. So we ran close under Cape Adare, anchored near the shore, removed our four-ton broken rudder, and replaced it with a spare one. Fortunately, the weather kept very fine, and we have special contrivances for facilitating the fitting of a new rudder. The whole business took only about twelve hours.

From Cape Adare we tried to push our way round Cape North in order to connect up that coast with Adélie Land, discovered by Dumont D'Urville. But the pack-ice and bergs were too dense to permit it. The nights now were very dark, large numbers of gigantic icebergs surrounded us and made navigation extremely dangerous. Soon after leaving Cape North a heavy gale came on with thick weather, during which we parted company with the *Terra Nova*, and we did not see her again until we met in the Auckland Islands.

After parting we steered a course for the Balleny Islands, sighted them on 2nd March and passed in between two on a due west course. The day was fine and we could easily see five distinct islands. From

Balleny Islands we steered for Wilkes Land, and passed right over his mountain peaks and capes. It evidently does not exist. After spending two or three days on the top of Wilkes Land, we headed north for Auckland Islands. We were then in Long. 153° E. The Antarctic Circle was crossed on 5th March. After that most boisterous weather was encountered with headwinds (N.W.) and a heavy sea. The *Discovery*, having very little ballast, rolled and plunged incessantly, sometimes rolling as much as fifty degrees on each side, but she is one of the best sea-boats ever built, and we were as safe as could be, although uncomfortable.

Ross Harbour, in the Auckland Islands, was reached on 15th March, but there was no sign there of either the *Morning* or the *Terra Nova*. We had expected both to be there long before us, for they had had a considerable start, but we had some advantage in going so far west and making a fair wind of the persistent north-west gales. In Ross Harbour we cleaned up our battered old tub, took in fresh water, and shot fresh meat ashore: rabbits, pigs, ducks.

On the 19th the *Terra Nova* turned up, and next day the *Morning*. They both had had a very rough time and had been driven far to leeward of these islands. The *Morning* especially had suffered. One of her boats had been washed away out of the davits and the bridge nearly washed overboard. Her engines also had broken down at times. She had been in a precarious position.

The New Zealand Government steamer *Hinemoa* put into Ross Harbour on 26th March, and we then heard of the outbreak of war between Russia and Japan.

Later—2nd April.
We have just reached Lyttleton and received a great ovation from the inhabitants. So after more than two years within the Antarctic Circle we have returned to civilization, and although our manners and habits may be rather primitive, we are, at least, little the worse for our long and adventurous journey, and enjoy the very best health.

*　*　*　*　*　*　*

This letter, which I found some years ago amongst my father's papers, written in the Antarctic and now printed word for word as written, requires some expanding and explanation, especially in connexion with the summer sledge journeys of 1903, which resulted in some of the most valuable work the expedition accomplished.

Whilst in the previous summer Captain Scott and his two companions were struggling southward over the barrier, Lieutenant Armitage with another party had gone west to attempt to pierce beyond the mountains, which appeared an impregnable rampart. With little or no difficulty they had found a pass at a height of some 6000 feet, leading to a large glacier now named after Ferrar, our geologist. Following up the frozen stream of that ice river at an altitude of some 9000 feet they had reached the Polar Plateau, proving beyond a doubt that the mountain rampart guarded a great ice-covered land area.

Armitage and his party can claim to be the discoverers of the polar plateau, and their route disclosed problems of considerable interest, not only from the point of view of a practical route to the interior, but from a geological one, for specimens collected showed strong probability of the existence of sedimentary deposits which could serve to reveal the geological history of the Southern Continent. Excellent pioneer work had been done but, unfortunately, the journey had lasted only seven weeks and progress had been very slow.

It was by this trail, blazed by Armitage, that in the second summer Scott made his western journey, so rich in geological and geographical discovery.

Early in October Scott was ready to set out with a large party for the west—a combination really of three parties.

Veterans now, the immense difficulties which, in the previous year, would have brought them hopelessly to grief were successfully met. Careful preparations had been made during the winter and all were in a hard and fit condition. This time there was no scurvy. Scott writes: "I am bound to confess I have some pride in this journey." The region of their work was not only interesting but probably the most beautiful in Antarctica. Certainly this is indicated from the magnificent photographs taken by Skelton, who accompanied the expedition most of the way.

At setting out, on 12th October, everything looked favourable, and with great speed and in fine weather, a spot in the western mountains had been reached in six days, where Armitage had taken twenty-seven. Describing his first impression of those mountains with their large but terribly rough glaciers, Scott writes: "To describe the wildly beautiful scene that is about us to-night is a task that is far beyond my pen." But on the 17th Scott's strangely fatalistic number, Dailey, the carpenter, reported that the German silver protection over the sledge runners was split to ribbons and the wood beneath deeply scored. On further examination it was found that of the four eleven-foot heavily laden sledges only one was unsplit and sound. It was a horrid revelation.

There was nothing for it but to return to the ship. The return over nearly ninety miles, on half rations, for nearly all provisions and gear were left behind with the solitary sound sledge, was a record in Antarctic travelling, and proved what could be done by fit men, light loads and no dogs. Twenty-seven miles the first day, twenty-four the second, and the third thirty-six miles to reach the ship— eighty-seven miles in three days! Scott himself outstripped them all. The attitude of Petty Officer Kennar, who, like Scott, came from the West country, had been that of "grieved astonishment"—"If he can do it, I don't see why I can't; my legs are as long as his." Although material in the second year had become very scarce, in five days' time one sound eleven-foot sledge for Scott's party was produced out of the various broken bits, and two short seven-foot sledges for the geologist, Ferrar, who with two others was to branch off on his own to carry out a geological and glacier survey. It was characteristic of Scott that he was always thoughtful of the scientists and their work, in this respect quite unselfish.

In a few days, with grim determination, they were back again in the mountains and on the glacier surface, but the runners continued to give trouble and required constant watching and repairs throughout the journey. In a valley named the "Vale of Winds" and which equally might have been called the "Vale of Tears", at breakfast, and before anyone could move, a sudden gust of wind swept down upon the tent, and sleeping-bags, socks, finneskoes, and other garments lay scattered and skidding about the ice. But they were nearly all retrieved. The "Vale of Winds", the arm of a large glacier, was responsible, too, for a very serious loss—that of Scott's *Hints to Travellers* containing the essential data and tables for finding latitudes and longitudes. A sudden gust had taken it off.

"The gravity of this loss can scarcely be exaggerated," Scott writes, "but whilst I realized the blow I felt that nothing would induce me to return to the ship a second time." Scott's fine knowledge of Nautical Astronomy, however, enabled him to compile certain data, slender, perhaps, from his own knowledge and the observations already taken and worked out in his diary. So they decided to push on and gained a height of 7000 feet on the glacier in the face of bitterly cold winds and frostbites. But owing to the slippery hard surface of the glacier it took nearly an hour even to pitch a tent; again and again the poles of the tent were blown flat. Gale after gale raged unceasingly, and there were long days of inactivity within the tent. The occasional calm and fine days revealed a scene around them utterly glorious. On the passage up the glacier, in some of the most unattractive areas, carcasses of the Weddell seal were found, one at nearly 5000 feet above the sea. "It grows more than ever wonderful how these creatures can have got so far from the sea," and again, "Unless we had actually found these remains it would have been past believing that a dying seal could have transported itself over fifty miles of rough steep glacier surface."

At Cape Adare, some years before, we had found the carcasses of the crab-eating seal, thirty-five miles inland and 3000 feet high. Some primitive instinct must impel these seals towards this habit, when very old or dying.

Long spells of bad weather pursued them, but on 13th November they at last won the fight and found themselves on the summit at nearly 9000 feet. They had five weeks' provisions in hand.

No sooner had the ice-cap been reached when trouble began once more. The winds were strong, temperatures fell to below -40° F., surfaces became extremely hard and slippery, and crampons had to be worn over and under their fur boots. But the unknown was before them and they decided to push on. Pulling was not easy—they were at over 9000 feet, and some of the men began to show signs of distress.

For some days they marched on a straight course due west, with no landmarks. Magnetically they found themselves in an interesting region; they were directly south of the South Magnetic Pole, the error of their compass had passed from east to west and was nearly at its maximum of 180°. The north end of the compass needle was pointing almost due south.

It was at this stage that Scott decided to carry on with two others only and to instruct the rest to return homewards; these were Lieutenant Skelton, Boatswain Feather, and Seaman Handsley. Dailey, the carpenter, Williamson and Plumley had returned some time before. The two men left behind with Scott were Petty Officer Evans and Leading Stoker Lashly. Evans, who later was to die with Scott on his last expedition, was a man of Herculean strength—very long in the arm and with splendidly developed muscles. He had been a gymnastic instructor in the navy and weighed 12 stone 10 lb. in hard condition. Lashly was deceptive in appearance. He was not above normal height, and did not look abnormally broad, but he weighed 13 stone 8 lb. and his was one of the largest chest measurements in the ship. He was a lifelong non-smoker and teetotaller. Scott's weight at the time was 11 stone 6 lb. Scott writes: "My companions are undefeatable." No matter how gloomy the outlook there was always something to jest about. Incidentally, Scott learned a great deal about lower-deck life, for in the evenings within the tent there were long arguments about naval matters, and it was generally agreed that they could run the service a great deal better than any Board of Admiralty. These three, working together like a living thing, pulled on patiently through the long days and hours, with scarce a word between them and never a halt between meals. The surface was not easy. High and formidable sastrugi caused by the wind, were crossed and brought about frequent capsizes of the sledge. It was distressing work with a high wind in their faces and a temperature frequently forty degrees below zero. Footgear was getting thin and worn, but all were in excellent condition and health. No sign of the scurvy fiend appeared. And so they continued until the end of the month in this scene of awful desolation, with nothing to be seen in the vast expanse of snow—neither tree nor shrub, nor any living thing nor even inanimate rock; three little human insects crawling out over this desert and now bent on crawling back again.

"The interior of Victoria Land must be considered the most desolate region in the world. There is none other that is at once so barren, so deserted, so piercingly cold, so windswept or so fearsomely monotonous." Poor Scott and Evans were to know more of it some years

SCOTT'S CAMP IN THE WESTERN MOUNTAINS

SCOTT'S PARTY TO THE WESTERN MOUNTAINS

BARRIER SLEDGE PARTY
Left to right:— (top) Cross, Royds, Bernacchi
(bottom) Plumley, Marine Scott, Kennar

later on their last epic march to the South Pole. As Evans expressed it, they "would have to leg it" back again. They were seventeen days out from the glacier head and now had fourteen days' full rations left with twelve days' oil supply. They started back on 1st December. The return was an ordeal with very low temperatures and, consequently, frostbites. Light was bad and direction-finding baffling, but, worse than all, food had to be cut down drastically.

At last land was sighted—the edge of the plateau—but exactly where they did not know. They pulled ten hours a day and became gaunt shadows of their former selves, but still they kept fit. Fifteen days after starting back, trouble came suddenly while passing over the edge of the plateau on disturbed ice surfaces. They were wearing crampons on the slippery slope when Evans, owing to a sudden strain, was thrown off his feet and in turn the other two with sledge complete were hurtling down at the speed of an express train. They fell 300 feet on the incline, but beyond severe bruises no damage was done and the sledge was intact, but with its contents distributed over the ice cascade. On picking themselves up the welcome and familiar sight of the smoke-capped summit of Erebus could be seen far away to the eastward. Whereas a few moments before they had been completely lost, now, as if a curtain had been raised, all the well-known glaciers and landmarks lay before them, and down the valley could be seen the high cliffs of the Depôt Nunatak, where rest and plenty awaited them. But they were not to get off so easily. Starting off again badly shaken, quite unsuspicious of further danger, with Scott in the middle but a little in advance, Evans and Scott suddenly stepped into space and disappeared from sight. By a miracle Lashly stopped himself from following and sprang back, throwing his whole weight on his trace. The loaded sledge dashed by and jumped the crevasse down which Evans and Scott had disappeared. One side of the sledge frame cracked through in the strain which followed, but providentially the other held.

Scott states he remembers nothing until he found himself "dangling at the end of my trace with blue walls on either side and a horrid-looking gulf below". Evans was dangling just above him. Asked if he was all right, Evans replied, in his usual matter-of-fact tone, that he was.

Fortunately, both were wearing their steel crampons, and by swinging his feet Scott was able to get a grip on a projecting ledge of ice to which, after a struggle, he managed to reach and get Evans to the same position.

Lashly above held on grimly to the half-submerged sledge, which he dared not leave since immediately he relaxed his strain it began to slip down the crevasse. So, unaided, Scott with his thick clothing, heavy crampons and frostbitten fingers, commenced what appeared to be an impossible task—to swarm up the harness rope. It was a nightmare climb, but, by an almost superhuman effort, he reached the top exhausted, and for several minutes was completely helpless. His hands were white to the wrists. Then harness was lowered to Evans and he was heaved up.

Lashly's position, holding on with all his strength, had perhaps been the worst of all, His comment on Scott's reappearance was "Thank God!" All Evans said was "Well, I'm blowed!" It was his first and only sign of astonishment in the face of a terrible crisis and an amazing recovery.

With ample food at the various depôts the journey down was relatively easy. Even a little running water was found trickling from a glacier and their small provision measure was used, luxuriously, as a drinking cup. Passing through superb scenery, full of geological interest, fascinated by the strange new sights around them, at lunch quenching their thirst at the tiny stream, and running warm sand from the moraine rubble through their fingers, "it seemed impossible that we could be within a hundred miles of the terrible conditions we had experienced on the summit".

The valley they descended was wonderful with indications of colossal ice and water action, now long past, but no living thing was found, not even a moss or a lichen. It was certainly a valley of desolation with even its once great glacier withered away.

Discovery was reached on Christmas Eve. It had been a wonderful journey. In the eighty-one days of the whole western expedition, Scott, Evans, and Lashly had covered 1098 miles, averaging over fifteen miles a day, notwithstanding being forced by blizzards to remain in camp nine days, and they had climbed heights which totalled nearly 20,000 feet. To this satisfactory journey were added

Ferrar's independent geological survey, rich in results, and Skelton's most excellent photographic work.

Ill-fortune, however, had dogged the survey expedition of Mulock and Barne to the south. They had been hampered by continual gales, dreadfully low temperatures, and long days spent in their tent. Notwithstanding, Mulock had used his theodolite indefatigably, with the result that this long stretch of Victoria Land is more accurately plotted than any other, and the height and position of over 200 mountain peaks fixed. Indications of the movements of the Great Ice Barrier were found for the first time.

Of the many shorter journeys those of great endurance and exposure to cold were Lieutenant Royds' four trips to Cape Crozier, in the first instance to fix the record which told *Morning* of our position, and, secondly, to visit the known rookery of the Emperor penguins on the sea-ice off the Cape. On one occasion he was accompanied by Wilson, who found the first-known eggs of the Emperor (actually found by Blissett—a marine who was with the party), and on another occasion by Skelton, who obtained the first photographs of the rookery and the young chicks.

Royds' pioneer journeys to Cape Crozier, especially the one commencing in the first week of September, deserve to stand very high in the records of Antarctic Winter Sledging.

Meteorologically, it was the coldest month in Antarctica when the sun had hardly returned. The usual fierce blizzards blew, it was dark, and temperatures well below -60° F. were experienced.

A similar journey to Cape Crozier was made on Scott's second voyage to Antarctica, which is now known as "The Worst Journey in the World".

Of my own Barrier trip to the south-east with Royds, Scott writes: "It deserves to rank very high in our sledging efforts, for every detail was carried out in the most thoroughly efficient manner."

The party which set out early in November consisted of six—a naval officer, Royds; a scientist, myself; a naval Petty Officer, Jacob Cross; a marine corporal, Scott; a leading stoker, Plumley; and the ship's cook, Clarke, who had replaced our former unsatisfactory one. We were thus an heterogeneous lot. Starting off with a total load of 1037 lb. on two sledges, we therefore dragged 173 lb. apiece over the flat monotonous surface of the Great Ice Barrier, for thirty-one days, covering a total distance of 356 geographical miles. Dragging was fearfully heavy most of the time, the wind persistently strong and the temperature for a sea-level journey fairly low. The rather staccato entries in my diary tell a similar story day after day:

November 16th.—Turned out at 6 a.m., blowing hard from S.W. and temperature -9° F. during the night. Dragging very heavy due to new drift and fairly deep sastrugi running S.W. and N.E. The wind is very cold and unpleasant and the sky overcast, hence we are slipping in our steps because we are unable to see the irregularities. All land below the horizon and we have been unable to get sights to-day for position. Steering very difficult due to bad light.

November 17th.—Turned out at 6.30 a.m., blowing hard from S.W. with drifting snow. Under way at 8 a.m. Very unpleasant marching day after day in this cold strong wind. Have to wear ski boots instead of fur "finnesko" on account of slippery surface, hence feet get frozen. I took sights at apparent noon for latitude and sights for longtitude at 5.30 p.m. After supper I took a complete set of magnetic observations. These series of magnetic observations taken on a prolonged line will be very helpful in calculating the position of the South Magnetic Pole, as they are free from local attraction. Had a clear view of the horizon all around this afternoon, and there is absolutely nothing in sight but the same uniform comparatively level and smooth barrier.

December 3rd.—Same routine as before and same wretched weather. Feeling very hungry all day even immediately after our very scanty meals which consist as follows:

Breakfast—each 1 pannikin of pemmican, mixed and boiled with a few spoonfuls of red ration (ghastly unknown ingredient), oatmeal and pea soup and ¾ of a navy biscuit.

Lunch—1½ navy biscuits and a small piece of Dutch cheese, tea mixed with a few spoonfuls of plasmon and seven lumps of sugar.

Supper—1¼ pannikin of pemmican, boiled with a little seal meat and a few spoonfuls of oatmeal, ¾ of a navy biscuit and one pannikin of cocoa.

Suffering from a painful attack of snowblindness in my right eye, due, no doubt, to taking off my snow goggles. Faces and lips blistered and cracked by sun and wind. It is uncanny travelling day after day over this white plain with no land in sight. One is entirely dependent upon astronomical sights for position. In this respect similar to a ship on the open sea. At noon took sights for latitude which gave 78° 57½′ agreeing almost exactly with our assumed or dead reckoning. Taking sights with sextant and artificial mercurial horizon in this weather is miserable work. It is difficult to use mitts when handling the small tangent screws, and both fingers and feet get frostbitten. Also the instruments and the mercury get covered with drift.

*   *   *   *   *   *   *

And so the days continued full of monotony and heavy pulling—occasionally the wind dropped, the sun shone warmly, and sleeping-bags and wearing apparel could be put out to dry at lunch or in the evenings. But always we thought of food as the rations grew shorter and shorter on our return journey. "Food, food, food" is what one thinks about all the livelong day. Visions of all kinds of delicacies passed before one's mental vision—seal liver, roast beef, mutton, game, French rolls, fresh butter, jam—*ad infinitum*, in procession like the ghosts before Macbeth. A fairly good memory of luscious dishes of the past is not an ally. Sledging in such circumstances is a trying business. Just as the barrier was a desert, our brains, too, became dull. We lived in an imbecile world of our own. As Leading Stoker Quartley put it:

> The noontide or the nightfall knows
> The pitching of our tents.
> The flung down harness, the tired repose,
> The talk of the days events.
> We camp, we go, and care no jot
> How soon, how far we roam;
> But every camp has marked a spot
> That men have called a home.

But we were all persistently cheery. There were no grumblings. There is an Arab saying that during a journey a man's character is weighed and revealed and to complain of one's hardship, except to God, is a humiliation. You cannot bluff on an Antarctic sledge journey.

In sledging you are harnessed to a cycle of things—chiefly unpleasant—which there is no avoiding, starting with the struggle, amounting at times to a fight, with the erection of the tent, and its collapsing poles and flapping canvas; the unloading of frozen sleeping-bags and food-bags, with contents partly frozen into solid ice; the filling of the large aluminium cooker with pressed-in snow, when fingers stick to the cold metal with the risk of leaving a part of the skin behind. Handling tins, spoons and pannikins white patches soon appear on fingers. The crest on a spoon may be reproduced in pink and white. The tea-strainer leaves a fine network impression much admired. Then comes the refractory Primus, especially refractory at high altitudes. You pump it and prick the nozzle and coax and swear at it, but in 40 degrees below it seems never to boil. A ridiculous number of what are humorously called "thermal units" are required to convert snow into water. But these are mere preliminaries.

Crawling into the small tent through a small circular opening is an art in itself, when you feel like a competitor in a sack race. Inside, the three stiffly clad figures absorb all the floor space, but by that time the warm comforting pemmican "hoosh" awaits you-—and although it is not a dish you would select in an ordinary bill of fare, you even treat the paraffin in your food with Antarctic disdain.

After a comforting smoke comes the ordeal of changing footgear, and getting into thick bed socks. No other garments are removed. The sleeping-bags, frozen hard and pressed together, stubbornly resist entry. With the persistency of a human ramrod you at last succeed, but your garments do not permit much comfort. Then the shivering fits start, which persist for one or two hours, and with chattering teeth you busy yourself stuffing up nooks and corners about your person, whilst showers of tiny icicles from the tent roof pour down your neck. Sleep only comes in the early hours. In the morning the first concern is your footgear. You gaze sadly at your fur boots, soft and pliable when you took them off—now stony imitations of those articles— you ram *saennegras* into these petrified *finnesko*, push your feet with frozen socks laboriously into them, and hope the recording angel is conveniently deaf. Then to fix your cross-gartered Burberry leggings of stiff gaberdine, and tumble out of the tent looking like a rumpled Malvolio.

One of the nightmares of sledging in Antarctica is the daily hygienic ceremony. No books, apparently, make reference to this, perhaps from a sense of delicacy, or fear of committing a rudery. Yet friends—male friends—frequently inquire, "What did you do?" You tell them.

On turning out of the tent in the early morning, heavily clad, for it is usually blowing with varying intensity and a temperature below zero, you are haunted by a vague trouble which you realize must be faced. There are no facilities within the tiny tent; latrines are impossible. They take too long to build and in any case are useless since they fill in immediately with drifting snow. Temporary shelters are merely places for whirling drift, and so there remains the open snow spaces.

Feeling like a ham in a sack, you go through various preparatory antics of loosening garments—preferably within the tent, and prowl around some distance away facing always the biting wind, and watchfully awaiting a temporary lull. The rest is a matter of speed and dexterity, but invariably the nether garments are filled instantly with masses of surface-drifting snow, which you must take along with you and suffer the discomforts of extreme wetness for hours.

Degree of discomfort is in direct ratio to the quantity of drifting snow, which, in turn, is in direct ratio to the velocity of the wind. It is a ghastly business.

Low temperatures, painful though they be, are not serious, but there have been cases of quite unpleasant frostbite.

A little slapping exercises in the open air, filling of cooker again with snow, ferreting in the food-bags on the sledges, and breakfast. If there are dogs and the temperature is below -40° F., they probably have been whining piteously all night. You pull them to their feet shivering, with lowered heads and tails tucked in under their stomachs, and you think of the fine Arctic pictures you have seen of galloping quadrupeds with erect curly tails.

You struggle with the harness kinked and frozen, break free the sledges from the piled-up snow around them, and with a disconsolate—One—two—three, off you are once more.

Six

Release

WHEN *Discovery* left England, the idea of a Relief Expedition had not been considered. Polar relief expeditions have only too frequently resulted in more harm than good. Lives and money have been extravagantly squandered in spectacular efforts which might have been husbanded for useful work. The story of polar exploration of recent days is not without its contribution of unnecessary and even disastrous "relief" expeditions. *Discovery* was a powerful ship, fully equipped for a polar sojourn of, at least, two to three years. Our second winter, it is true, was wearisome, but never were we in any danger. In fact, knowledge gained by experience, particularly in relation to food, made us more fit when summer dawned in 1903 than we had been the previous year.

Nevertheless, although there could be no reason to suppose that *Discovery* was in distress, the authorities at home, who had dispatched so valuable an expedition on such a long voyage beyond the limits of communication, could not be blind to the dangers attached to a prolonged programme of exploration in the tempestuous ice-infested ocean of the Antarctic regions. Everything possible had been done to avert mischance as far as the ship was concerned, even to the extent of instructions to leave cylinders containing messages at agreed landmarks along the Antarctic coast—footsteps that could be traced at some future period, if necessity arose.

So it came about that soon after *Discovery* had departed, the burden of responsibility had been realized, and the necessity of safeguarding the expedition.

To raise the funds for what amounted to a second venture was no light task, but the President of the Royal Geographical Society, with his customary energy and pertinacity, at last accomplished it. Subscriptions came from the King, the Prince of Wales, from Longstaff again, the City Companies, the New Zealand Government, and many private individuals. At last about £22,500 were raised, and a small stout barque-rigged Norwegian whaler, with mild auxiliary steam power, was purchased—she was less than 300 tons, but facetiously known by those who sailed in her as the *Dreadnought*. Command was given to my old colleague Lieutenant William Colbeck, R.N.R., who had been already in the Antarctic regions and spent a winter with us at Cape Adare. He was chosen as the most fitting person to command this new supporting venture—a quiet, capable, bold, and most resourceful seaman. He selected some of his officers and most of his own men, with whom he was personally acquainted, amongst them, Captain Rupert England, R.N.R., who was first officer, and, some years later, was to sail with Shackleton as Captain of the *Nimrod*.

Three young junior officers were permitted to join— Evans and Mulock, sub-lieutenants in the Royal Navy, lent by the Admiralty, and Gerald Dorley, a sub-lieutenant in the Royal Naval Reserve. Evans and Dorley had been "pals" in the old merchant marine training ship *Worcester*. They were in the same term and competed in the same year for the two principal prizes, one, a cadetship into the Royal Navy, the other the Queen's Gold Medal, awarded annually to the boy who showed qualifications likely to make the finest sailor, decided by a ballot of the cadets. Evans won the cadetship—Dorley, the medal. Their names are printed in gold abreast each other on the coveted scroll on board. They were known in the *Morning* as the "Evanly twins". Much tidal water has passed under the old *Worcester* since then. Evans, the cadet, is now Vice-Admiral Sir Edward Evans, K.C.B., D.S.O., famous for his exploits during the Great War. Dorley, the medallist, is a Harbour Master of one of our great overseas Dominion ports.

They were a cheery, happy crowd, those lads of the *Morning*, able to write, in their leisure hours, Antarctic verses and put them to original music.

Mulock was a young hydrographer, who could plot and make exceedingly fine charts. He was transferred later to *Discovery*, and may be regarded as the pioneer of Antarctic cartography.

On board *Discovery* the idea of a supporting ship, for no clear reason, had steadily grown during the first winter, and many false alarms of "smoke to the North" were given in the summer, so when a ship actually did appear late in January, very little excitement or even surprise was evinced.

"JOY COMETH IN THE MORNING"

CHEERING THE APPROACH OF THE MORNING

RELIEF SHIPS APPROACHING DISCOVERY

The gallant little *Morning* reached the fast ice within ten miles of *Discovery* on 24th January, and brought us nothing but good news from home and some fresh stores and luxuries. "Joy cometh in the Morning", and "We bring you in the Morning bread to the full", said our cheery visitors. Small as she was, with little ability to force her way through heavy pack-ice, her voyage to find and reach us was full of difficulties only overcome by steady perseverance. A tiny volcanic island, 600 yards long, 250 yards wide, and 130 feet high, had been discovered on Christmas Day almost on the Antarctic Circle; a mountain peak in the middle of the wide ocean, with 1000 fathoms of water around it. The *Morning* had gone ashore on one of its hidden outlying rocks, and only the fact that she was a wooden ship and the coolness and prompt seamanship of her commander had saved her. The island was called Scott Island.

A record had been found at Cape Adare, and later at Cape Crozier, where it was learnt that the object of their search was somewhere in the mysterious depths of McMurdo Sound.

The *Morning* was able to remain with us until 2nd March, when, due to the lateness of the season, she was compelled to leave. She had reached to within a mile of *Discovery*, and at one time, when the ice was rapidly breaking up with a northerly swell, our release looked to be in sight, and bets were freely made. But the swell did not last and all was quiet again. And so we were faced with another long winter. A list was sent round for the names of those who desired to quit. This read: "Any man who does not care to face the possibility of another winter can submit his name and his case will be considered." There were eight names on the list.

Scott writes: "Of course, all the officers wish to remain, but here, with much reluctance, I have had to pick out the name of one, who, in my opinion, is not fitted to do so. It has been a great blow to poor Shackleton, but I have had to tell him that I think he must go, he ought not to risk further hardships in his present state of health. But we cannot afford to lose officers, and Colbeck has already kindly consented to replace Shackleton by his naval sub-lieutenant, Mulock, and the latter is most anxious to join us."

Thus it came about that Shackleton returned—in due time organized his own great expedition in the *Nimrod* notwithstanding the lack of official geographical support at home, subsequently took out his expeditions in the *Endurance* and the *Quest,* and ended up with a knighthood, international decorations, and gold medals from nearly every Geographical Society in the world. To-day, looking at that strong bronze statue by Jagger set in its niche in the outer wall of the Royal Geographical Society, it is difficult to avoid an amused smile at the irony of fate.

The expedition of the "relief ships" of the second year, after it was known that *Discovery* was tightly gripped in the ice behind Hut Point, can best be described as the "canker in the damask". In the words of Captain Scott, who, with Wilson, first sighted the two ships from their tent on Cape Royds, where they were having a "picnic" near the edge of the fast ice to study the habits of penguins and gulls: "Our tent door was open and framed the clear sea beyond, and I was gazing dreamily out upon this patch of blue when suddenly a ship entered my field of view. It was so unexpected that I almost rubbed my eyes, before I dared to report it, but a moment after, all became bustle, and we began to search round for our boots and other articles necessary for the march. Whilst we were thus employed, Wilson looked up and said, "Why, there's another," and sure enough there were now two vessels framed in our doorway. We had, of course, taken for granted that the first ship was the *Morning*, but what in the name of fortune could be the meaning of this second one?"

He was soon to learn. That night Scott was a very unhappy man. Although, in his official report of the previous year, he had made light of the position of the *Discovery* and the prospect of our detention for a second winter, a sort of panic, quite unjustified, seemed to have seized the authorities at home. The *Morning* was available and ready and capable of reaching us, as she had indeed proved, and very little extra money was required for this purpose. But Sir Clements Markham, who was now seventy-three years of age and had had some years of constant work and worry over the Antarctic Expedition, took a hasty view of the situation, and made a feverish appeal—perhaps truculently—to the Government to come to the rescue with funds. The reaction of the Prime Minister and First Lord of the Treasury (Mr. A. J. Balfour) is told in *Hansard.* His reply to questions in the House was as follows:

HUT POINT AND A FINAL EXPLOSION

DISCOVERY FREE AT LAST

EREBUS IN ERUPTION

This photograph was taken in moonlight with an exposure of ten minutes

The Government are prepared to contribute to the relief of the officers and men on board the *Discovery* which is now ice-bound in the Antarctic seas. The course taken by the two learned Societies responsible for the expedition in respect to the contribution of money (Government had already contributed £45,000) and men made by the Government is greatly to be regretted. I have always leaned towards the principle of extending the very limited aid which the British Government have been accustomed to give towards the furtherance of purely scientific research. But such action can only be justified so long as the Government are able to feel absolute confidence that the scientific bodies approaching them have placed before them all the information in their possession as to the estimated cost of their proposed action, and the limits within which they intend to confine it. That confidence has been rudely shaken by the present case.

Balfour's reply was a little unjust. The Balfour *cum* Markham *cum* Royal Society broil, as will be seen, was to have its repercussions— chiefly on the heads of those who had done such splendid work in the Antarctic. The Royal Society, one of the "learned societies" referred to by Balfour and which, no doubt, had been little consulted by Markham, indignant at being involved in the scene, withdrew within itself, and Scott, on our return, was left alone to fight any battle that might arise on behalf of his people.

Balfour sent an ultimatum to the Royal Geographical Society demanding the instant handing over of the whole expedition, and in turn handed over the "relief" to the Admiralty. It proved a most wasteful business, just as Government relief expeditions had been in the past. The Admiralty from the word "go" did things with its usual thoroughness, efficiency and speed. The finest Dundee whaler afloat—the *Terra Nova*—was purchased, refitted, provisioned, and a whaling captain and crew engaged to navigate her, and then towed out by relays of warships through the Mediterranean, the Suez Canal and the Indian Ocean. Never in history had a wooden whaler moved so swiftly. What a "to-do" about a handful of men and a small ship, known to be comfortably and safely ensconced in McMurdo Sound! At Hobart, in Tasmania, *Terra Nova* was joined by the *Morning*, and Captain Colbeck took over command of both.

Hence it came about that on that gloriously fine Antarctic morning Captain Scott and Wilson saw two ships where only one was expected, carrying peremptory orders for him to abandon *Discovery* in the ice after the end of February. Happily, this ordeal did not occur, for on 16th February "*Discovery* came to her own again—the right to ride the high seas", and we were able to bring our good ship home— through the long stretch of ocean towards Tierra del Fuego, where we were able to complete our magnetic survey, which was thus carried out around the greater part of the circumference of the Antarctic area. Other tasks of importance, too, were accomplished; such as soundings which showed fairly uniform depths of about 2000 fathoms, with a maximum of nearly 3000 fathoms. An island called Dogherty Island on the charts had been reported on two occasions previously, approximately in Lat. 59° S., Long. 120° W., but we sailed over the spot in clear weather in 2318 fathoms of water. We passed through the beautiful Magellan Strait, also in glorious fine weather, spent three days at Port Stanley in the Falkland Islands, where food and coal were replenished and the last series of our magnetic observations taken, and then, rather wearily, but slowly and surely, we sailed north and homewards across the Atlantic, arriving in the Channel on the 9th September, 1904, where "all Nature was smiling to welcome us", Scott writes.

They were golden days, and their memories are fraught with joy.

*   *   *   *   *   *   *

The expedition had returned after more than three years' absence, with the richest results geographical and scientific ever brought from high southern latitudes. A vast new land (King Edward VII Land) had been discovered. Many hundreds of miles of unknown coast, with ranges of mountains of great height and immense glaciers emptying into the Ice Barrier, had been seen and plotted. The Antarctic Plateau, averaging nearly 10,000 feet in height, had been found and partly transversed where, subsequently, the South Pole itself was found to be situated, proving that the Antarctic Continent was almost all under ice without vegetation or animal life of any kind.

Never had a polar expedition come home with so great a harvest of original research work, nor have such original results been surpassed by subsequent polar expeditions, carrying, in some cases, duplication of scientists in speciality branches.

The specialists of *Discovery* were lone-handed and were confronted with many unknown difficult problems. Hodgson always must be regarded as the pioneer of Antarctic marine biology. His work was prolific. Ferrar is the pioneer of Antarctic geology. The extensive physical work, part of an international programme, for which I was responsible, was one of the principal objects of the expedition. It was completed. In due time the scientific work was reduced, discussed and published in many large volumes by the Royal Society. No funds, however, were available to employ the scientists who for over three years had carried out the observations in the field, and this comprehensive and important work had to be undertaken chiefly by scientists in Government departments.

A polar medal was struck and awarded to all alike who had returned in *Discovery*. Captain Scott was made a Commander of the Victoria Order (C.V.O.) (a personal honour from the King), and awarded a special gold medal by the Royal Geographical Society, of which officers and crew received silver replicas. Like Llewellyn Longstaff, who had contributed in all £30,000 to make the great expedition possible, *Discovery's* scientists received an expression of thanks from the Learned Societies and a niche in polar history.

THE SHIP'S COMPANY

OFFICERS

ROBERT FALCON SCOTT, C.V.O., Captain, R.N.
Albert B. Armitage, Lieut., R.N.R.
Charles W. R. Royds, Lieut., R.N.
Michael Barne, Lieut., RN.
Ernest H. Shackleton, Sub-Lieut., R.N.R.
George F. A. Mulock, Sub-Lieut., R.N.
Reginald W. Skelton, Lieut. (E.), R.N.
Edward A. Wilson, Surgeon, artist, vertebrate zoologist.
Reginald Koettlitz, Surgeon and botanist.
Louis C. Bernacchi, Physicist.
Thomas V. Hodgson, Biologist.
Hartley T. Ferrar, Geologist.

WARRANT OFFICERS (All R.N.)

Thomas A. Feather, Boatswain.
James H. Dellbridge, 2nd Engineer.
Fred E. Dailey, Carpenter.
Charles R. Ford, Ship's Steward.

PETTY OFFICERS (All R.N.)

Jacob Cross, P.O.1.
Edgar Evans, P.O.2.
William Smythe, P.O.1.
David Allan, P.O.1.
Thomas Kennar, P.O.2.

MARINES

Gilbert Scott, Private, R.M.L.I.
A.H. Blissett, Private, R.M.L.I.

CIVILIAN

Charles Clarke, Ship's Cook.

SEAMEN

Frank Wild, A.B., R.N.
George B. Croucher, A.B., R.N.
Thomas S. Williamson, A.B., R.N.
Thomas Crean, A.B., R.N.
James Dell, A.B., R.N.
Arthur Pilbeam, L.S., R.N.
Ernest E. Joyce, A.B., R.N.
Jesse Handsley, A.B., R.N.
William L. Heald, A.B., R.N.
William J. Weller, A.B.

STOKERS

William Lashly, Ldg. Stoker, R.N.
Arthur L. Quartley, Ldg. Stoker, R.N.
Thomas Whitfield, Ldg. Stoker, R.N.
Frank Plumley, Stoker, R.N.

In addition to the above who returned in the *Discovery* there were three naval seamen, viz. Bonner, Vince and Macfarlane. Bonner was accidentally killed on leaving Port Chalmers by falling from aloft. Vince was lost in the blizzard near Winter Quarters, and Macfarlane, who had suffered severely from scurvy, returned voluntarily. Hare, who acted as a ward room steward, was a young civilian from New Zealand who volunteered for one year only and had to return. Buckridge, Walker, Duncan, Hubert, Page, and Peters were merchant seamen employed in various capacities on board. In addition there was a cook. All returned to New Zealand in the *Morning* after the first year.

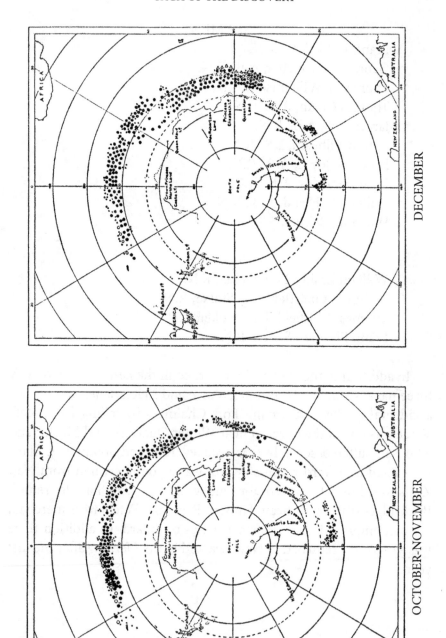

Seasonal Distribution of Antartic Whales

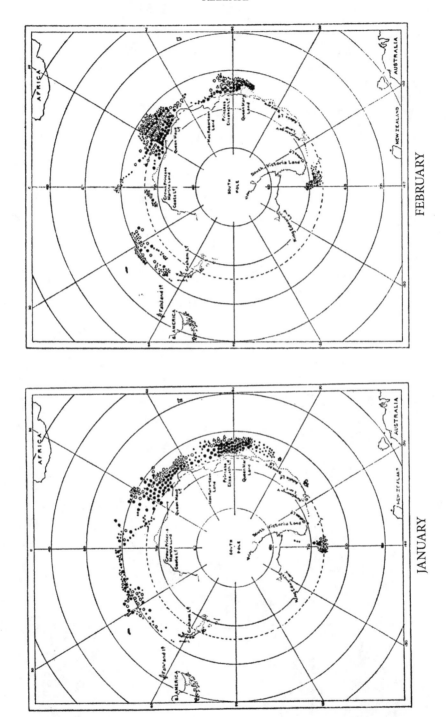

Dark spots indicate Blue Whales. Light Spots indicate Finner Whales.

Seven

Cetacean Research

DISCOVERY'S first great voyage of exploration was ended. The sturdy little ship which had survived so many perils was soon forgotten. For some months she lay neglected in the docks, and then, as so many brave explorers before and since have done, she went into trade. In 1905 the Hudson's Bay Company acquired her, and in June she sailed from West India Dock laden with supplies for Charlton Depôt, in James Bay—somewhere in the region where Henry Hudson had been set adrift from that first *Discovery* nearly three hundred years before. In dull routine voyages from London to Hudson's Bay carrying supplies, and back to London loaded with furs, she continued for six years. Then once more she went into dock, and all through 1912, 1913, and the spring of 1914 she mouldered, all but forgotten until an assassination at Sarajevo sent the world to war.

Ships of every kind were needed in ever increasing numbers, and *Discovery*, late in 1915, made a voyage to the White Sea carrying munitions for Russia and returning with alcohol for the manufacture of gunpowder. Chartered to the French Ministry of Commerce, she served until 1916, when she was returned to the Hudson's Bay Company, which placed her at the disposal of the Admiralty to carry out the rescue of the members of Sir Ernest Shackleton's *Endurance* crew, stranded on Elephant Island after their ship had been crushed in the ice. That was work for which she was preeminently fitted, and in August, 1916, she sailed for Port Stanley in the Falkland Islands—only to find when she arrived there that her services were not required, as Shackleton's untiring energy had already effected the rescue of his men. *Discovery* returned from Montevideo with a cargo of grain to France, and post-war shortage of ships kept her on coastal service there for transporting grain from incoming steamers to the smaller ports of France till 1920, when once more she was docked. In 1923 the Crown Agents for the Colonies purchased her "for the purposes of scientific research in the South Seas".

As far back as 1773 when Captain Cook's *Resolution* penetrated into Antarctic waters, one of Cook's staff had written: "If the Northern ocean should ever be cleared of whales by our annual fisheries, we might then visit the other hemisphere where these animals are known to be numerous. However, there seems to be little necessity to advance so far as New Georgia in quest of them, since the Portuguese and North Americans have of late years killed numbers of them on the coast of America, going no farther than the Falkland Islands. It should, therefore, seem probable that though Southern Georgia may hereafter become important to mankind, that period is at present far remote and perhaps will not happen till Patagonia and Tierra del Fuego are inhabited and civilized like Scotland and Sweden."

A century had scarcely passed before the improbable state of affairs envisaged by the paragraph above was approaching realization, and when Sir James Ross reported sighting numbers of whales in the Antarctic seas the northern whale fisheries which had flourished since 1600 were already showing signs of depletion. Whalers lost no time in visiting the far southern seas, but although the first adventurers found nothing to justify their effort, the Norwegians, true to Viking tradition, knew no discouragement and persisted in their search until they discovered the great whale pasturage in the neighbourhood of South Georgia and the South Shetlands. In 1904 the first whaling station was established in South Georgia, and the following season that innovation in the industry, a floating factory, visited the South Shetland area. So successful were these enterprises that in 1911 there were eight companies working in South Georgia and twelve floating factories in the South Shetlands. The outbreak of war in 1914 gave the trade new significance, and the colossal proportions of the market for whale oil as a source of glycerine for munitions encouraged slaughter on a scale heretofore undreamed.

With its migration to new hunting areas so far afield, the industry had been compelled to evolve new hunting technique. The commercial Antarctic whales—the Humpback, Rorqual and the Blue whale— were much too active to be captured by the old open-boat methods. Moreover, they were most vulnerable on the borders of the pack-ice which held up their southerly journey in search of food, and ships able to navigate the stormy seas which sailors had named the "Roaring

Forties", and capable of manœuvring among the ice-floes, were too large and too noisy to approach near enough to take their victims. Necessity bred invention, and the new whale-catcher evolved, a small steamship of 100 tons or more, working either from a land station or a floating factory, quick enough to follow the whale, yet not so noisy as to frighten it unduly. By skilful manipulation and long experience the skipper was able to manœuvre close enough to use the new harpoon gun, fired from the bow of the ship.

But there was another problem to solve. The southern whale, attaining sometimes a length of 100 feet and weighing roughly 100 tons, was too powerful and tenacious of life to be captured by a mere harpoon. The bomb-harpoon resulted. The gun was fired just as the whale came up to breathe, and, if well directed, struck somewhere in the vast body momentarily exposed, fixing itself in the vital organs where the bomb exploded. Seldom was so direct a hit scored as to result in immediate death, but never was the inevitable end long delayed. The giant of the seas was soon exhausted from loss of blood. The line to which the harpoon was attached was then hauled in, the carcass pumped full of air to keep it afloat, a flag fixed in it so that it could be more easily located, and the catcher went in search of another victim. Towards the end of the day the carcasses were collected and towed to the factory ship or land station, according to circumstances.

The results render almost ludicrous the ideas of extensive slaughter prevalent at the end of the nineteenth century, when I wrote in my account of the *Southern Cross* expedition:

"It is stated that in 1843 the whale fishers of New Zealand alone employed 85 boats and 750 men, and the oil taken amounted to tons . . . after this period the decline in the take became rapid." By 1911 the factory ships in the neighbourhood of the South Shetlands alone were averaging some 400 barrels of oil per day, or something like 2000 tons a month. And in the season of 1915-6 the record number of 11,792 whales were captured, yielding a vast fortune of over £8,000,000.

Even when the war ended the wholesale massacre continued. The possibility of extinction of the species became a matter of international concern. Regulations looking to some sort of protection clearly were necessary, but in order to prove effective must be based upon exact knowledge of the habits of the whale. An International Council for the Exploration of the Sea was already in existence, having among its objects a study of the laws governing the supply of whales. But nothing constructive had been done up to 1911, when Dr. William S. Bruce, the leader of the Scottish National Antarctic ("Scotia") Expedition, reported that "a most profitable scientific investigation would be a cetacean expedition which devoted its whole time with two or three ships to the study of these Antarctic whales, and indeed to the study of whales all over the world." By 1923 the time had come when Bruce's suggestion was to be given effect.

By a strange trick of fate, although Norway led the world in whaling enterprise, it was Britain which owned the world's most prolific whale-producing areas. The Falkland Islands Dependencies, the most southerly colony in the Empire, extended south to the Antarctic continent itself, embracing the barren, storm-swept islands of South Georgia, the South Shetlands and the South Orkneys. The rugged, rocky Falklands, once of value for the true fur seal, and as a naval base and a coaling station, discovered first in 1592, forgotten and from time to time rediscovered by the explorers of the nations, claimed in turn by England, Holland, France, Spain and Argentina, almost at one time in their history the cause of war between England and Spain, had become a self-supporting colony, its revenues largely derived from Antarctic whales.

The British Government, as far as was in its power, had undertaken to restrict the whale fisheries within its territory with a view to cetacean preservation. But factory ships had rendered futile most of the regulations. It was possible to exercise some measure of supervision within the three-mile limit of the scattered islands of the southern colony, but outside territorial waters the factory ships might proceed without let or hindrance. The Norwegians, theoretically, were not opposed to preservation of the goose which laid such golden eggs. But whaling was a commercial proposition. The £ s. d. of necessity governed the situation. The crews of whalers received only the smallest wage, counting on a bonus from the catch to pay them for their efforts. It was inevitable that wasteful slaughter should result. A whale of 100 feet length gave twice as much oil as a whale of 80 feet, which in turn produced twice as much as a whale of 60 feet. But a 50-foot whale was better than no whale at all. Females pregnant with young and immature males were being captured on a scale that spelt ultimate extinction. If the industry proceeded on the basis on which for years it had been operating, the repetition of the disaster of depletion already experienced in the Arctic would not be long delayed.

It was in 1917, the year of the great catch of nearly 12,000 whales, that the Secretary of State for the Colonies constituted an Inter-departmental Committee to advise him on research and development in the Dependencies of the Falkland Islands— "To consider what can now be done to facilitate prompt action at the conclusion of the war in regard to the preservation of the whaling industry and to the development of other industries in the Dependencies of the Falkland Islands; and to consider not only the economic questions above referred to and the scheme for the employment of a research vessel, but also what purely scientific investigations are most required in connexion with these regions, and whether any preliminary inquiries by experts in this country should be instituted."

In due course, the Inter-departmental Committee reported, and the old *Discovery* was bought to be reconditioned and equipped for the scientific work in view. Although it had been decided that it would be more economical at that time to acquire *Discovery* than to build a new ship, yet even the task of reconditioning proved a lengthy and expensive work, and it was not until 1925 that she was ready for her new employment. The battering she had experienced in the Antarctic ice had badly strained her. The lack of air courses had caused deterioration of her inner timbers. These defects must be made good. New masts, spars, sails and rigging were also necessary, and although the machinery generally was in excellent repair her main boilers had suffered considerably from corrosion.

Apart from replacement and repair there were also alterations to be made. Remembering her slow progress under sail, the fore and main masts were moved forward, and an increase was made in her sail areas, and to facilitate handling the sails, upper and lower topgallant sails were fitted in place of the single topgallant of the original construction. Wireless equipment was installed, a new biological laboratory built on deck, and winches and machinery necessary to deal with deep-sea investigations. A ten-ton evaporator and fresh-water distiller and an electric generating plant contributed to general modernization, as well as a large refrigerator—undreamed of in the days of her service with Captain Scott.

Dr. S. W. Kemp, as Director of Research, was in command of the expedition with three qualified zoologists and an hydrologist under him. Commander J. R. Stenhouse, D.S.O., D.S.C., R.N.R., who had had experience in Antarctic waters under Shackleton, was the Captain of the ship with six officers under his direct control.

On 5th October, 1925, *Discovery* sailed south from Falmouth, calling at the Canary Islands and Ascension en route for Cape Town, the first lap of her journey, and testing her gear in tropical waters as she proceeded. Tow-nets and buckets came up from depths of 2000 to 3000 metres filled with fantastically shaped tropical fish, scarlet crustacea and deep-sea medusæ patterned in reds and blues like Turkey carpet. Phosphorescent jelly-fish in which hundreds of tiny individual animals were embedded, each glowing with a bright blue-green light, swarmed like incandescent gas-mantles in countless millions in the warm tropic seas, or were replaced by wide areas of an even stranger animal which gave off its light in instantaneous flashes, so that she seemed to steam through a sea filled with submarine rockets, bursting in thousands just below the surface. Her new work already bade fair to surpass in biological interest even her early explorations.

But these phenomena were only by the way, and after a stay at Cape Town she sailed again on 17th January, calling at the lonely island of Tristan da Cunha to leave its isolated inhabitants one of their periodic supplies of stores and mail, and thence onward to South Georgia. Her first Antarctic iceberg in more than twenty years was sighted on 16th February, lonely and serene, sailing northward to its doom, and four days later the snow-clad peaks of South Georgia rose above the blue waters of the sunlit sea. Dropping anchor in Cumberland Bay, the grim settlement of Grytviken built around its malodorous whale-reducing factory lay on her right, and on her left the tiny wooden houses of the British settlement were grouped closely on King Edward's Point. Before her rose Mount Paget, towering 9000 feet above the shore.

It was on the opposite shore of Cumberland Bay that Norwegians, years ago, had landed some reindeer, and there they have flourished

A WIDE-ANGLE INTERIOR VIEW OF UPPER LABORATORY, LOOKING TO STARBOARD

FLENSED BLUE WHALE ON DECK OF A FACTORY SHIP

and increased so amazingly that annual shoots are organized from Falkland to prevent overpopulation.

Winter was already closing in. The snows had crept down from the barren mountain sides to meet the stormy sea. The Marine Biological Station was a tiny spot on the white landscape. The lonely grave of Sir Ernest Shackleton, marking the scene of the culmination of his greatest effort, was blanketed in spotless white. That great explorer had been buried in a fitting mausoleum. It was on the rocky South Georgia shore that Shackleton had landed with his small picked crew, after their 800-mile voyage in an open boat, to get help for his *Endurance* party stranded on Elephant Island. Shackleton had landed on the western shore, only fifteen miles away if one disregards the perpendicular distance, and had climbed over the rugged snow-clad mountains and down again to Grytviken. When in his little *Quest* he returned to the Antarctic in 1921 to die, the rocky land set in the stormy sea again received him.

The shore scientists who had been sent out by the Discovery Committee were established at King Edward's point and were already well through their second season's work, which consisted in examining the whales brought in to the Grytviken factory, in order to gather data which would assist in reconstructing the life-cycle of the giant of the seas. Each whale was measured, and when it had been flensed and the blubber removed to the oil-reducing boilers, and dismemberment of its body for the fertilizer plants began, its organs were examined. Day after day, month after month, the huge carcasses passed in hundreds under the eyes of the marine biologists, who pieced together the information gathered to make up the life story of the whale. The age of maturity could now be judged, the season of mating, the period of gestation and the time of parturition, all questions of incalculable importance to the problem of preservation of the species. And the conclusion that reproduction occurs probably only once in two years, that pregnancy lasts somewhere near a year, and that only very seldom is more than one young whale produced at birth, all indicated the slow replacement taking place in the Antarctic herds and the necessity for regulation of their slaughter.

A systematic exploration of all the economic resources of the Falkland Island Dependencies was the ultimate aim of the Discovery

Committee, but the primary investigations were to be directed to the whale, with a secondary and closely related work—the execution of coastal surveys in the dangerous and largely uncharted seas in which the industry flourished. Many aspects of the biological problem were being dealt with ably by the land scientists. But the effective study of the whale extended to the food of the whale and the food of the food of the whale, which in turn involved investigation of ocean currents and deep-sea conditions that might affect the cetacean food supply, and, therefore, the annual migration. That was *Discovery's* task.

One of the few facts about whales which was definitely established was their habit of migration, but where their wanderings led them was a closed book. During the southern winter they were almost entirely absent from the sub Antarctic whaling grounds. Where did they go? If the Antarctic whale was a distinct species, migrating only within the limits of the Antarctic seas, then in order to protect it the industry need be regulated only in those high latitudes. If, on the other hand, it migrated to tropical and sub-tropical waters then the same groups were hunted all the year round, and diminution in the temperate seas spelt diminution in the farthest south.

It was more or less definitely known that one species at least found in the Antarctic seas—the Humpback whale—did travel northward to the temperate seas along the coast of Africa in the Antarctic autumn, returning southward in the following spring. There was good reason to believe that the Humpback paired and bore its young during its sojourn in the north, and such information as was available seemed to suggest that the Fin whale and the giant Blue whale also had similar habits. It was most essential to establish definitely whether this was indeed a fact.

In tracing the migration of fish the method most generally adopted is that of marking. Fish are caught, suitable marks with a reference number attached to them, and they are then liberated. A proportion of these marked fish are recaptured in the course of commercial operations, and the offer of a reward increases the chance that the mark, together with the necessary data, will be returned to the fishery authority. For obvious reasons this is a difficult method to apply to whales. A system had been evolved of shooting metal markers, somewhat like a drawing-pin, with a barbed point, but this work was done by the other ship, an auxiliary whale-catcher type sent out by the Discovery Committee, the *William Scoresby*. *Discovery's* efforts were confined to other phases of the problem.

An intensive survey of the waters in the neighbourhood of South Georgia was planned, which it was hoped to repeat annually, and in which observations should be taken on plankton and hydrology. In the study of the plankton, the minute floating life of the sea, vertical and horizontal tow-nets worked on a scheme to give comparable results would be employed, while for the hydrological work "water-bottles" would be dropped, designed to supply the fullest information regarding temperature, salinity, hydrogen-ion concentration and phosphate and oxygen content of the sea. And since even such intensive surveys could not yield all the necessary information, a study of the mass-movements of the surrounding ocean was also planned, with a view to ascertaining alterations in the direction of currents and intensity of movement, since this would in turn involve alterations in the physical and biological environment of any small area situated in their path. Little hydrographic work had been done in those Antarctic seas. Of the known harbours few had been surveyed, the position of many of the islands was doubtful, and those which were charted were often shown as much as twenty miles from their actual position, a factor which might spell disaster to whale-catchers caught in sudden storms, and whose only safety would be in some protected harbour.

The South Georgia whaling grounds comprised only a small part of the Falkland Island sector, which extended from Grahamland to Cape Horn, and when one considers the weather conditions likely to be encountered in these regions it is evident that *Discovery's* construction was not in every way ideal for the work in hand. Since it was necessary, because of the "tumble home" of the ship's side, to operate nets and trawls from outboard platforms, the hazardous adventure on which *Discovery's* scientific staff was engaged is evident. Only the "water bottles" could be worked in safety as they were sent down from the forecastle head.

Before explaining the details of *Discovery's* work, some idea should be given of the nature of the creatures with which she was concerned. The whale is the largest animal in the world, probably the largest animal which ever has existed in the world, and although its habitat is the ocean, the whale is a mammal and not a giant fish. It is a unique creation. It is warm-blooded, as are land animals—the fish is cold-blooded. It breathes air, as do land animals— the fish does not. And it is this characteristic which renders it peculiarly helpless when the hunter is on its track—it must come up for air at regular intervals. It reproduces in the same manner as land animals, giving birth to its fully developed young, suckling them and caring for them until they can care for themselves. In the case of fish the female lays its eggs, which are later fertilized by the male, and the outcome is left to fate. The whale is thus in yet one more respect rendered vulnerable, for the mother whale will not desert her young, and at one time it was the practice of whale hunters to kill the slow and inexperienced baby whale, knowing that the mother, in the throes of cetacean grief, would then be captured more readily.

Whales of different species attain in maturity different sizes; the largest type and that most eagerly hunted because it carries the most blubber and consequently produces the most oil and is, therefore, the most lucrative, is the Blue whale, which sometimes grows to a length of about 100 feet, with corresponding bulk. The scientists at the Marine Biological Station at King Edward's Point occasionally measured even larger whales on the flensing planes at Grytviken. The young of the Blue whale, at birth, are about twenty feet in length. The Fin whale is next in size and importance for commercial purposes. But there are several other species, including the Humpback, also commercially hunted, and on down the scale in size to, perhaps, the smallest, but also the most vicious, the Killer whale—*Orcinus Orca*.

This beast, more commonly called the Orca Gladiator, averages only about twenty feet in length, but it is the terror of the seas. To offset its disadvantage in size it hunts in packs of anything from three or four to from fifty to one hundred. Unlike the larger whales which are hunted for their blubber, and which are toothless, its powerful jaws are fitted with rows of three-inch teeth, and, although it feeds chiefly on seals and penguins, it will attack man. Its greatest delicacy is the tongue of the baleen, or toothless whale. In order to indulge in this epicurean feast, the Killer resorts to carefully planned attack on monsters ten times its size. A group of Killers will hurl themselves upon a huge Blue whale, like thugs attacking an unwary pedestrian.

Two Killers will seize either side of the hapless Blue whale's lower jaw, hanging to it by the aid of their cruel teeth, while their bodies beat it like flails. Other members of the pack then hurl themselves upon its back again and again until it becomes exhausted, and when that occurs the whole gang of Killers turns attention to the great toothless mouth, and forcing it wide open, they callously eat out the living tongue, leaving the giant to die a slow and painful death.

Not content with what he finds in the sea, the Killer attacks also the dwellers on the ice-floe. His steel-jawed head rises through the pack leads, six or eight feet above the ice. His cruel eye takes in the scene. And if he finds a likely victim, he hurls himself from below against the ice. The whole vicious crew joins, the ice is shattered, and the object of the attack precipitated into the sea. Mr. Ponting, the photographer with Captain Scott's second Antarctic Expedition, had a narrow escape from death through ignorance of the Killer's methods of attack. A pack of six or eight Killer whales had been skirting the ice on which two sledge dogs were tethered. Their beautifully marked black and cream bodies, perfectly streamlined, shot up again and again above the surface of the sea, as they planned their attack. Ponting thought it a good opportunity to obtain a photograph, and seizing his camera ran to the edge of the floe. The Killers suddenly disappeared and the next moment the whole floe under him heaved and split into fragments, as one after another the brutes rose under it, striking it with their backs. Fortunately for Ponting he was able to keep his feet and scramble from the broken floes to safety, and fortunately too for the dogs the ice broke around them. One by one the hideous heads of the astonished would-be assassins shot above the surface to see what had robbed them of their expected feast, but before they could repeat the manœuvre both Ponting and the dogs were out of reach.

The commercial whale, unlike the Killer, is not a beast of prey— else probably there would be no other ocean life, for what could stand against it? One of these monsters followed Sir Douglas Mawson's *Aurora* for several hours, and since *Aurora* was only 160 feet in length, with a register of 380 tons, Mawson wondered what would happen if the giant were to charge. But the larger the whale the smaller its food, and indeed it appears that during the mating and breeding season in the temperate regions it does not eat at all, feeding only during the

Antarctic summer, and fasting until its next season in the southern seas. It is an astounding fact that the largest species of whale feed almost exclusively on a shrimp-like creature, *Euphausia superba*, only about three inches in length from the tip of its feelers to the tip of its tail—the Norwegians call this deep-sea shrimp *Krill*, and since the whale fisheries are preponderantly Norwegian, krill it has become in common parlance. It is obvious that only immeasurable quantities of krill can make up to the browsing leviathan for its comparatively minute size, and it is only in the cold Antarctic waters that these quantities are found. Hence the annual influx of whales to the very edges of the pack-ice—farther they can not go as only in open water can they come up to breathe.

The preponderance of krill on the east coast of South Georgia appears therefore to account for the richness of that area as a whaling ground. In these vast cold pastures of the sea the toothless whales, whose upper jaws are furnished with rows of jagged whalebone, dripping like stalactites from a cavern roof, swim open-mouthed to collect their tiny victims, breathing by means of a specially designed wind-pipe and air passages into the lungs. The mouth is eventually closed, the strange tongue inflated to force out the water, and the food remains, entangled in the whalebone of the upper jaw.

But the krill, too, must have its food, and although it swims and therefore is not completely subject to the ocean currents, the diatoms on which it lives are minute floating unicellular plants, swept hither and thither as the ocean follows its own laws. The krill must follow the diatom and the whale the krill.

> Big floes have little floes all around about 'em,
> And all the yellow diatoms couldn't do withoute 'em:
> Forty million shrimplets feed upon the latter,
> And *they* make the penguins, seals and whales much fatter!

It is evident that in order to elucidate the conditions affecting the recurrence of whales it is necessary to examine also adjacent seas where they are seldom found. Thus a detailed survey of the waters around South Georgia showed that the island lies in the path of currents of some complexity originating in the Weddell and Bellingshausen seas,

DISCOVERY IN PORT LOCKROY, PALMER ARCHIPELAGO

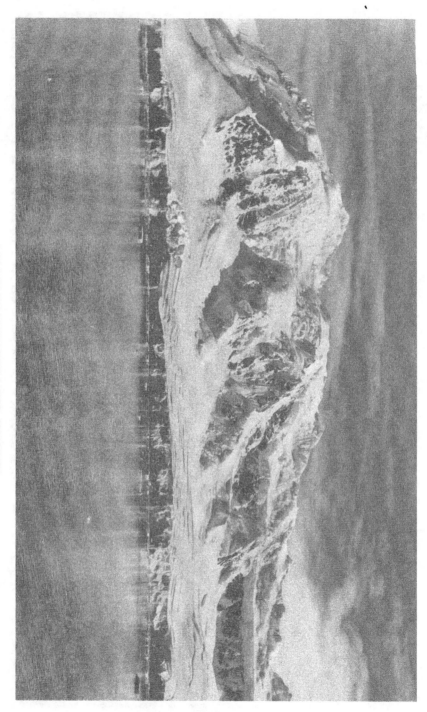

MT. WILLIAM IN NEUMAYER CHANNEL

and giving rise to conditions favourable to a rich growth of diatoms and krill, especially to the north-east and east of the island. It is here that the whales are found. So *Discovery's* discoveries proceeded.

On 17th April she sailed northward from South Georgia to the Falkland Islands, for winter had already come. But as she journeyed north she made a line of "stations"—a station being a pause of the ship, usually for something like three hours, while complete sets of observations are taken. Deep-water bottles went down from the forecastle head. From the outboard platform nets were dropped, nets of graded mesh and varying size, from 75 centimetres in diameter, with 200 meshes to the inch, to nets of 4½ metres in diameter of mouth, and in shallow waters huge otter trawl nets of 40 feet. Vertically, horizontally or obliquely the hauls were taken and the speed of the ship regulated to keep the cables taut — vertically when the ship was stopped, horizontally and obliquely with the ship steaming at only about two knots, for if she steamed too fast the nets fished too near the surface. Sometimes nets and bottles became entangled and long weary hours of labour in the biting cold were necessary to free them. And then the whole task must be commenced again from the beginning. Apparatus was attached for closing the nets at any desired position, so that whatever they contained could with assurance be ascribed to the depth at which they had been fishing. And so the hidden ocean life gradually became known.

Only from the contents of nets or trawls or water sampling bottles can an attempt be made to piece together the geography of the sea— to say here lies a great plankton "jungle", there a barren area, here a comparatively warm spot, there a cold zone that retains the effect of contact with the polar ice. And always it must be borne in mind that these characteristics are not definitely fixed, as is a forest area or a desert on land, but are moved by ocean currents and increased or diminished in size and density from time to time by climatic conditions. It is, therefore, impossible at first to do more than sketch out roughly the probable limits of various zones, and endeavour by repetition of investigations over many years, in all states of weather, to acquire sufficient data to say with assurance that, in such and such conditions at such and such a depth in such and such an area, such will be the state of ocean life.

The Falkland Islands were reached in due course. In the land-locked harbour of Port Stanley a halt was made, and after a series of stations around the islands and some trawling and dredging, *Discovery* returned to Cape Town and went into dry-dock, where special sister keels were fitted in an endeavour to temper her rolling proclivities. For that feature of the old ship, which in Scott's expedition had been no more than an unpleasant inconvenience, was a great handicap in the work in which she now was engaged. Considerable improvement resulted, and in the autumn of 1926 she steamed once more from civilization, this time directly southward, to investigate the waters in the neighbourhood of Bouvet Island and the shores of the Antarctic continent itself. Weather, shortage of coal and ill conditions prevented her reaching the mainland, and from Bouvet Island she continued westward through fog and myriad icebergs, reaching Grytviken once again on 5th December.

The summer lay ahead, and observations started immediately, *Discovery* and *William Scoresby* working night and day, in close wireless communication. Only a rough analysis of the "take" was possible, both because of the time factor and because the rolling of the ship, not yet overcome, made elaborate examination impossible. But the deck laboratory became the busiest place on board as fixation and preservation of specimens was carried out, the smaller organisms being stored in tubes and bottles, the larger in stoneware jars and steel and cast-iron tanks, and then labelled with information as to the station number, the data, the depth of the net, and type of net.

In February both ships left South Georgia, *William Scoresby* for another trawling survey of the Falkland Islands and *Discovery* for the farther south—the South Orkneys, South Shetlands and Palmer Archipelago, and the pack-ice once more. Passing Elephant Island where the *Endurance* party had been marooned, she made Whalers Harbour on Deception Island, a harbour unique in the world. It is the crater of a sunken extinct volcano into which the sea has poured, but a volcano not so completely extinct that the adjacent land has cooled. Surrounded by gale-driven icebergs, with a background of snow-covered mountain slopes, the hot beach steams, the still sea boils along the shore, and sulphur fumes are almost overpowering.

But *Discovery's* most difficult work of the season was still in store.

She was to run a line of stations across Drake's Strait, as the expanse of sea between the South Shetlands and Cape Horn is called. Over 400 miles in width, it is hardly a strait in the accepted understanding of the word, but it is the narrowest channel between two great oceans, and the line of stations was valuable because the currents flowing through from west to east have a profound influence on the whaling grounds of the Falkland Island Dependencies. The area is notoriously tempestuous, but *Discovery* was fortunate in finding exceptionally fine weather interrupted by only one storm. She completed a set of six full vertical stations from the ocean bed to the surface, intermediate stations of towed nets, and a continuous plankton record. In the shelter of St. Martin's Cove, just inside Cape Horn, where the beech forests that clothed the hills were a welcome change from the icebergs and barren islands of the South, a pause of three days was made before continuing to Port Stanley.

Discovery's second year's work was done. She had brought to a successful conclusion the largest and most important oceanographic expedition which had sailed from England since the *Challenger*. It was intended that she should again go south the next season to continue her investigations. But the British-Australian-New Zealand Antarctic Research Expedition under the leadership of Sir Douglas Mawson was looking for a wooden ship. The results of the work which *Discovery* had completed showed that the next stage of Antarctic ocean research should be in the open sea. The immense strength of hull which rendered her so suitable for work in the ice would not be necessary there, and a larger, faster ship would carry out more expeditiously what was to be done. Therefore when the Australian Government offered to charter her for Mawson's expedition, the offer was accepted.

CETACEAN RESEARCH EXPEDITION

SCIENTIFIC STAFF AND OFFICERS, 1925

Dr. S. W. Kemp (In Command and Director of Research).

Mr. A. C. Hardy (Chief Zoologist).

Mr. J. E. Hamilton (Assistant Zoologist).

Mr. E. R. Gunther (Assistant Zoologist).

Mr. H. F. P. Herdman (Hydrologist).

Cmdr. J.R. Stenhouse, D.S.O., O.B.E., D.S.C., R.N.R. (Captain).

Lt.-Cmdr. W. H. O'Connor, R.N.R. (Chief Officer).

Lt.-Cmdr. J. M. Chaplin, R.N. (Navigating Officer).

Mr. T. W. Goodchild (Third Officer).

Eng.-Lt. W. K. Horton, R.N. (Chief Engineer).

Mr. A. Porteous (Second Engineer).

Dr. E. H. Marshall, D.S.O. (Surgeon).

Eight

The B.A.N.Z.A.R.E.

WHEN in 1907 Shackleton took his own famous expedition to the Antarctic, there went with him a young Australian mineralogist and physicist called Douglas Mawson, who shared with Professor Edgeworth David and Dr. Mackay the honour of reaching the actual position of the South Magnetic Pole. Mawson returned to Australia, took his doctorate of science, and settled down to the life of a professor of geology at Adelaide University. He had no thought of returning to Antarctica. But as years passed the land of ice and silence called him, and in 1911 he went south again as the leader of an Australian Expedition. His splendid work in a new area, his courage, his powers of endurance and his ability in the three years which followed won for him a place on the Antarctic explorers' scroll of fame. He stood now with Shackleton and Scott; with Bellingshausen, Balleny, Biscoe, Wilkes and others, those early adventurers in the days of sailing ships.

The Australian Expedition marked the end of what Gordon Hayes has called the "heroic era" in Antarctic exploration—the era of man-hauled sledges, insufficient and improper food, the days when exploration meant isolation and suffering and sometimes death—the days when, at times, it was conducted "by guess and by God". The Great War had intervened. Aeroplanes, wireless, new methods of preserving food, a fuller knowledge of the food necessities of the human machine in order to keep it fit, all had developed in the interval, and Dr. Mawson's expedition of 1911-4 marked the close of the "heroic era" as Sir Douglas Mawson's voyages of 1929-31 were in the vanguard of the mechanical age.

The great Antarctic regions to the south of Australia were now deemed by Australians their own peculiar heritage. The expedition of 1911-4 had been only a precursor of effort to come. But while the area was peculiarly Australian, New Zealand also was interested, and through those two great dominions, the British Empire as a whole. Therefore, when in 1927 Australian plans for a new expedition began to take shape, "to more completely chart and scientifically investigate" the wide sweep of unknown Antarctica lying west of New Zealand's Ross Sea Dependency south of Australia, both New Zealand and the British Government were invited to participate. The result was the expedition known as the British-Australian-New Zealand Antarctic Research Expedition—for short BANZARE.

Although the years since the 1911-4 expedition had resulted in immeasurable advances in modern science, although wireless might now keep an expedition in communication with the world, although aeroplanes might now give their invaluable scouting aid, although vitamins had been acknowledged, and scurvy was no longer to be feared, yet for accurate investigations nothing, so far, had superseded the wooden ship for pack-ice work, as nothing had surpassed dog transport for detailed land investigation. The work of the BANZARE was to be confined to the sea, no dogs were necessary, and for service in the ice-strewn Antarctic seas *Discovery* was still the staunchest ship available. But she was to go south this time with all the auxiliaries which science had developed. She was equipped already with wireless, electricity and other improvements undreamed of when she was built. But once more she was overhauled and refitted, and when in August, 1929, she sailed for Cape Town she carried with her also that innovation in polar exploration—an aeroplane.

Mawson already had made an effort to utilize air transport in 1911, but his machine had proved useless, except the engine which was used for tractor purposes. In the intervening period, however, heavier-than-air machines had developed beyond the dreams of 1911. In 1928 Sir Hubert Wilkins had made spectacular flights to the south of Graham Land. Admiral Byrd's expedition was equipped for extensive flying. The Norwegian whaler-explorers already were taking aeroplanes south. And in packing cases, stowed amidships, *Discovery* carried a De Havilland Moth, fitted with alternative float and ski undercarriage, for use in reconnaissance.

In August, 1929, she sailed down the Thames for Cape Town with Captain John King Davis in command, a veteran of Mawson's Australian expedition. Sir Douglas Mawson with most of his scientific staff, travelling by mail steamer from Australia, met her in South Africa, and on the morning of 19th October, after a final overhaul

SIR DOUGLAS MAWSON, D.Sc., F.R.S.

A TOAST IN THE WARD ROOM, JAN. 1st, 1930

From left to right (standing):—Johnston, unknown, Williams, Steward, Simmers, Child, Fletcher, Harley (seated):—Marr, MacKenzie, Howard, Falla, Moyes, Colbeck. Ingram, Douglas, Mawson

and final coaling, her journey south began. As before, *Discovery* was a happy ship, both in the wardroom and forward, the high spirits of the younger members being particularly marked. Practically everyone had a nickname. Owing to the limited crew some of the scientific staff were called upon occasionally to man the yards, and Marr, Summers and Douglas, in particular, became quite competent seamen and useful both on deck and aloft.

A course was set south-eastwards towards the Crozet Islands, and on 2nd November *Discovery* dropped anchor in American Bay on Possession Island. The stern grandeur of Antarctic scenery was hinted at even here. Snow-clad peaks rose high above low moorland vegetation, and on the rocky shores sea elephants lolled stupidly, in a shambles created by a company of sealers collecting blubber, unmoved even when their mates were clubbed to death and flayed within a few feet. Giant albatross were nesting on the rocky shores, the young so far developed that they were almost ready to begin their ocean wanderings. And, alas for human frailty, the hut and stores landed many years before by a naval ship for shipwrecked sailors were found to have been broken into and rifled, the store empty and the substantial hut in disrepair. Magnetic observations were taken, the naturalists made their first shore collections, plans of the bay and anchorage were made, and after two days the voyage continued to Kerguelen.

The Crozets are desolate and windswept, but all that the Crozets are Kerguelen is to an infinite degree. Fogs enshroud it, the " Roaring Forties" sweep across it, its boggy peatlands and bare hills, rising tier on tier to the extinct snowcapped volcano of Mount Ross, have earned it the title "Island of Desolation". Kerguelen is only now emerging from the glacial age, which still holds the Antarctic continent within its grasp. Kerguelen announces what Antarctica may be many thousands of years from now. Glacial valleys, cutting from the highlands to the sea, are deep erosions, spreading at intervals into icy lakes, and ending in long fjords between which the dark volcanic rocks protrude in long peninsulas that end in trailing islands, growing smaller and ever smaller till they are lost in the boisterous ocean. This is not a coastline to be approached without great care, and now as *Discovery* drew near a gale arose, so that it was only after a week's battling with wind and wave that she made anchorage at Port Jeanne D'Arc in Royal Sound.

Kerguelen, though so desolate, has more history than most Antarctic islands. It was first sighted on 12th February, 1772, by a French explorer, Yves Joseph de Kerguelen-Tremerac, who commanded the French frigate *Fortune*. He thought he had discovered the great Australian continent and hurried back to France to tell the news. France, to maintain her right to this stormy outpost, sent out the ship *Eure* in 1893 to take formal possession. And in order that her claim should remain undisputed, established there at Gazelle Bay one hardy Frenchman, to hold his country's title by "squatter's right". The treaty of Versailles, recognizing Kerguelen as French territory, removed that necessity, and the lonely builder of French Empire was relieved, the island given over to seals and sea-birds and whalers. Port Jeanne D'Arc is a monument to whaling days—an abandoned whaling station on a sheltered fjord, twenty-five miles from the sea, complete with factory building, storehouses and living quarters for one hundred men. For *Discovery's* purposes it was a coaling station, for the South African Whaling Company had undertaken to transport thus far four hundred tons of coal.

All hands, except the scientists, turned to, filling every available space with Cardiff briquettes. Once more meteorological observations were taken and the naturalists were busy with the life peculiar to the island—the strange insects which, lacking other methods of protection, feign death at the approach of danger, and drop from leaves and shrubs, to mingle with the gravel from which they are almost indistinguishable—lichens, moss and fungi, and the fleshy-leaved plant called by the sailors of the southern seas Kerguelen cabbage, a storehouse of health in the old days of sailing ships, because of its anti-scorbutic properties. Eaten with teal, in which the islands abound, it provided a welcome change of diet in *Discovery's* wardroom, though on the mess-deck, where a deeper conservatism reigned, it was treated with scorn, as something new and strange, and the ratings insisted on their usual tinned meat.

For nearly two weeks *Discovery* lay at Port Jeanne D'Arc, while the scientific staff explored the shores. The old encampment of the Transit of Venus Expedition of 1874 was visited, and the living-hut found to

HOISTING OVER THE DE HAVILLAND SCOUTING SEAPLANE, OFF PRINCESS ELIZABETH LAND

PROCLAMATION ISLAND (ENDERBY LAND), FROM THE NORTH

ALOFT, MANNING THE FOOT ROPES

be still in good repair, while adjoining it, and built over the base upon which the transit instrument had been mounted, was another and new building, monument to the optimism of a certain M. Bossière, who had built it for his shepherds when he leased the island to raise sheep. Sheep-raising on Kerguelen was a failure, and the shepherd's hut, like the whaling station at Port Jeanne D'Arc, exists now only as a memento of disappointed hopes. An unfortunate memento is the introduction by man of rats, rabbits and dogs. The dogs, now wild, are said to be descended from odd sledge dogs left by the German *Gauss* expedition of 1902.

On the morning of 24th November, laden with coal, *Discovery* sailed from Royal Sound, steering for Heard Island, nearly 200 miles due south and set in the stormiest sea in the world. Its sheer black cliffs, rising from a grey sea, were soon in sight, its rocky ledges flecked with snow, its permanent ice-cap. Then a surf-pounded beach of black volcanic sand came into view, from one end of which a majestic mountain called Big Ben rose to 7000 feet above the sea, its lower slopes shrouded in cascades of glaciers that pushed out in blue ice cliffs far from the land. As recently as March, 1910, the summit of Big Ben was in complete volcanic activity with immense clouds of smoke rising from it.

Once more the scientists were put ashore. But the swell was too heavy for the ship to remain, and she put out for safety as well as in the hope of being better able to chart the coastline. In an abandoned sealer's hut the scientists lived in comparative comfort until the ship returned, but the stormy weather prevented any survey of the coast, and as soon as winds permitted *Discovery* returned, signalling the shore party to come aboard as soon as possible. There were high seas running, but orders must be obeyed, and soon a heavily laden motor-launch, thickly decked with frozen spray, brought out the sorriest collection of wet, sick scientists that could have been imagined. Even Kerguelen now seemed, in comparison, clothed in richest verdure, for the shrieking winds that swirl around Heard Island have kept it for the most part free of growth, and only in sheltered coves may poor moss and coarse tussock grass be found. But the unremitting storms which prevent the existence of vegetable life were balanced by the wealth of life from the sea, for, by keeping off marauding sealers, they make a natural sanctuary for penguins and sea-elephants.

On 4th December, Heard Island was left behind. The purpose of charting its coastline more correctly had failed, and *Discovery's* next endeavour was to trace a rise believed to exist in the ocean floor. The echo-sounding apparatus installed by the Admiralty was now brought into play, and the journey south proved beyond doubt the existence of the Kerguelen-Heard Island Ridge, theretofore only conjectured, the land beneath rising to within 350 fathoms of the surface.

Although a few stranded icebergs had been sighted even as far north as the Crozets, the sea had been thus far free of ice, but on 7th December the first floating bergs appeared, to be followed in another day by the pack. Twisting and turning and following open leads through the floes, *Discovery* worked her way slowly southward for three hundred miles until, on 15th December, the ice became impenetrable. There was no choice but to commence her westward journey. A few days before Christmas a gale opened up the pack so that on Christmas Day, when the wind abated, progress in a south-westerly direction was possible. Soundings showed that the sea-floor was rising rapidly. Everything indicated the near approach to land. But a day later the way was once more barred by heavy close-packed floes, though with the closing of the sea, as if to mock mere human effort, smooth slopes of land ice appeared thrown up in mirage, and dredgings with a large Monagasque trawl brought up quantities of rock of continental type.

So far the aeroplane had not been used, as there had been too much wind for a take-off from the sea. It was possible only to guess at what lay beyond the range of vision from the crow's nest. But now in the midst of the pack a calm and ice-bound pool was reached where there was ample space to take off. The ship hove-to for three days while the packing cases were opened and the Moth assembled, and then when all seemed ready colder weather set in and the pool froze over. Once more the ship worked westward, and again an ice-locked pool was found. The great moment had come. But fate had more disappointments in store. The engine refused to start. Hour after hour Flight-Lieutenant Campbell and Pilot Officer Douglas "tickled" and "doped" the engines, switched on and off, swung the propeller, tried everything they knew. The engine remained lifeless. It was discovered that during the long sea voyage the magnetos had become damp. There was nothing to do but take them to pieces and dry them in the galley oven for twenty-four hours. And meantime *Discovery* continued westward.

The magnetos were dried and replaced, but still the engine would not start in the intense cold, until a pre-heater was rigged on the main deck, comprising a large Primus stove from which the heat was carried in a fireproof canvas chute to the engine cowling. This worked fairly well, although later it exploded with a report that brought everyone on deck, and embedded bits of torn brass deep in the wooden bulwarks, indicating how fortunate it was that no one had been near. The engines were run up, all was in readiness. But now evening was falling, and the flight was postponed until the morning. Again fate intervened. Shortly after midnight the wind freshened; by four o'clock it was blowing a full gale. For four days the blizzard howled, and when the storm abated it was the last day of the year. Another effort was decided upon. The lifting tackle was rigged, the engine started, and the plane at last lowered over the side.

She took off splendidly, and rose quickly to 6000 feet. To the south lay the unbroken pack, with its monotonous flat surface broken here and there by giant bergs. But to the west were darker shapes, standing out boldly against a world of white—too large, too dark for icebergs— islands, or perhaps the continental coast itself. The Moth alighted and was hoisted aboard with a report of probable land and a sketch of ice conditions. For a distance of some forty or fifty miles the pack extended almost solidly. It would be too wasteful of coal to attempt to push through, and *Discovery* turned north to skirt it. Changed times from the old hit-and-miss methods of following a likely lead and hoping for the best, finding herself at the end of, perhaps, twenty miles in a hopeless *cul-de-sac*, and being forced to retrace her course.

Within a few days the open sea about the pack again trended south-west, and on 5th January land was reported from the crow's nest. As soon as a reasonable calm and ice-free area was reached the Moth was again lowered over the side, Campbell took off with Sir Douglas Mawson, and from a height of 2000 feet an indubitable line of black mountains could be seen projecting through the ice and snow of the continent itself. Only about fifteen miles of pack separated the ship from shore, but the ice cliffs rose sheer from the sea. No landing-place could be found. It was intended to make another flight the next day to map out the new-discovered land, but again a blizzard blew up from the south, and *Discovery* fled before the storm, while Mawson contented himself in christening the landfall MacRobertson Land, in honour of Mr. MacPherson Robertson, an Australian whose large contribution had made the expedition possible. They were sailing now over the Wilkes Land of the old charts, as they were to sail in their next season's work over their own charting of MacRobertson Land. All the discoveries of science had not yet overcome the distortions of Antarctic atmospheric conditions, nor even Mawson's experience of atmospheric phenomena in the frozen south enabled him to gauge accurately the position of the rocky continental outcroppings seen on his flight.

Gradually the storm abated and the swell decreased. The pack became less congested, the ship was able to make a southing, and in a few days came once more from the masthead the welcome cry of "Land". But though there was land there was still no landing-place, and for sixteen hours *Discovery* coasted along inhospitable cliffs, rising one hundred feet above the sea, until persistence brought its reward. Numbers of small rocky islands led to a large dark patch of rock, rising to 800 feet, separated from the mainland only by a narrow frozen bit of sea not much wider than a ditch. It was a striking feature of the coastline and the landing was easy, and christening it Proclamation Island, Sir Douglas Mawson and a party went ashore to raise the Union Jack and claim it with the land behind for the British Empire. Fat Weddell seals basked in the sunshine, the slopes were crowded with chattering Adélie penguins, and above their clamorous settlement a party stood in thrilled silence while the proclamation was read and placed in a casket at the foot of the flagpole in the cairn that they had built.

Three cheers were given for the King, and thus formally was added to his territory the vast slice of frozen land discovered first by Captain Biscoe and named for his employers Enderby Land. MacRobertson Land, Kemp Land, Enderby Land—there could be no doubt now that they were all parts of one great Antarctic salient, and who knew how valuable it might be in the years to come to the great Empire of which it had become a part. The ceremony of proclamation ended, the scientists set to work. Magnetic observations, as usual, were taken, and geological and biological collections made. But as the day wore on the ice began to pack closely between the outpost islands, and the party was forced to leave in haste, to avoid being cut off from the ship.

Discovery was nearing now the westerly limit of the voyage for which she had set out—to investigate the coastline as far as the 45th degree of East Longitude. The journey already had added stores of knowledge as it had added vast realms of new territory to the Empire, and sailing westward in the sparkling sunshine behind a great breakwater of tabular icebergs, a feeling of work well done permeated the whole ship. One after another of Biscoe's landfalls was identified— his Cape Ann, behind which rose a mighty mountain which was named Mount Biscoe. Range after range of rugged peaks rose on the horizon. The Tula Range was named for Biscoe's tiny vessel, the Scott Mountains for Captain Robert Falcon Scott, and in fitting proximity Amundsen Bay, commemorating forever in the communion they deserved the two rival discoverers of the South Geographic Pole.

Two days more and the westerly limits of the cruise would be reached. But now, to the amazement of everyone on board, a ship appeared out of the west. Who was she? What was her nationality? What could her business be? It could be seen that she had two aeroplanes aboard, and soon she was identified as the *Norvegia*, belonging to the Lars Christensen whaling interests in Norway, and sent south each season to carry out exploration, whaling research, and to look for new whaling grounds. By eight o'clock in the evening the two ships were abreast. Captain Riiser-Larsen came aboard *Discovery*. Not for the first time had explorers representing different governments found that their efforts in Antarctica converged. It might have meant an international situation. But after an hour's conference with Sir Douglas Mawson, Captain Riiser-Larsen agreed to wireless for permission to turn back into the sector he had left. Antarctica was large enough for both. *Discovery*, in any case, was almost on the point of returning. The next day her farthest west marine station was made, and on the 16th the officer of the watch reported the *Norvegia* steaming westward. Her new instructions, apparently, had come. And in memory of the friendly arrangement the highest peak of the Tula Range was named Mount Riiser-Larsen.

Following this friendly conference on the high seas a practical joke was played on *Discovery's* chief engineer. Most people had started to grow beards as soon as the ship had left Cape Town, and now were hardly known in their clean-shaven condition. Douglas and Fletcher were particularly hirsute. A few days after meeting with *Norvegia* these two shaved, dressed themselves in flying kit, and accompanied by Campbell as guide, paid a visit to the engine-room, to be introduced to the chief, Griggs, as two Norwegian airmen who had landed alongside. As the ship was not under way Griggs had no suspicion, and it was not until he accompanied his visitors on deck, after courteously showing them round his domain, that he realized he had been duped.

Ice conditions had changed even in the few days since *Discovery* had visited her landing-place in Enderby Land. She was able now to sail much closer to the coast. But the inevitable gale arose, driving her 150 miles out to sea, and it was not until 22nd January that the weather had cleared sufficiently to take her position. Once more she worked back to the vicinity of the Scott Mountains, with the intention of making a survey flight, but the heaving sea continued too rough for a take-off. On the 24th and 26th, however, as she steamed eastward, short flights were possible, unrolling before the eye of man for the first time an endless series of rugged mountains rising from an ice-covered land. Two hundred peaks were counted, a flag was dropped on the inland ice-plain, and on the 25th the proclamation was read again claiming all the land as far as the 45th degree East Longitude for the British Crown.

The voyage had reached the peak of exciting work. It was the height of the Antarctic summer. Ice conditions were improving every day, and there seemed no limit to what might be done. But the supply of coal had shrunk until it was unsafe to remain. Immediate return was necessary, and, regretfully, the explorers headed towards Kerguelen to recoal for the journey to Australia. Nothing more could be done that season in the way of exploration, and the journey home was occupied in the duller if more immediately useful routine of running a series of deep-sea stations with the echo-sounding apparatus. On 21st March

LOOKING EAST NEAR CAPE DENISON, SHOWING THE 1911-1914 HUT (JAN., 1931)

SEA ELEPHANTS AT CROZET ISLANDS

they were off Albany, but *Discovery* continued to Melbourne, where she was soon in the dockyards for a winter's overhaul.

The great problem throughout the voyage had been fuel. The measure of the dependence upon steam for progress in the pack-ice had brought a new appreciation of the work of those indomitable sailors in the days before steam was known who had unveiled the frozen southland, theretofore a myth. Now sail was only an auxiliary, useful as a fuel-saving device in an ice-free sea. Then sail had been the only means of progress, and with tiny ships, primitive gear, inadequate and improper food the early adventurers had made their epic voyages. Cook, in 1773, with his *Resolution* and *Adventure*, the first to cross the Antarctic Circle; the Russian expedition sent out in 1819, in the grand manner of the old Czarist regime, under Captain von Bellingshausen, discovering Peter I Island and Alexander Land, both within the Circle; James Weddell with his two small sealers, who had penetrated far within it, discovering the great sea which now bears his name—though he had seen no land; John Biscoe, in 1830, with his *Tula* of 150 tons and the tiny cutter *Lively* of only 50 tons, who had first seen the lands of which *Discovery* had recently taken formal possession, his the first sight of Antarctic continental land. He had made his landfall after six weeks' struggle with wind and ice, and writing on 4th April: "The vessel, now a complete mass of ice, only three of the crew who can stand." Yet the homeward voyage still had to be made, and when he reached Hobart Town only one man could stand, while of the *Lively's* crew of ten only three were left alive. Balleny, another whaler, in turn made his discoveries, and Wilkes the American, Dumont D'Urville, sent out by France, and James Clark Ross, who discovered South Victoria Land and the Great Ice Barrier. All had relied on sail alone. Their hardships, their determination and their supreme seamanship could only be imagined.

Of his plans for the next season's work Sir Douglas Mawson wrote: "It was essential that additional coal supplies be available at intervals throughout the cruise." In order to provide for such supplies every effort was made to arrange for refuelling from time to time from whalers and floating factories, but without signal success. Only the *Sir James Clark Ross*, one of the Norwegian giant floating factories, agreed to provide 100 tons of coal to be available somewhere in the

SAGA OF THE DISCOVERY

vicinity of the Balleny Islands. Coal supplies would, therefore, be more limited than on the previous year's cruise.

On 22nd November *Discovery* sailed once more. Captain J.K. Davis had returned to his duties as Director of Navigation to the Commonwealth Government, and his place was taken by Captain K. N. Mackenzie, who had been First Officer on the previous journey. Lieutenant W. R. Colbeck, son of Captain W. Colbeck of the *Southern Cross* and *Morning*, was now Navigating Officer. Because of the necessity of making contact with the *Sir James Clark Ross*, the course was set south-easterly from Hobart by way of Mill Rise in the direction of the Macquarie Islands, which had aroused my first interest in Antarctic exploration, when in 1896 the ketch *Gratitude*, in the service of sealers on the Macquaries, put in to Louisville, my home in Tasmania. The captain of the ketch regaled us with strange tales of the sub-Antarctic seas, stories of seals and penguins and even of a hybrid unknown animal, developed from inter-breeding cats and rabbits. The captain asserted that he had eaten "rabbit-cats" and described, most realistically, their huge whiskers and fine fur coats. At that knowledgeable age I appraised the story as a sailor's "yarn", but Mr. Burton was different. Mr. Burton was a taxidermist, en route to the Macquaries to make zoological collections, and intended to remain there alone during the six months season until the *Gratitude* returned. That was an adventure which fired imagination, so that I wrote to the Hobart *Mercury*—which, miraculously, published the letter—with suggestions for extensive Antarctic exploration. "Why should not the Australian colonies organize, by subscription, an expedition to the Antarctic seas?" I asked, and went on to give details of ideas for such an expedition. It should be "composed of three ships, one fully equipped for scientific purposes and commissioned to proceed as far south as possible, and the other two to act as escorts to a certain extent, but also to be used for the purpose of whaling and sealing, and so defray the expenses of the expedition and reimburse the subscribers". At that early age, it would appear, I had a practical mind!

Now after thirty-five years the Australasian Dominions had organized their expedition—though on somewhat different lines *Discovery* was sailing for the Macquaries as her first port of call, and if she did not find the legendary "cat-rabbit", she found something almost as strange, for the roaring sea-elephants could be heard half a mile at sea as she approached. In 1916 all sealing licences for the islands had been suspended by the Tasmanian Government, with the laudable intention of making this outpost a sanctuary for wild life. The success of the move was evident. In the intervening years the islands had become a wonder spot of sub-Antarctic life. Sea-elephants bred unmolested on their shores, and the raucous babble of penguins echoed far inland in the secluded valleys. But it was interesting to discover from papers in an abandoned sealer's hut, and a grave with an inscription dated May, 1918, that some daring sealer had found a happy hunting-ground two years after all licences had expired.

The call at Macquarie was brief, for *Discovery's* real work lay in the farther south, but it was out of her course to visit the Balleny Islands, and Sir Douglas Mawson wished to make an inspection of the wireless installation and living-hut established in Lusitania Bay by his 1911 expedition, with a view to their possible utilization during the programme of the International Polar Year scheduled for 1931-2. The wireless station was a complete wreck, and the gales had played havoc with the living-hut so that it was uninhabitable, and when the scientists went ashore, tents were erected for their shelter, while the ship dredged along the coastal shelf. But fog and rain flung a curtain of invisibility over the whole group, and little could be done. In a few days the journey south continued. Soundings soon showed a rise in the ocean floor which was traced for several hundred miles, and excitement rose at the thought of locating the almost mythical Emerald Island shown on the older charts, the existence of which is now generally discredited. When the latitude assigned to the islands was reached, there was every indication of the proximity of land, but fog and gales shut out the view, and delay in the southward journey until the weather should clear could not be considered.

Now came another disappointment, for the *Sir James Clark Ross* wirelessed that owing to the scarcity of whales in the vicinity of the Balleny Islands it had been necessary to move eastward near the 180th Meridian. At a cost of sixty tons of coal *Discovery* followed, a cost hardly balanced by the hundred tons she had been promised, but necessary now since she was so far from her objective. The only compensation was that the oceanographic observations were carried farther east than had been anticipated.

Icebergs became numerous, and the loose pack had been met already, when on 18th December the *Sir James Clark Ross* was sighted. *Discovery* was soon moored alongside, Captain Nilson did everything in his power to facilitate the coaling, and in a few hours the fuel was aboard. Those new to modern whaling methods found the giant factory a revelation as a constant stream of whales were hauled through the stern tunnel to the flensing deck, and monsters of 100 tons and more were disposed of in less than an hour.

Bidding good-bye to the whalers, *Discovery* continued on her way, having the good fortune ten days later to sight the *Kosmos*, another pelagic factory, and obtain another fifty tons of coal. And six days later, battling a stiff gale, a landing was made on 4th January in the miniature landlocked harbour at Cape Denison, that "Home of the Blizzards", where Mawson had wintered for two seasons twenty years before. There stood the hut, with the skeleton fuselage of the first aeroplane ever taken to the Antarctic still lying in the snow. Snow was banked so deeply about the walls that entry had to be made through the roof. The soft fibres of the exterior timbers above the protection of the snow were eroded in some places to a depth of more than half an inch from the action of the constantly recurring blizzards, while the inside, clothed in festoons of delicate ice crystals, had been transformed into an ice-fairy's cave. Otherwise all was as it had been left. A bottle standing on the table still contained Mawson's message to the next comers, and the food which had been abandoned was in such excellent preservation that it was eaten with gusto on board *Discovery* that night. But in spite of appearances there had been one great change, for magnetic observations, taken as usual whenever a landing was made, showed that the wandering South Magnetic Pole had moved so much in the interval that it was now probably not more than two hundred and fifty miles away.

At noon on 5th January the Union Jack was hoisted, and the proclamation read claiming formal possession of King George V Land, extending from the 142nd to the 160th degree of East Longitude, and the next day the voyage westward was resumed.

So the second season's work continued in much the same routine as that of the year before, with twistings and windings through the pack-ice, and long detours to northward when it became too dense, with reconnaissance flights from time to time that sketched out the continental coastline and the condition of the ice. And always the recurring ice-laden gales which poured down from the great inland plateau, driving the ship before them, far off her course. But after each gale she worked south again, and the map of Antarctica began to bristle with new names. Balleny's Sabrina Land was once more charted, and a hitherto unseen land given the conglomerate name Banzare, in commemoration of the expedition.

On the morning of 25th January, after days of fog and gale, a change in the sky conditions to the south suggested the proximity of still more land. This was the neighbourhood of the charted position of Knox Land, and Mawson was most anxious to make another flight before passing from that part of the coast. The weather was unfavourable. Both wind and current were against him, and the ship was being carried always westward. For two days, at the cost of considerable coal, *Discovery* kept her position, but instead of improving the weather showed signs of changing for the worst. He decided to take a chance. The take-off was accomplished, and rising to 6000 feet above the clouds the Moth flew southward. All view below was obscured, but far to the south-west a break appeared, and through it the undulating plains of land ice. Kemp Land had been proved a reality.

The machine had been an hour only in the air, but the wind had increased to dangerous proportions, and when a landing was made a wave caught one of the wings, nearly capsizing it. The motor-boat, always in readiness when a flight was made, rushed to the rescue, Mawson and the pilot and then the Moth were brought aboard, though she looked a total wreck. Both wings now were crumpled, and the petrol tank was completely flattened. But as the gale freshened and *Discovery* sped before the storm through the berg-infested waters, all hands turned to in an endeavour to make her air-worthy again. The damaged wings practically had to be rebuilt, mainly from bits of packing-cases, and then re-covered. That work the two aviators undertook, while the photographer, Hurley, who proved to be also a mechanic, rebuilt the petrol tank. The result was perhaps the flimsiest

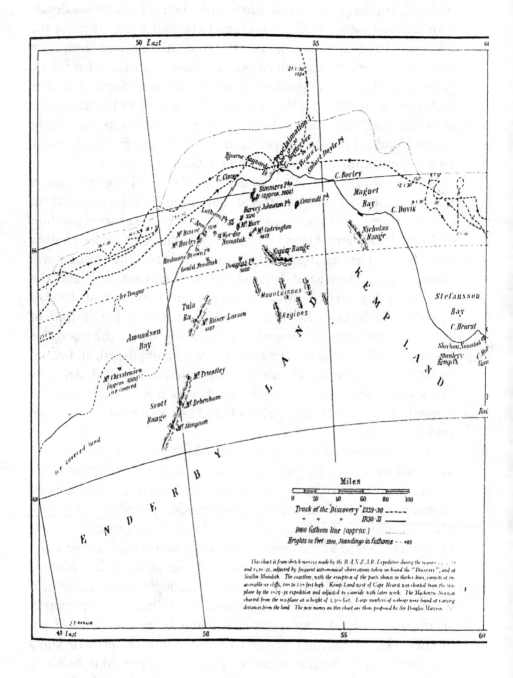

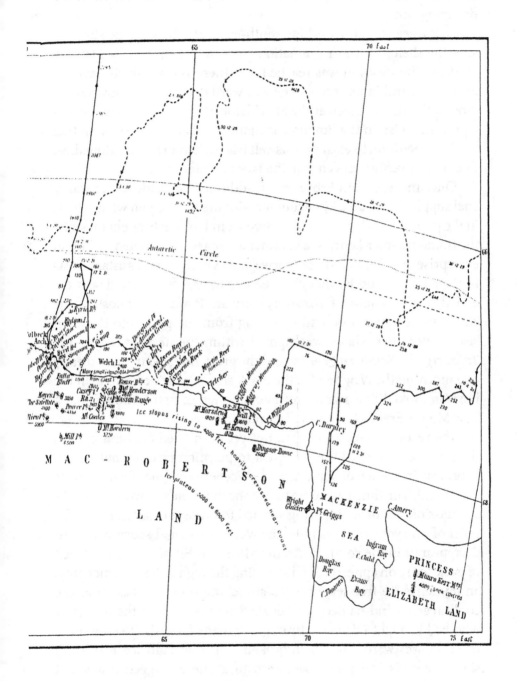

aeroplane that ever tempted Antarctic air, but it flew, though with a drooping wing.

Discovery was now working south-eastward through the storm to seek the shelter of the Termination Ice Tongue, charted by Mawson in 1911. The position was reached, but there was no shelter and no ice tongue, and in its absence the westward drifting pack now surged around the shoal known as the Shackleton Shelf, so impenetrable that a proposed visit to the Emperor Penguin Rookery, discovered in that earlier expedition to exist on Haswell Island, had to be abandoned. So does even twenty years change the face of Antarctica.

Once more, on 6th February, an addition was made to the scanty coal supply due to a lucky encounter with the Norwegian whaler *Falk*, in the process of taking aboard a cargo from Durban brought to her by the tramp steamer *Lestris*—a summer auxiliary. No jealousy of British enterprise ever hindered the Norwegians giving what assistance was in their power, and by that chance encounter a few more days were added to the length of *Discovery's* cruise. It was the midst of the Antarctic summer now, and emerging from the pack into the open sea, whaler after whaler was sighted within the next few days—the *Tafelberg*, the *Southern Princess* and the great *Thorshammar*, and early one morning the *New Sevilla*, the black smoke of which rising on the horizon looked like a great volcano, and led at first to hopes that a new Mount Erebus had been discovered.

The reconstructed Moth had not yet been tried out, and here in the open sea the swell was too great to permit a take-off, but on 9th February, in the lee of some stranded icebergs, a quiet field of water was found. The time had come to test the machine's airworthiness. As she took off her drooping wing seemed to presage disaster, but to the relief of everyone she was none the worse for it, and soaring upward disappeared in the south to discover Princess Elizabeth Land. A belt of pack-ice soon appeared, and steaming through it the next morning, an immense ice-free sea was seen stretching southward as far as eye could reach—and named Mackenzie Sea in honour of the navigator who had brought *Discovery* through so many hazards. Twenty miles or so to westward smooth unbroken slopes of land ice rose from sheer ice cliffs and rolled backward to a line of rugged peaks, but the southern limits of the sea were veiled in mist. Once more a flight was made over some forty or fifty miles of open water, but the mists remained too heavy to permit a sight of the southern coastline. Only to the south-east was there a break in the clouds, where white ice plains glittered in the sun. Flying inland for several miles the Union Jack was dropped, but no place could be found where a landing might be made, and, on returning to report, the already severely tried little aeroplane met with yet another accident. The sea was not as free of ice as had appeared, and as a landing was made she struck an almost submerged block of clear floe which tore away her undercarriage. Once more the motor-boat hurried to the rescue, and once more the aviators had to face the unpleasant task of making repair in weather always below freezing-point.

Tempting as the open water was, the advancing season and decreasing coal supply made further investigations of the coastline seem unwise, and the ship again headed north by west. By midnight the scene had changed. She had entered a great field of grounded bergs that might have been a giant graveyard. Standing in the crow's nest, one hundred feet above the deck, the lookout was overtopped by towering walls of ice, their dark shadows in the moonlight accentuating their ghostly shapes, the stillness only broken, from time to time, by the loud report of falling pieces, or a splitting berg. Winding in and out among the shadowy giants an uncanny other world seemed to have been reached. The water took on the consistency of glue. Progress was hampered and the ice walls seemed interminable. To be frozen in, in such a place, would be certain death. But with the daylight there came also the welcome lift of the open sea. In a wide lead in the pack sail was set, and in a freshening breeze from the south-east *Discovery* sped once more to safety, the giant bergs behind her taking on a hundred glittering colours in the morning sun.

She was sailing now along the coast of MacRobertson Land, located somewhat vaguely during her last cruise. "What a difference in the two seasons," Mawson wrote. "Last summer when we traversed the area the sea was rendered unnavigable by dense pack. This season from the 70th Meridian to the west there was practically no pack-ice south of lat. 67½°. Now steaming along the coast, we were able to chart the features accurately. Last year the MacRobertson Land coast, which for the most part was seen only at a distance, was but approximately located. The clarity of the Antarctic atmosphere gives a wonderful degree of visibility, easily misleading in regard to distance. Thus it is not surprising to find in cases of objects observed last season from the aeroplane at an elevation, the distance was under-estimated."

Capes and bays, islands and mountains were now taking names upon the map in quick succession. Rounding each headland the whole ship's company waited eagerly to learn what might be ahead. Scientists and crew alike formed lookouts. Passing inside a surf-beaten reef they entered an archipelago of islands large and small, extending for twenty-five miles from the coast, and, more amazing still, in that ice-gripped land, a long stretch of rocky coastline came into view. Precipitous black headlands rose from the sea. Ranges of rocky mountains and unnumbered peaks protruded from the age-old ice-cap. A landing was made on a headland called the Scullin Monolith, and once more the flag was raised and the proclamation read.

But the barometer began to fall, and it was evident that a blizzard was approaching. In a sea studded with islands and grounded bergs *Discovery* was in a hazardous position. There was time for no more than a glimpse of this ice-free coast. Before she was clear of danger the hurricane was on her, and for eighteen hours she drove before snow-laden winds, rising to gusts of eighty miles an hour. Again and again the cry of "Berg ahead" or "Berg abeam" rang out. Visibility was so bad that they could not be seen until she was almost upon them. It seemed miraculous that she escaped, and more miraculous still when suddenly, as if a curtain had dropped upon the storm, she ran into a strangely calm area, only the shriek of the wind overhead telling that the tempest still persisted. She had accidentally found the lee of some giant iceberg, it was thought, but they could not see. Only feeling their way by the strength of the wind, as the ship drifted from shelter, could they regain it again. Three days and three nights passed, and when at last the snow lifted they were astonished to find themselves safe in a veritable Druid's circle of stranded bergs. Ninety-two were counted from the masthead, and they were almost as safe as behind a harbour breakwater. Anxiety was ended, there was now an opportunity for sleep.

With the moderation of the weather *Discovery* again pushed

A LARGE 4½-METER NET FOR PLANKTON

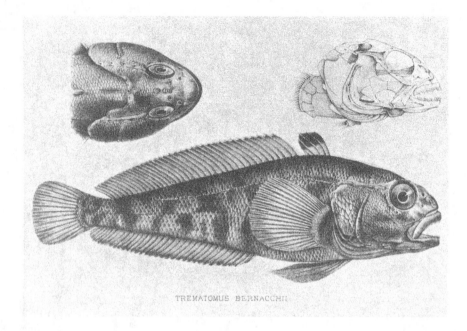

TREMATOMUS

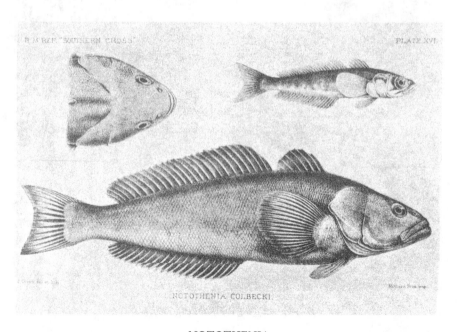

NOTOTHENIA

eastward, and to the charts were added more new names—the Mawson, David, Casey and Henderson mountain ranges, named for members of the Committee of the expedition, and Mount Hugh Robert Mill, after the well-known authority on Antarctic exploration. One last landing was made, and once more the flag was raised on a rocky point which was named Cape Bruce. It was fascinating work. The sea was free of ice. A final effort was made by wireless to contact a whaler with coal to spare, but without success. There was no choice but to return. 1000 miles of new land had been charted. Mawson in 1911-4 discovered 1500 of new coast, making now 2500 miles—a great and outstanding achievement.

THE BANZARE EXPEDITION

OFFICERS AND SCIENTIFIC STAFF
Sir Douglas Mawson, D.Sc., F.R.S. (In Command).
Captain J. K. Davis (Master and Second in Command). [1st voyage]
K. Mackenzie (Mate). [1st voyage]
Captain K. Mackenzie (Master). [2nd voyage]
A. M. Stanton (Mate). [2nd Voyage]
Lieut. W. R. Colbeck (Second Mate).
J. B. Child (Third Mate).
J. H. Martin (Boatswain).
W. J. Griggs (Chief Engineer).
B. S. F. Welch (Second Engineer).
A.J. Williams (Wireless Operator).

Commander M. H. Moyes, R.A.N. (Survey Officer).
Professor T. Harvey Johnston (Chief Biologist).
J.W. S. Man (Zoologist and Plankton Specialist).
R.A. Falla (Ornithologist).
H.0. Fletcher (Assistant Scientist).
Dr. W. W. Ingram (Medical Officer and Bacteriologist).
R.G. Simmers (Meteorologist and Physicist).
A.Howard (Hydrologist and Chemist).

Flight-Lieut. S. Campbell (Aviator and Assistant Scientist).
Air-Pilot E. Douglas.
J.F. Hurley (Photographic Artist).

With officers, scientists and crew the ship's company totalled 39.

Nine

Antarctic Phenomena

MARINE LIFE

ALTHOUGH the Antarctic seas are replete with low forms of marine life such as krill, those shrimps upon which the baleen whales feed, relatively few species of fish are to be found in those cold waters, and they are not numerous and are generally small of size. The majority live at the bottom in shallow or moderately deep water, and are valuable and delectable as food, although rather sweet. They somewhat resemble small rock-cod.

Nearly all those found near the coasts of Antarctica belong to a single group, the Nototheniiformes, characteristic and peculiar to those southern seas, so much so that they seem to point to the conclusion that the Antarctic may have been isolated and its coasts washed by cold seas throughout the Tertiary Period. They certainly do not support the idea that the Antarctic continent connected America with Australia during that period, nor does the distribution of other groups of animals confirm this view. There is another genus of fish known as *Trematomus*, first found by the *Southern Cross* expedition in Robertson Bay, and a few other genera of considerable interest. Nevertheless, over ninety per cent are Nototheniiformes. The fish in the waters of the sub-Antarctic island areas are quite different.

The invertebrate fauna of the Antarctic seas is very abundant and varied, more so than anywhere else in the world. *Plankton* is a Greek word which means "that which is drifted", and is a general term to cover all those forms of life, both plant and animal, which are passively carried along by ocean currents or driven on the surface by the wind. Some, like jellyfish, are very large. The largest ever found, eight feet across, came from the Arctic, and at Cape Adare in the *Southern Cross* we secured one weighing ninety pounds, and twenty-nine inches in diameter. But by far the majority of the plankton organisms are microscopic or only just visible to the naked eye. It is upon the single-celled plants of the plankton that practically all the animal life of the sea ultimately depends, for "the rule that animal life depends directly or indirectly upon plant life for its subsistence is universal and holds in the sea as on the land". Plant growth in turn is dependent upon oxygen, carbon dioxide, mineral salts and sunlight. The necessary gases are dissolved into the sea from the atmosphere, the mineral salts from the land, and the rays of sunlight penetrate the upper layers of the water. Each speck of plant life which multiplies into countless millions has its own device for existence—such as for flotation and propulsion. All the different stages from the single-celled protozoon are represented in this world of drifting life, and there are many queer forms found in Antarctic waters. It is possible to bring up a hundred different species in one trawl, including curiously shaped deep-sea fish; purple sea-slugs a foot long; sea spiders with ten legs; sea cucumbers; deep red spiny crustacea; molluscs and brachiopods; sea-lilies and sea-anemones; monstrous gelatinous sea-squids; isopods resembling trilobites and sea-urchins and crimson starfish. Such a list obtained by a dredge gives only a poor idea of the hidden beauty and wealth of life in south polar seas. Where ice-barrier and glaciers reach the sea there are deposits of debris and mud with, in turn, their own peculiar animal communities.

What is the cause of this rich growth? There is a striking similarity between the plankton of the two poles. The long days of polar summer and sunlight may be one cause. Perhaps, too, there may be more essential salts in the cold than in the warmer waters. Again, the uneven distribution of surface waters due to hot and cold layers may be a contributory cause, since plankton, especially diatoms, are unevenly distributed and some localities, where the whales congregate, are richer than others.

By far the most important of all this small life are the small crustacea—little shrimp-like creatures which occur in great variety and numbers. They feed the myriads of herrings in the northern seas, and build up the huge bodies of the "Whalebone" whales in the south. Captain Scott relates that "the shrimp-like amphipods are a kind of submarine locust, for myriads of them exist and devour everything that is edible". These live on the bottom in shallow Antarctic waters

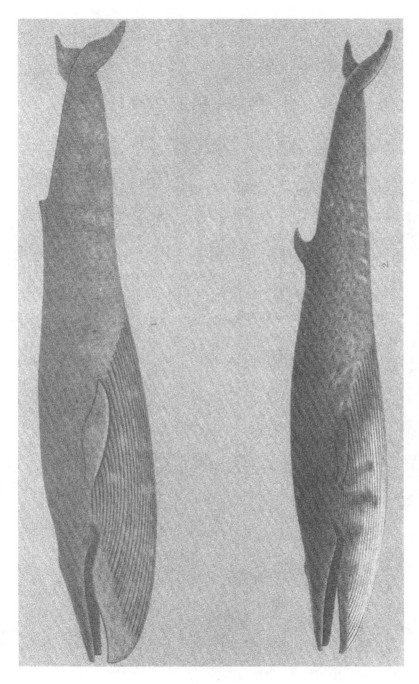

(Above) THE BLUE WHALE (Balaenoptera musculus)
(Below) THE FINNER (Megaptera)

WEDDELL SEAL AND CALF

and are sometimes called "sea-lice". Carnivorous in their habits, they are good scavengers and can be utilized for cleaning skeletons and skulls of seals that are to be preserved. The most valuable, however, is the sort of shrimp called *Euphausia*. Feeding on diatoms, it is itself the food of fish, penguins, and whales. Diatoms are excessively prolific in Antarctic seas, staining the ice yellow in places where they live, and forming a diatomaceous scum on the surface of the water.

Inasmuch as all the small copepods and larger euphausians feed directly upon tiny plants, their study in the polar seas is not only fascinating but of increasing importance.

On the sea-bottom are found many species and varieties of sponge peculiar to the Antarctic, including good examples of siliceous pale cream-coloured sponge with glassy spicules looking like glass wool, and amongst them are various forms of life: tube-dwelling worms with beautiful flower-like heads of tentacles; delicate shells, almost invisible to the naked eye; hairy worms with a double row of phosphorescent lamps, flashing in succession from head to tail. Corals and seaweeds are also fairly well represented. On the coasts of Adèlie Land Mawson found "giant" seaweed, dense, rank and luxuriant, known as "kelp" types, similar to those found around the sub-Antarctic islands and the Australian seaboard. On the more sheltered spots of the Antarctic shores small frozen pools or miniature lakes are found, formed from the melting snow on warm summer days. These are alive with myriads of microscopic living things, animal and plant, which, however, can scarcely be described as marine.

There, in and around the green algae gambol rotifers, infusoria, rhizopods, thread-worms and water-bears—the latter scratching among the debris or fiercely "pawing the air" with great curved, dangerous-looking claws; the thread-worms, like snakes, twisting in and out and lashing their tails, but nearly all so tenacious of life that it is not cold enough in the Antarctic to kill them. They can be frozen in temperatures as low as procurable, thawed, dried, and immersed in boiling water and yet they live. Some of the rotifers were still alive on reaching England. By what means do they survive? Whence is this microscopic fauna derived? Are they survivors from the remote time when a milder climate prevailed in Antarctica?

FAUNA

One of the most outstanding peculiarities of Antarctica is the entire absence of land mammals; none at present are known, living or fossil. This is strikingly different to the Arctic Regions, where conspicuous and numerous forms are to be found, such as the polar bear, reindeer, musk ox, wolf, fox, hare, ermine, lemming and other less important kinds.

Whales.
Whales and seals, however, abound, and most of the species and genera are peculiar to the regions. Whales are divided into two classes—toothless whales, provided with a sieve of horny plates (baleen) suspended from the roof of the mouth and no teeth in the jaws; and the tooth whales, with no baleen but with teeth present in one or both jaws. Both types are represented in the Antarctic ocean. To the former class belong the giant Rorquals (*Balænoptera*), and Right whales (*Balæna*), and the Humpback and Finners (*Megaptera*). To the toothed class belong the Sperm whale or Cachalot, the Bottlenose, the Porpoise, the Dolphin and the famous "Killer" (*Orcinus orca*), which hunts in "packs". Tyrants of the sea, these ferocious beasts prey on the seals, penguins, dolphins and whales. The large whales live in dread of the Killer, for their great bulk cannot save them from those swiftly moving twenty- to thirty-foot beasts, with their fearsome jaws and three-inch teeth. Only the Sperm whale, with its equally fearsome jaws, is immune from their attacks.

Amongst the rorquals is the famous Blue whale (*Balænoptera musculus*), sometimes over 100 feet in length, and, occasionally, weighing nearly 150 tons. It is the largest animal known to have lived on the globe, and is eagerly hunted by the whaling companies because of its size and its richness in oil. It is easily distinguished by its broad blue slate-coloured back and its very small dorsal fin. Its spout rises twelve or fifteen feet into the air. Whales do not inhale water and then blow it into the air as is sometimes supposed. Being mammals with lungs like most mammals, the spout is the exhalation of the air, though some water may be sprayed upwards by the breath. Their normal speed in the water is about eight miles per hour, but when disturbed they can swim much faster. They perform great annual migrations from the Antarctic seas northward to tropical and even equatorial waters for the purpose of breeding, returning to the south in the spring to feed on the prolific surface organisms or plankton, which they separate from the water by means of the sieving apparatus of baleen plates in the mouth.

We have now some knowledge of the breeding conditions and the growth in their earlier years of these whales. The female of both the Blue and the Finner whale has a calf about every second year; the calf of the Blue whale is about twenty-one feet long at birth, and it is suckled from two mammary glands for about seven months. Actually the milk, of cream-like consistency and oily sweet, is pumped into the youngster. At the age of two the whales are sexually mature. We do not know to what age they live.

When I first visited the Antarctic in 1898, the baleen whales of those seas had practically no value, and no one did or could have foreseen the great industry which has developed, and which arose from the shortage of glycerine during the War. To-day it threatens extermination to those splendid Cetaceans, just as the Right or Whalebone whale was exterminated years ago in the Arctic. The Blue whale and the Finback are the mainstays of the Antarctic whaling industry, and already their numbers have very noticeably decreased. Blue whales especially are increasingly difficult to find, and there is very little doubt that the time is not far distant when human rapacity will bring about not only a complete collapse of the profitable business, but the practical extermination of the whales.

The whaling industry to-day provides the world annually with some 400,000 tons of good oil which is of great service in the manufacture of margarine, soap and glycerine. The whale, too, is the source of various extracts for the purpose of vitamins and of at least one valuable drug.

The total value of whale oil taken from Antarctic seas, since 1900, must be in the vicinity of £100,000,000! The onslaught for the past few years has been terrific. To a certain extent this valuable international asset is, by mutual agreement, internationally controlled, but as some countries are at present outside the agreement, and are ruthless "exterminators", the attempt at protection seems somewhat futile. So that the vast expenditure of the Discovery Committee of the Colonial Office since 1925 in research work on the environment of the whale, breeding times, rate of growth, food of whales and migratory habits may be wasted, excepting from a purely scientific point of view, if in a few more years there are no more whales. Indeed the information collated to date may even prove helpful to piratical countries.

The Killer whales are sufficient in themselves to keep in check the number of baleen whales without the aid of man.

Seals.

Excluding the seals of the sub-Antarctic shores, there are only three different kinds peculiar to the ice. They are all fairly large species distinguished from each other chiefly by the character of their skulls and teeth and by their habits. Those seals of the kind known as true seals are distinguished by the absence of external ears, merely having small holes leading through the skin to an internal ear. The hind feet, like flippers, which are extended behind when on the ice or on land, take no part in the animals' progression, and the palms and soles are hairy. They are completely adapted for an aquatic life and are, apparently, the highly modified descendants of that primitive carnivorous stock which gave rise to dogs and bears, and which, in a far remote period, like the beaver and the water-rat of the present day, gradually took to water as a source of food supply, and thus, by habit continued through a long series of generations, became adapted for a water rather than a land life, and, finally, have reached the form in which we now see them.

The best known, and most numerous, is the Weddell (*Leptonychotes Weddelli*), named after its discoverer, James Weddell, an early explorer. It is a large hairy seal, sometimes ten feet long, fat, floppy and handsome, with a darkish coat richly marked with black, grey and silvery white, and with large, soft brown eyes almost human in expression. It is slow, quiet, entirely inoffensive, devoid of fear, and an invaluable source of food and even fuel, when required, to the explorer. It is a coastal non-migratory species, and in the summer thousands can be seen lying on the shores and land ice surrounding the various Antarctic lands. They feed on crustaceans, cuttle-fish and the shallow water cod-like fish found there, and are very fond of gathering together, and sometimes

ADÉLIE PENGUINS

EMPEROR PENGUIN WITH CHICK

EMPEROR PENGUINS

can be seen in hundreds basking in the sun along the cracks and lanes in the ice. Due to their "longshore" habits they are not so exposed to the voracious Killer as the other seals. They share with the small Adélie penguins the honour of being the comedians of Antarctica. Their skins always seem a size too large, and when walking through a sleepy community one witnesses endless amusing habits. One may be scratching his nose with the very tip of the forefinger nail of his front flipper, or scratching one hand with another, or twisting himself into knots to scratch his back (for they harbour flea-like parasites), or sleepily stretching himself in a prolonged yawn. The expression of open-eyed surprise and bewilderment when aroused from slumber, as if awakening from a bad dream to a worse reality; their weird noises, bubbling, gurgling, snorting, sighing and especially whistling, for they possess remarkable vocal chords, afford endless entertainment.

The babies are born on the ice in the springtime (November in those latitudes). Small, soft, yellowish fluffy creatures, that "baa" like lambs, make a dreadful uproar when touched and rush to their mothers for protection. A month after birth they must be taught to swim. This is like teaching babies to walk, for the calves do not take kindly to water. They make a fuss and the mother gets very angry. She frequently pushes them in from behind! Perhaps the old habits of the land animal of which they are descendants persist in the young.

In the dark winter, owing to the bitter cold on the surface, these seals remain for months in the relatively warm water beneath the ice, breathing through open blow-holes. Since the sea ice, in places, is as much as fourteen feet in thickness and the surface temperatures, at times, fifty degrees below zero, causing the holes rapidly to freeze over, it is a remarkable feat to keep them open. Sometimes the freezing overtakes them and they must work vigorously to keep them open. This is done by opening the mouth very wide, baring their fine strong curved teeth, and biting into the ice from beneath, spinning round upon themselves all the time.

A very different type is the slim, active, long-snouted crab-eating seal (*Lobodon carcinophagus*).

These light-coloured species are also fairly numerous, but rarely found in communities. They haunt the pack-ice of the open sea singly or in pairs and are comparatively rarely found along the actual coastline. They are more timid than the Weddell, shorter and lighter in weight, and also feed upon crustaceans. In the early spring their coats are a beautiful silvery white; later in the season this turns more creamy, and, later on, a dirty stained grey.

Cruel scars often disfigure the body, probably caused by the Killer, and also, no doubt, by quarrels and fights amongst themselves.

The third and last true Antarctic seal is the Ross (*Ommatophœa rossi*), a rare beast, seldom seen and nearly always quite solitary far out on the floating pack-ice. Consequently, little is known about it. It is short and bulky, from seven to eight feet in length, with small weak teeth which, apparently, enable it to feed only on soft squids and jelly-fish. The skull is different to any known seal in the world, and the head ridiculously short with an extraordinary bloated neck, like a pouter pigeon, into which it has a way of drawing the head back, making it appear like the face of a pug dog or the pictures of the little pig that Alice nursed in Wonderland. This swelling is stated to be due to an abnormal development of the larynx which gives the creature a peculiar tenor voice.

All these Antarctic seals are true hair seals—the flesh is eaten extensively by polar explorers and is very good food, the liver especially being considered a delicacy. They hate the cold biting winds, love to bask in the sun, and after enjoying a good square meal may take some days to sleep it off and dream, as dogs appear to dream, snorting, gnashing their teeth and quivering all over their sloppy forms. They have only one real enemy, the dread Killers—those bandits who hunt in packs, chasing them under the water and under the ice, and even tipping them off the ice-floes by bumping their shadows seen from beneath.

Like other wild animals, they retire to most remote places to die.

The sea-leopard (*Ogmorhinus leptonyx*), which frequents the Antarctic seas, chiefly in the summer, is a solitary predaceous beast, spotted like a leopard, and a visitor from sub-Antarctic waters. It has a long agile body, as much as twelve feet in length, with a large flat head, massive jaws, and most formidable teeth. He is a thoroughly nasty fellow, and a bad character. Very fast in the water, he lives chiefly on penguins. Penguins are terrified when a leopard is seen nearby, and refuse to dive into the sea from the floes. No wonder, for no less than twelve Adélie penguins have been found in the stomach of one sea-leopard. He has no fear of man, and various members of expeditions have been chased by them. I have an unpleasant recollection of a fight with one of these enraged beasts on an ice-floe in the pack during the *Southern Cross* expedition. But the sea-leopard in turn has one enemy to fear, again the dread Killer.

Birds.

Another peculiarity of the Antarctic is the complete absence of true land birds. Indeed so essentially marine is the Antarctic avifauna that only two species, the skua gull and the giant petrel, appear capable of recognizing food substances except in the sea. This is remarkably different to the Arctic. On the other hand, Arctic birds are of small average size and there is almost complete absence of petrels and albatrosses which are such a feature of Antarctic bird life. No penguins are found in the Arctic and no auks in the Antarctic, and whereas many plover-like birds occur within the Arctic Circle none are known from the Antarctic. However, several members of the gull family are common to both regions.

Some thirty-two species have been recorded south of Lat. 66½°, but a large proportion of these are only wanderers and do not habitually visit these inhospitable latitudes, so that as far as is known at present there are only five species—the Emperor penguin, the Adélie penguin, the Snowy petrel, McCormick's skua gull, and Wilson's petrel—all of which breed on or near the Antarctic continent.

The penguins are the most pronounced varieties. They are a primitive type of diving bird related to the order of the northern auks, without the power of flight, but able to swim with fish-like activity. So much has been written about them that it is somewhat superfluous to describe them fully here. Staff-Surgeon Murray Levick's book on Penguins and his zoological volume on the Natural History of the Adèlie Penguin make not only fascinating reading but give a very complete description of the species. Dr. Edward Wilson's Reports, too, are very complete.

All species of penguins are restricted to the Southern Hemisphere. Even fossil forms do not occur north of the Equator. Fossil penguins have been discovered in Patagonia and in New Zealand. There is little doubt they were separated from other birds early in history. The largest known type, the Emperor (*Aptenodytes Fosteri*), has primitive leg bones in which the three parallel shank bones are still distinct, though in all other birds they are fused.

The Emperor is perhaps the most unusual of all living birds. Standing about four feet high and weighing as much as ninety pounds, glossy, richly coloured and handsome, he is one of the most dignified birds in existence. He walks erect with a proud, slow and deliberate shuffle, and being of great antiquity may have more reason to be solemn, important and pompous than descendants of those humans who came over with the Conqueror or who are of Roman patrician origin. Inasmuch as these Emperors take not the slightest notice of the small hooligan-like Adélie penguins, they behave like the best so-called "Society" human creatures of pre-war days, treating such inferiors with true Antarctic disdain.

Quite unsuspicious and slow to take alarm, apparently they think explorers are a type of large penguin and are interested to be in their company, tamely standing around, and, perhaps, making comments on their appearance. They refuse, however, to be hustled or stroked, and, in such circumstances, can be very obstinate, otherwise they seem perfectly peaceful, and no sign of quarrelling was ever noticed amongst them—so different in this respect to the quarrelsome and pugnacious Adèlie. If hustled or chased by dogs their great powerful flippers are used with resounding whacks, striking forward and backwards with equal facility. It is well to keep clear of that flipper, for it is very powerful and might break an arm or make great bruises on legs to last for weeks.

Possessing the manners of a perfect gentleman, the Emperor receives human explorers with great politeness and much ceremony. Waddling up to them, his mode of address is stately, and accompanied by many grave welcoming bows until the beak almost touches the breast. Keeping his head bowed, he will make what appears to be a speech in a muttering manner. Could we but understand this earnest talk in its age-old language, it might prove enlightening to those unhappy people who to-day are wallowing in a sea of international and political vexations. The Emperor penguin is not only a strange bird of great antiquity and rare intelligence, but, having lived for

EMPEROR PENGUIN ROOKERY AT CAPE CROZIER

ADÉLIE CHICKS AND PARENTS

A PROPOSAL

endless generations, he may have left behind him all the foolishnesses in which we humans to-day are involved and have acquired, in that germ-free and healthy atmosphere, a quiet philosophy, tolerance, a curiously open and interested mind, and, above all, excellent hospitality and courtesy to others. Apparently they have no vices and their virtues are simple.

Nevertheless, the Emperor has a topsy-turvy breeding arrangement, for instead of laying its single egg in the summer it chooses the middle of the fiercest winter on earth, when it is dark and temperatures fall to nearly as much as -80° F. Furthermore, it does not lay its egg on the snow-covered land. It has no nest but remains out on the frozen sea close to land, and the egg is carried on the broad flat feet. Thick feathers just above the feet and a fold of abdominal skin envelop the egg, keep it warm, and incubate it in that position. Both males and females do the hatching, and when the young one comes it is carried in the same manner, the parent bird standing upright both with egg and chick. The egg is large and white, weighing over one pound, and takes about eight weeks to hatch. It is amusing to see the chicks, covered with white down and with black marks on the head and throat, peeping out through the feathers to have a look round. As would be expected there is a heavy mortality amongst the eggs and chicks, due to the awful cold and blizzards of the Antarctic night. Not more than twenty per cent can survive. Many are killed by the possessiveness and kindness of parents or would-be parents. As there are so few young, unemployed mothers and fathers wait around ready to pounce upon any chick who happens for a moment to find itself alone. There is a wild dash for its possession, like a football "scrimmage".

Should they manage to survive all the difficulties of their childhood they slowly grow up like their parents, taking in the process about two years, and probably live to the ripe old age of fifty or more.

In common with nearly all Antarctic animals, these penguins live on the delicate and luscious crustaceans of those waters which are found in the lanes and cracks of the ice, and regurgitate the partly digested food into the throats of the chicks. At present only two rookeries are known, one at Cape Crozier on the sea ice where the Great Barrier commences, discovered in 1902, and the other in

Queen Mary Land, discovered in 1912. No doubt there are many others.

The cry of the Emperor is loud and prolonged. It is a musical, defiant trumpet call, and can be heard at a great distance over the ice-floes.

The relatively small Adélie penguins (*Pygoscelis adeliæ*) are met with almost immediately on entering the pack-ice. Quaint little black figures with spotless white breasts and a comic white circle around the eyes, toddling along on short, fat legs, with a stiff little tail which is dragged on the ice and seems to support them. Possibly the scientific name (Pygo-scelis, tail-leg) refers to this habit. They stand about two feet high, are devoid of fear and intensely curious. On sighting a ship or men they hurry forward, faffing into water lanes and over projecting pieces of ice and even tobogganing on their breasts in their anxiety to see what it is about. On reaching men they solemnly stand around inspecting them, and even come right up to their feet, looking them up and down, ogling up and squinting in a most comical manner. Then quite suddenly they lose all interest; remain "put", flap their short wings, ruffle the feathers of the head, and close their eyes— completely bored.

Generally they are most friendly and affable, but should any liberty be taken, such as gently pushing them backwards on to the snow, they immediately become furious and indignant, boil with anger and outraged dignity, rush upon the offender and peck and smack his legs with their strong flippers and beaks until he is glad to beat a hasty retreat.

During the winter these birds probably live on the edge of the pack-ice some hundreds of miles north of the lands where their rookeries are situated. Nearly the whole of the Antarctic polar lands are very high and are deeply buried under ice, but here and there close to the sea there are bare spots where, in the summer, these little penguins come in millions, forming what are known as "rookeries". It has been estimated that some of the largest colonies contain as many as three-quarters of a million birds. Long distances must be travelled over the ice, where it is still unbroken, to reach the shores. Early in October long streams of them are seen, like people in a queue, gravely and persistently toddling along for days and days, many with

SKUA GULL CHICKS

THE RAPACIOUS SKUA

THE BEACON SANDSTONE FORMATION PENETRATED BY A DOLERITE SILL

sore and bleeding feet, until, at last, they reach the shore, very tired and bedraggled. Soon the rookery is like a great society function; incessant cackling and rejoicings; jubilations and gambols. Finally, they settle down to the serious business of the season. Nests have to be built, eggs laid, baby penguins reared. The mating commences with a definite "proposal" to the hen, and the lady only too frequently is extremely difficult to please and thoroughly enjoys a good fight between two rival cocks. These fights are not unlike modern boxing. The birds stand up to one another, breast to breast, in the orthodox and picturesque human fashion, delivering resounding blows with their powerful flippers. Smack, smack, smack, with astonishing rapidity, the fight will sometimes continue for half an hour until one is entirely exhausted and vanquished.

When two birds have agreed to pair they assume the "ecstatic" attitude, raising their bills vertically and rocking from side to side, looking extremely ridiculous.

The nests are crude affairs consisting of small round pebbles and stones, and the males generally collect them whilst the females mount guard over the construction. Some are very industrious, busily collecting and making circular nests with plenty of stones; others, extremely lazy, are content with just a few pebbles and generally are shameless thieves, sneaking stones from the more industrious. Should the owner, however, observe the crime, the thief will drop the stone and gaze around in a perfectly bland and innocent manner. Cherry-Garrard writes: "The life of the Adélie penguin is one of the most unchristian and successful in the world." All manner of callous tricks are played upon each other. However, the partners in domesticity are mutually kind, for both husband and wife share the work, take it in turns to sit upon the eggs and, when the babies come, look for food. There are generally two white eggs, never more, and the period of incubation is about thirty days, during which the parents do not feed. The eggs are delicious and a valuable addition to Antarctic fare. The husband is really extraordinarily kind, considerate, and patient with his wife, although she is frequently exacting and irritable and even punishes him by knocking him down when he is careless and neglectful or flirts with the lady next door. It is wonderful to watch a hardy little cock pacifying a fractious hen by the perfect grace of his manners.

There is nothing particularly interesting about the chicks. Slaty grey in colour, they soon grow to look like bloated ninepins owing to their prodigious appetites, and the poor parents are kept busy fishing for shrimps and small marine life in the open lanes and cracks in the neighbouring sea ice. Although they are absolutely alike in colour and appearance, the parents can always find their children should they wander off—as frequently they do—among the throng. This, presumably, is done by the sense of smell. Their senses—hearing, sight, and smell—are highly developed. Hearing is very acute, and they seem quite interested in gramophone tunes, cocking their heads on one side and coming right up to the instrument to look inside. Eyesight is very true and sharp, and the sense of colour is surprising. If pebbles are painted different shades—red, green, blue—and put into a heap with ordinary dark ones, the red and green will be picked out first, and in a very short space of time will be found distributed even to remote parts of the rookery; the red in particular, stolen from nest to nest—a true communistic spirit. When the time comes and the stiff feathers grow which keep out the water, the chicks are taken down to the ice edge, pushed in by the parents, and taught to swim.

This is the great holiday period—sports, gambols, drilling squads, tobogganing with breasts on the snow, swimming, diving, pushing one another into the water and leaping out again—all carried out with great glee but with discipline and order.

The discipline existing must be seen to be believed. Squads of penguins will form up from the nests and at an apparent word or squawk of command will commence to shuffle towards the water; at another note they will turn together—right turn—left turn, and even right about turn. On arriving at the ice edge overlooking the sea they stop and hesitate for quite a long time before diving in, worried perhaps by the suspicion that a sea-leopard may be waiting to take the first that dives. Cruelly and selfishly a companion of meek character is gradually hustled to the edge, hastily pushed over, and, the sacrifice accomplished, helter-skelter they plunge in, leaping out of the water, chasing one another like merry children. Notwithstanding the discipline and order of the rookeries, there are, like other communities, the outsiders—regular outsiders, the hooligans of the place, dirty and unkempt, who live by themselves some distance away from the better-class penguins. These are chiefly young males unsuccessful in the matrimonial market, and are ignored entirely by the others on account of their continued brawling, thieving and general low habits. Late in the Antarctic polar season these small penguins, with their families, leave the land and return to the pack-ice until the following early summer.

Apart from the penguins, the Skua gull (*Cacheracta maccormicki*) is the most prominent and important bird and is ubiquitous over Antarctic shores. It is a large brown bird of prey with a white patch on each wing, measuring five feet or more from tip to tip. It breeds all along the shores in hollows in the rocks and in the vicinity of the penguins' nesting colonies, where it takes a heavy toll of the eggs and young. It is a freebooter of the worst kind and flourishes the farthest south of any bird. Like the small penguin, it spends the winter in the pack and arrives on the shores early in November. Two eggs are laid in December, and these are brown, with black and tawny flecks on them, but only one chick is ever reared, for the adults devour the offspring as readily as they do that of the penguin, thus simplifying the home life. The chicks, beautiful little grey creatures with greenish feet and bill and blue eyes, have the fighting instinct from birth, for, like the adults, they quarrel and fight furiously without any provocation. Skuas are savage, voracious, and disgusting creatures. Their raucous screaming never ceases, their ugly big beaks are always scavenging into some filth, and the spilling of blood attracts them in large numbers. They will steal any object that they think may be edible. Their gluttony is beyond belief, and they frequently must disgorge the contents of their overloaded stomachs.

Explorers, when in the vicinity of their nests, are invariably most viciously attacked and even vomited upon by these disgusting birds. Uttering piercing screams they swoop down from behind upon the intruder's head, striking savagely with the wings. Ponting relates how, on one occasion, he received two blows in rapid succession, one on the back of the head and the other in the right eye, from an infuriated bird. He lay on the ground for an hour suffering acutely, his eye streaming with water. Only the brim of the hat saved the sight. Ponting affirms that the skuas scream with sardonic laughter on observing the effect of their assaults, as if these birds were the embodiment of filthy demons.

The rapacious bandit walks calmly up to a nesting penguin, and, in the most barefaced manner, extracts an egg from beneath it, impaled on the end of its bill. The poor penguin, when robbed, looks up at the disappearing treasure in an extremely ludicrous and disconsolate manner. The only "skua" virtue is its personal appearance and love of cleanliness. In fresh water, which sometimes appears in the snow lakes on warmer days, they will cleanse themselves for hours, splash, stretch and flap their wings and ruffle their feathers whilst squawking their harsh notes in delight. As already related, the Skua is occasionally seen far inland over the continental ice. Scott saw one as far south as Lat. 87° 20′ when the distance was as much as 600 miles from the sea. As they are strong fliers and can fly up to 200 miles an hour, it is quite possible that they fly across the continent from sea to sea. The distance would be about 1750 miles, and, resting on the snow as they do from time to time, they would be quite capable of performing this journey.

The pure white Snow Petrel (*Pagodroma nivea*), with black eyes, bill and legs, is the most beautiful bird of its kind in Antarctica. It is about the size of a pigeon, and, like the small penguin, is seen almost immediately on entering the pack-ice. It nests high up in the cliffs of the Antarctic mountains in long tunnel-like holes under the large slabs of rock. It lays a single white egg, nearly as large as that of the domestic hen, which is very good eating. Although they are tame enough to catch, they eject the usual yellowish red matter of gulls at intruders. They are able to eject this most obnoxious fishy fluid to a distance of eight feet, and its smell will cling to garments for many days.

The Wilson Petrel (*Oceanites oceanicus*), too, has similar habits to the snowy species, and is said to nest only on Antarctic or sub-Antarctic shores. It is one of the smallest of the petrel family, being only a little larger than "Mother Carey's chicken" with very long legs. Although Antarctica would seem to be its natural home, it appears to wander farther afield than any other bird, since it has been seen in Labrador, the coasts of Western Europe, and even in the British Isles.

The brown-backed Antarctic petrel (*Thalassorca antarctica*) was well known in the pack and on the Ross sea coasts in the earlier *Southern Cross* and *Discovery* days, but its nesting-place was not discovered until Mawson found large rookeries in Queen Mary Land and the adjacent coasts. This applied also to the blue-grey Fulmar petrel (*Priocella antarctica*), which had been regarded as rather a rare bird, but is now known to haunt the lands of the Mawson district in fair numbers, and there the nesting-place of the bird has been found.

However, like the albatrosses, most of the well-known southern petrels do not go beyond the edge of the pack-ice. Exception must be made of the Giant Petrel (*Macronectes gigantea*), an enormous bird about thirty-two inches in length, and having a wing span of at least sixty-six inches. Consequently they are very ungainly on the ground, and need a run of twenty to thirty yards before being able to fly. It does not breed on the Antarctic continent, but is a visitor during the autumn and the summer, and is seen as far as the Great Ice Barrier. Like the Skua it is a scavenger, and will devour an almost incredible quantity of offal, and it takes a heavy toll of the baby Adélie penguins.

FLORA

Unlike the Arctic, Antarctica is almost sterile in vegetable life on land. Its appalling poverty in comparison is very striking, for whilst many species of flowering plants are found in high northern latitudes, only the minutest forms of non-flowering plants, such as lichens and mosses, have been found in high southern latitudes, and so scanty as only to be seen in a few places near the immediate seaboard, where their existence is ever menaced by the insatiably curious penguins which occupy nearly every spot of ground during the breeding season. It is a country where no flower ever blooms. In past ages it enjoyed quite a genial climate—but to-day it is the glacial age there, with an inadequate summer and remarkably low temperatures.

The predominant feature of the vegetation is the number of lichens, not as species but as individuals. They are found over the rocks and stones not permanently covered with snow, and frequently show a touch of colour. On the continent itself Cape Adare is one of the richest localities, and farther north, on the islands, such as the

South Orkneys, this vegetation is comparatively rich. Although most forms are endemic in Antarctica, some are common to the Arctic and to South America and Australia. The accounts, however, of Antarctic lichens are very incomplete. Grasses and ferns are entirely absent within the circle, but there are various species of mosses and these show a fairly vigorous growth. They grow in small colonies in which a number of different kinds may be found together. Small red insects are sometimes found among the moss and under stones. Important seeds, however, will certainly germinate under glass in the Antarctic, but even a few handfuls of local soil is very difficult to find. Dr. Koettlitz grew a luxuriant crop of mustard and cress in the native soil in boxes under the wardroom skylights of *Discovery*, and some hyacinth bulbs planted in sawdust flourished in the hut of Scott's last expedition.

CLIMATE AND GEOPHYSICAL CONDITIONS

Extreme cold is usually associated with the polar regions. Although every winter in Northern Canada, Russia and Scandinavia temperatures fall far below zero, the periods of such cold are relatively short, whilst in the polar regions it is not so much the intensity of the cold that matters as its persistence throughout the year, and the lack of heating means to counteract it. There are no means of getting warm except those that men carry with them.

The lowest temperatures ever recorded come not from the polar regions, but from Northern Siberia, but the cold which is most prolonged and most severe is on the high plateaux of the Antarctic continent and of Greenland.

Generally speaking, the Arctic is warmer than the Antarctic. The snows on the land masses around the Arctic Ocean melt during the summer, and the relatively bare lands attain quite high temperatures on account of the continuous sunlight. Temperatures rise as high as 60° F., and from these warm land masses winds blow on to the circular ocean and raise the temperatures there. The mean July temperature *everywhere* within the Arctic Circle is above or near the freezing-point, even at the North Pole itself.

Conditions are entirely different in the Antarctic. The Antarctic lands are too heavily glaciated to get warmed up, and there is, therefore, no bare land. Instead of being surrounded by warm lands, Antarctica is surrounded by a cold ocean, and bitterly cold winds blow outwards from the high plateau surrounding the South Pole. Consequently, a conspicuous feature is the low summer temperature. Probably everywhere within the South Polar Circle the average temperature of the warmest month (December) is below freezing-point. With low summer temperatures at the coast, it is not surprising to find very low temperatures in the heart of the Antarctic, where the snow-covered surface rises to between 9000 and 10,000 feet. Amundsen found the mean temperature near the South Pole in December to be -9° F. (41° of frost), while Scott a month later found a mean temperature of -19° F., and temperatures as low as -40° F., on his return journey. After making full allowances for altitude, the regions surrounding the South Pole must be at least 20° colder in summer than those of the North Pole.

Barrier temperatures are, of course, much lower than coastal temperatures—where the sea, even when frozen over to a depth of twelve feet, has considerable influence. A remarkable feature of the Barrier temperatures is the large daily variation—an amplitude of 20° F. being not unusual. Considering that the difference between the maximum and minimum altitudes of the sun during twenty-four hours is only about 20°, this variation may be considered enormous, and compares with large variations obtained in India.

Winter temperatures, north and south, are more difficult to compare. Speaking generally, the winter temperatures at sea-level during the winter are not appreciably lower in the Antarctic than in the Arctic. Temperatures of lower than -60° F. are commonly recorded in both Arctic and Antarctic lands. The lowest Antarctic temperatures recorded are: -76° F. by Scott, and -80° F. by Byrd, on the Ross Ice Barrier.

Very low temperatures usually occur when the air is dry and invigorating, and are not dangerous or even uncomfortable if there is no wind. The presence of even a slight wind becomes alarming, and steps must be taken to avoid frostbites on fingers, face and toes. Condensation of one's breath on one's face and headgear becomes a nuisance; condensation in sleeping-bags, and, thereby, their gradually increasing weight, and the inability to smoke a pipe because the stem blocks up are minor troubles. The real enemy of the polar traveller is the wind. Wind conditions are very different in the Arctic and Antarctic. The seas surrounding Antarctica are among the stormiest regions of the globe.

Arctic wind conditions are a veritable calm as compared with the Antarctic. During the three years' drift of the *Fram* across the Arctic Ocean the mean wind velocity was only ten miles per hour. No place in the world has such high wind velocity as some parts of the Antarctic. These high winds, sometimes blowing with a velocity of over 100 miles per hour, are caused by the air getting thoroughly chilled in the high plateau and slopes and "slipping off" towards the relatively warm surface of the surrounding seas to the north. Sir Douglas Mawson, at his winter quarters near Cape Denison, recorded an average wind velocity of fifty miles an hour for the whole year.

The prevailing winds are from the south-east, probably owing to the earth's rotation acting upon the air currents which flow at a high level towards the south. The smoke from Mount Erebus, 13,000 feet high, frequently is observed streaming southwards, whilst the surface winds at the same time are blowing northwards. Local conditions, however, such as high mountains, valleys, glaciers and low temperatures of barrier surfaces set up local circulations. Notwithstanding the meteorological stations of various expeditions of the past, all very carefully and scientifically conducted, there still remains a great deal to be learned about the general circulation over the vast Antarctic areas. We have no knowledge at all of the winds on the inland plateau except during the midsummer months.

The general distribution of pressure in the southern regions is as follows: over the Pacific, Atlantic and Indian Oceans anticyclones or areas of high barometric pressure are found with their centres in about Lat. 30° S. From these anticyclones the pressure falls steadily southward until, in the vicinity of the Antarctic Circle, it is only about 29.0 inches. This belt of low pressure completely encircles Antarctica and reaches a maximum low-pressure area close to the high Antarctic shores, where "pressure waves" travelling outwards from the centre of the high continent meet it and possibly cause the well-known furious blizzards when and where the local pressure conditions are receptive.

At one time it was thought that atmospheric pressure decreased from the belt of high pressure, right up to the South Pole itself, but it has now been shown to rise again. So much so that it has been assumed that an anticyclone covers most of Antarctica, but information available is not yet sufficient to say whether a true anticyclone exists there or only a very shallow one. Two eminent scientists, Professor W. Meinardus, a German, and Professor H. W. Hobbs, an American, have advanced diametrically opposite theories on Antarctic circulation; the former, that of a cyclone which occupies the region about seven thousand feet high and which is fed with constant westerly winds at that level, carrying along the large supply of snow in order to maintain the ice-cap, glaciers, and the constant drain of drifting snow and icebergs which break off around the margin. Hobbs favours an anticyclone which he calls "a glacial anticyclone" over a very high ice-cap around the South Pole (which actually exists) at about 10,000 feet, descends fairly slowly most of the distance and then steeply near the sea (also actually the case). Both theories are somewhat technical, but the principal objection to the latter is the enormous supply of snow required, which, however, Hobbs contends is provided by the continuous deposit of ice crystals from the cirrus clouds, which may easily be the case, since there is certainly very little snow fall, as such, in Antarctica. Sir George Simpson, the eminent meteorologist, who accompanied Scott on his "Last Expedition", has offered another solution which, in part, combines the theories of Meinardus and Hobbs. Hobbs may have over-emphasized his points, but there may be more in his theory, and in the dynamic power of cold-producing condensation of air and a downward and outward flow from the Antarctic, than is generally accepted by meteorologists. However, little further advance can be made by spasmodic meteorological observations. We now need first-class permanent geophysical stations in the Antarctic to combine with simultaneous observations in other parts of the southern regions. The interplay between masses of air of tropical and polar origin is the prime factor in the development of storm depressions. Since the advance in our knowledge of the dynamics of the atmosphere, we are much more humble than we were before *Discovery's* first voyage when meteorologists thought they knew all about the general circulation of the atmosphere.

The great transparency of the atmosphere in polar regions, due to absence of dust and humidity, results in remarkable visibility. It is quite common to see mountains over 100 miles away, and even more. On one occasion, from the slopes of Mount Erebus, a mountain was seen 300 miles away. Extreme effects of mirage due to temperature stratification in the atmosphere frequently occur and produce distortion and magnification of distant objects. Icebergs and ice-floes, distant lands, ships and sledge parties appear on the horizon, looming largely, although many miles away.

The exceptional visibility in the polar regions, due to absence of moisture and dust and to temperature inversions, has perhaps not always been correctly understood. In the old sailing-ship days it was not advisable to approach too closely to unknown ice-encumbered lands. New coast-lands discovered or claimed may have appeared much too near, and have been charted in positions much too close, to the observer. Consequently, later explorers, with steam power and more accurate nautical instruments, have, in some cases, sailed over charted lands and have unjustly brought the earlier explorers into discredit. The greatest caution, therefore, should be exercised before discounting the earlier claims.

Such phenomena as the solar and lunar halo and corona, fog-bow, iridescent clouds, prismatic sunrise and sunset effects are frequently observed. Although rain occurs in the high Arctic during the summer, it is practically unknown in the south polar regions, and even snow precipitation there is not heavy.

There are many problems in geophysics which can be best studied in the polar regions, such as terrestrial magnetism, atmospheric electricity and the aurora. Some of these studies are related more or less closely to the sun.

The study of the magnetic records taken near the Magnetic Poles (which do not coincide with the Geographical Poles) have thrown much light on the magnetic state of the earth. Magnetic storms occur which sometimes put out of action the telegraph lines of the world and have a pronounced effect upon radiations of certain wave-lengths used in wireless communication. These storms are probably caused by electrical particles shot out by the sun. Visible tokens of these electrical storms, which are drawn towards each pole by the earth's magnetic field and ionize the air, are the auroræ, one of the most beautiful of all nature's light effects. Science has measured the height of this radiant beauty as usually forty or fifty miles above the earth, though sometimes extending 400 miles into space. No completely satisfactory explanation of their cause has yet been made. Many observations have been taken in high latitudes where they are most frequently seen, but a great number of problems still remain to be solved.

But the more immediate and practical application of magnetic observations is the correction of navigation charts, making the sea safe for ships. Apart from determination of absolute values, it is essential to know all the changes and variations in forces taking place from year to year, and there is no better place for this than the polar regions. Indeed, it is desirable to have simultaneous observations at a number of places, properly distributed over the whole polar regions, of the meteorological, magnetic and auroral phenomena. To a certain extent this was done in 1882-3 by various nations, and termed the International Polar Year. In 1932-3 there was a repetition of the polar year. Many nations participated. Soviet Russia did particularly fine work in the Arctic region.

SEA ICE AND LAND ICE

Arctic forms of sea ice are really very little different from those of the Antarctic, although in the Arctic the sea ice is much more irregular and hummocky and closely packed. All sea ice is formed by the freezing of the seas on autumn and winter days. The depth of freezing depends on the surface temperatures, but generally, out at sea, it is from three to seven feet in thickness. In sheltered bays it can grow much thicker. *Discovery*, at the end of her second Antarctic winter, in 1903, was frozen in nearly fourteen feet of sea ice. Sea ice is of very low salinity, and when melted can be used for culinary purposes, and is even quite suitable for drinking. The salt appears to be mechanically pressed out, or perhaps the brine drains off through the spaces between the crystals. An interesting phenomenon in connexion with sea ice is the formation of most beautiful forms of ice flowers on the surface when it freezes rapidly in a low temperature. These are really salt, extruded on the surface of the newly formed ice, which accretes by moisture from the air. The heavy Arctic pack is driven about the polar basin by many currents, influenced by the great rivers which flow into the Arctic Ocean. Generally speaking, the currents flow from west to east as the earth rotates, with an outward tendency to move towards the lands. The whole of the Antarctic is surrounded during the winter by a great belt of frozen ocean. This breaks up in the spring and summer and drifts up north towards the Southern Ocean, so that, as there is land behind, there comes a time when it is possible to push through the zone of pack-ice and reach a comparatively open ocean to the south.

On approaching pack-ice, there is a distinct whitening of the sky on the horizon, which is called "ice-blink"; also when, well within the white pack-ice, a dark patch is seen on the horizon, one may be sure there is open water there, and this, in turn, is known as "water-sky".

Land ice practically all comes from the atmosphere in the form of snow, ice crystals, or rime, which, through lack of thaw, accumulates in the course of thousands of years to truly enormous proportions, forming the well-known ice-caps and glaciers. In the north the best example is the ice covering of Greenland, which has been crossed on various latitudes and is said to be in places as much as 8000 feet deep. Most of the Arctic lands, however, have no permanent covering. A very much larger ice-cap is that of the Antarctic, about which much less is known.

In Greenland the ice-cap has receded, and there is a belt of land free of ice around most of the coasts. In the Antarctic the supply is greater than the area of land can accommodate, and the land ice not only reaches the sea, but pushes out over the sea in the form of mighty tongues or floating glaciers.

The most famous glacier in the Arctic is the Humboldt, in Northwest Greenland, and that in the Antarctic—the largest in the world—the Beardmore, which is 120 miles long before it reaches the Barrier and eight to thirty miles wide. Almost every type of glacier can be found in Antarctica, and since the snow-line there reaches sea-level, the snow which falls upon suitable support forms, in the process of time, extensive flat areas known as "barriers". The Ross Ice Barrier, one of the wonders of the natural world, is the most famous. It is a snow-laden sheet of ice afloat at the seaward edge, which is over 500 miles in length from west to east, where the depth of the ocean is sometimes over 400 fathoms. Even under Little America, Admiral Byrd's winter quarters, at the eastern extremity the depth is over 300 fathoms. The Barrier edge extends in unbroken uniformity across the Ross Sea in approximately Lat. 78° S. as if cut by a giant knife. The height of its edge varies considerably, from well over 200 feet in places to only a few feet at its eastern extremity. Owing to later land discoveries behind, we now know it is triangular in plan, and about 500 miles deep to the apex of the triangle. It is, therefore, about 200,000 square miles in extent and averages about 150 feet in height over its whole area. Generally speaking, its thickness is still unknown, but it must be about 1000 feet in places. On Byrd's last expedition a number of seismic soundings were taken, chiefly at the known shallow end of the Barrier, which gave an average of 500 feet. Although water-borne over considerable areas, it is probably largely grounded and held in by ice that is grounded in many places. The temperature at the bottom of the Barrier is slightly below freezing-point. Its surface is slightly undulating, excepting where it approaches land, and then formidable pressure ridges appear sometimes 40 feet high and from one to two feet from crest to crest. The rate of movement in places is as much as 1400 feet a year, and judging by the accumulation of snow in six years over a depôt on the Barrier the annual excess of precipitation over denudation is in the vicinity of 15 inches of snow of 0.5 density. It carries within itself much of the overflow from the great Polar Plateau, nearly 10,000 feet high, for the mighty glaciers thrust themselves into it, expanding and flattening themselves outwards. When this ice reaches the sea, storms and tide break it off to float away as icebergs.

In Antarctica glacier ice covers almost completely the continent upon which it rests.

For the purposes of the layman glaciers can be divided into two classes: (1) mountain glaciers; (2) continental glaciers. They are of fresh-water ice, and fed by moisture in the form of snow, ice crystals, or rime. They differ essentially in their modes of nourishment, their inland movement and their reactions with the lithosphere.

Mountain glaciers are of modest proportions, and are held within rock valleys whose walls are higher than the contained material. They are nourished by moisture-laden air currents, and have rapid internal movements which cause a rugged surface topography. They have downward movements throughout.

Continental glaciers are of vast proportions, spread over vast areas uncontrolled by terrain. They assume a figure somewhat resembling the flattened dome of a glass watch cover. Fine snow and ice crystals fall over the continental glaciers from *descending* air currents, and are distributed and redistributed centrifugally by surface winds and carried outwards toward their margins in quantities measured by millions of tons. It is this centrifugal snow broom which brings about the watch-like shape of continental glaciers such as we have in the Antarctic. We know that internal movements, varying considerably in different localities, take place all around the *Marginal Zone* of the Antarctic glacier, but we have no evidence of what takes place at the back of the *Marginal Zone*, or evidence of any movement at all under or near the centre of the polar ice-cap, which is at an altitude of between 9000 and 10,000 feet.

The Antarctic plateau slopes gradually up from 7300 feet in the vicinity of the Magnetic Pole (72° 25′ S., 155° 16′ E.) to 9862 feet in the neighbourhood of the South Pole itself. We do not know how far the plateau extends westward, but it comes to a sharp and sudden end in a great escarpment which extends from Cape Adare in Lat. 71° S. for at least 1000 miles to the south, and then bends round towards the south-east. The South Pole is situated about 350 miles from the edge of the known escarpment. Antarctic glaciology owes a great deal to Scott. He was tremendously interested in its problems. Apart from the experts' reports, such as David's and Debenham's, of later expeditions, his own writings are full of accurate descriptions and lucid explanations of glacial phenomena.

The icebergs of the north come chiefly from Greenland, and are of hard glacier ice, sometimes very lofty, with beautiful towering pinnacles, due to pressure and melting. They are familiar as a menace to navigation off Newfoundland.

The icebergs of the south polar regions are not only much more numerous, but very much larger. Coming as they do chiefly from the "barriers", they are usually flat-topped, with a very heavy surface layer of snow which has not become completely compacted into ice. They are rarely more than 200 feet above the water-line, but they are frequently awe-inspiring in their immensity. They are often a few miles in length, and have been reported from thirty to one hundred miles in length, with a surface area of several hundred square miles. The cooling effect on the southern oceans of such vast masses of ice is considerable.

GEOLOGY AND FOSSILS

The first specimens of Antarctic continental rocks *in situ* were collected by the members of Borchgrevink's *Southern Cross* expedition at Cape Adare. Here and on the shores of Robertson Bay were found lavas, quartz-grits and slates. H. T. Ferrar, geologist to the *Discovery* expedition of 1901-4, was the first to discover traces of ancient plant-life in Antarctica. Ferrar showed that most of the coastline of South Victoria Land consisted of a foundation series of metamorphic rocks, and in the great glacial valleys which rise rapidly towards the plateau these basal rocks are soon hidden beneath later sedimentary and igneous rocks.

The basal rocks, such as gneisses and schists, which are rocks that have been changed by pressure and heat, and are similar to those of pre-Cambrian age found in the North, are probably universal throughout Antarctica. They exist at every locality so far explored. Silicified limestones and sandstones are found on the coasts of South Victoria Land with casts of radiolaria, which are organisms resembling corals that occur in deep-sea deposits, and in Robertson Bay are the greenish grey slates known as graywackes (cemented formation of small fragments of slate, quartz, &c.), which are extensive and differ considerably from those found in other parts of the Ross Sea area.

The thickness of the pre-Cambrian strata has been estimated at not less than 20,000 feet, but such estimates are rather futile, for no one can tell how much has been denuded throughout the ages. These rocks, it is stated by geologists, were originally sedimentary but, owing to the restless state of the earth's crust during the period which succeeded the igneous age, the conditions under which they were deposited were continually changing and fossils of low forms of life have been completely destroyed by pressure and heat.

Rocks known as Cambrian rest upon the metamorphic, but not very uniformly.

On Shackleton's journey south in 1909 he discovered not only the Beardmore Glacier but Cambrian limestone formation 7000 feet up in its valley, which contains traces of early organisms. These horizontal beds are several hundred feet thick and vary from pink to dark grey in colour. Beds of black limestone containing corals also occur in the Beardmore Valley. Similar fossils have been dredged from a depth in the Weddell Sea on the opposite side of the continent which indicate the great extent of these rocks.

Above these Cambrian limestones an extensive series of sandstones and shales almost level in their bedding are found, and of these the most remarkable and extensive is that known as the Beacon Sandstone, discovered on Scott's *Discovery* expedition, and so called after the Beacon Heights, hills named by Lieutenant Armitage on his western sledge journey across the Royal Society range of mountains. This formation, fully described by Ferrar, plays a very important part in the configuration of the mountains of Antarctica. It can be described as a dominant formation and extends to at least as far south as Lat. 85°, a distance of 700 miles, where it reaches a thickness of about 1500 feet. It is probably much more extensive. The Beacon Sandstone is classified as early Permo-Carboniferous and is hard, close-grained and very uniform in composition. No fossils have been found in the beds of the Royal Society Range, but ripple marks and sun cracks seem to indicate shallow lakes or pools during sedimentation. Charred woody stems have been noticed, due possibly to the intrusion of igneous rocks. The fact that no recognizable fossils have been found here must not be accepted as an indication of the paucity of vegetation. At Cape Bernacchi, a low rocky promontory, the geology is extremely interesting. The dominant type of rock is a pure white marble containing here and there small red garnets in granite rocks which have broken through. Veins of pure copper ore *in situ* also occur there.

But by far the most interesting geological discovery in the Antarctic is that of coal seams found by the Shackleton party on Mount Buckley at the head of the Beardmore Glacier within 300 miles of the Pole, and in which were found remains of fossil plants and fossil wood. These coal measures were estimated to be three hundred feet in width containing seven seams of coal from one foot up to seven feet in thickness, with sandstone and shale between them. The formation in which the coal occurs is the Upper Beacon Sandstone. Coal measures also have been found by the geologists of Scott's second expedition in Granite Harbour and in Terra Nova Bay, where fossil stems twelve to fifteen inches in diameter and impressions of even larger conifer trees were found. Possibly a great deal of coal exists under the polar ice-cap, but that so far discovered is of an inferior quality—a hard bright coal with a large amount of ash and containing about fifteen per cent of volatile constituents. The existence of coal and fossil wood in the most heavily glaciated land on earth presents some interesting problems, indicating that those regions enjoyed at one time a relatively warm climate, possibly due to different astronomical conditions, or to the fact that the earth's crust remained heated by its own internal state until the Carboniferous Age, or to quite different solar radiation conditions which brought about the glacial period.

It will be remembered that when the bodies of Captain Scott and his party were found on the Great Ice Barrier, after their heroic journey to the Pole, a bag thirty-five pounds in weight, containing rock specimens, was found beside the bodies in the tent. These specimens were from Mount Buckley and contained impressions of fossil plants of late Palæozoic Age occurring in other parts of the world, and proved to be of the highest geological importance. These plant-fossils were the best preserved of any yet found, and the notes made by Dr. Wilson in connexion with them were very complete. The impressions referred to are leaves of *Glossopteris* flora which, from the point of view of geological history in the widest sense, is of the greatest interest, as they are distinctive of the Coal Measure period on all the great continents in the Southern Hemisphere. These conditions demand a close connexion at one time between the different continents. The best impressions were found in the rotten lumps of weathered coal which split up easily with a sheath-knife and gave abundant vegetable remains. The bigger leaves were like beech leaves in shape, size and venation. Many years ago Hooker, in a letter to Darwin, wrote: "Nothing is more extraordinary in the history of the Vegetable Kingdom, as it seems to me, than the *apparently* very sudden or abrupt development of the higher plants. I have sometimes speculated whether there did not exist somewhere during long ages an extremely isolated continent, perhaps near the South Pole." The origin of the higher plants is still an unsolved problem, but, to-day, it is difficult to escape from the conclusion that the ancient hypothetical continent of Gondwanaland, placed in the middle of the present Indian Ocean, extended to within a short distance of the South Pole, and calls up a picture of an Antarctic land upon which were evolved the elements of a new flora that spread in diverging lines over a vast Palæozoic continent extending to Australia, South America, and South Africa, now separated by abysmal depths of water.

Various theories have been advanced from time to time to account for the general arrangements of continents. One in favour with some well-known geologists is that known as the Tetrahedral Theory, which seeks to show that the earth is a flattened sphere (geoid) slightly modified towards the shape of a tetrahedron or pyramid.

The antipodal arrangement of land and sea shown by more than ninety per cent of the land surface appears to support the theory, especially the contrast between the extensive elevated region around the South Pole. Most of the great continents are opposite the wide oceans. It is well known that when a hollow glass sphere is blown by the glassmaker it has a strong tendency to collapse to a perceptible tetrahedral shape as it contracts on cooling.

Another theory is that of drifting continents. Thus Antarctica, at one time possibly connected to the other continents by means of land-bridges which are now submerged, may have drifted apart from Africa and South America, and Greenland may even now be drifting from Europe towards America. However, these theories must be regarded as very speculative.

It has been shown that in Antarctica on a groundwork of metamorphic rocks, such as gneiss, rest Cambrian lime-stones and coal-bearing sandstones, but there are great intrusions too of recent igneous rocks, such as granite, lava-flows of basalt, and even some active volcanoes of which Mount Erebus is the best known. There are many outbursts of eruptive rocks in Victoria Land indicating great volcanic activity. There are several types of granites; some, such as the porphyries, are very old and their chemical composition indicates they are more an Atlantic type of rock than a Pacific. Quartz dolerites occur in the form of huge sills and have penetrated both the granites and the Beacon Sandstone. They were, in all probability, erupted in the Cretaceous Age. Kenytes and basalts are very abundant all along the west coast of the Ross Sea, especially on the small island built up by Mount Erebus and Terror, itself an extinct volcano. Here the basalts are conspicuous as dykes or flows on the flanks of the volcanoes, but the main bulk of the great Cone of Ross Island is built up of the remarkable lava called Kenyte, which is closely allied to similar series from Mount Kenya in East Africa. The chief characteristic of Ross Island Kenytes is the presence of large crystals of Anorthoclase felspar about an inch long.

In describing the vast quantities of large and perfect crystals found near the crater of Mount Erebus, Griffith Taylor writes: "On almost all the outcrops these felspars weather out of the fine-grained ground mass under the action of frost so that the surface of the Kenyte resembles a mediæval church door studded with huge nailheads."

There are very few data as to the period of these eruptions, but they are associated with great tectonic movements in this portion of the globe during late Tertiary times.

On the other side of the Antarctic continent there is clear evidence of a close connexion between the rocks of Graham Land and those of South America.

Adèlie Land and the region explored by Mawson exhibit much the same geological formations as those found near McMurdo Sound and Ross Island.

Raised beaches exist in South Victoria Land and in Graham Land, proving a recent uplift of the land.

The general conclusion arrived at by various geologists by studying the evidence of Antarctic rocks is that "glacial conditions have been the exception and not the rule in Antarctica", that it appears to have enjoyed a uniformly genial climate, and it was not until Mid-Tertiary times that glacial conditions appeared in Antarctica.

*   *   *   *   *   *   *

Although the results obtained by the three *Discovery* expeditions were magnificent they were really only first fruits. It is true, other expeditions such as Scott's last, and the expeditions of Shackleton and Byrd have added very materially to our knowledge, both geographic and scientific, of the great continent itself. Even so, over 3,000,000 square miles of virgin land and ice still remain unseen, unknown.

Investigations of the surrounding oceans, however, continue, for to-day *Discovery II*, a modern scientific ship, is at work under the auspices of the Discovery Committee of the Colonial Office, but she is not built for the ice. A tremendous amount of whaling research and general oceano graphic work has been done by the Norwegians, especially by the ships sent out by Lars Christensen. Many land discoveries have been made by them between Longitude 0° to 80° east, due south of South Africa. The scientific material collected is arranged by experts and gradually being published by the Norwegian Academy of Science and Letters at Oslo. The Whaling Museum at Sandefjord probably contains more information, practical and scientific, regarding Antarctica than any other place in the world. Antarctic literature there alone comprises 2000 volumes.

There remains the question of the future.

Owing to the great discoveries of Ross, Biscoe, Balleny, Weddell, Scott, Shackleton, Mawson and other British explorers, we now own a silent empire in the extreme south, the territorial rights of which are likely to be of high importance in the future, just as similar rights in the extreme north have proved valuable to Canada and to Soviet Russia. Our title to our Antarctic Dependencies must not in the future be questioned by an unfriendly Power. Discovery may not be enough to give a valid title to a territory. It must be followed by occupation. "I upon my Frontiers here keep residence," should be the policy. The hoisting of a national flag and a formal proclamation no doubt strengthens a claim, but such formal annexation should surely be followed by occupation and settlement. The dropping of a flag from an aeroplane over new land would appear to be entirely futile for purposes of establishing a claim. No doubt it is all a question of International Law.

The importance, therefore, of formal annexations by occupation by an Act of Government speaking on behalf of the State is evident, especially in the Ross Dependency, Graham Land and the quadrant of Mawson's discoveries.

Year by year Arctic Canada, Labrador, Alaska, Spitzbergen, Greenland, and Arctic Russia in particular are being developed economically. The Arctic has a positive future as an airway. Ownership of polar lands, therefore, must be of great importance in the future if only as sites for stations suitable for air transport.

It would be a bold man who would say that the Antarctic regions have no source of wealth. Agriculturally, this may be true, but what tantalizing vistas of other possibilities remain. The Antarctic land ice fields and plateau are ideal for aeroplane landings, as witness Lincoln Ellsworth's and Kenyon's splendid feat in crossing the continent from Graham Land to the Ross Barrier in 1935; so efficiently and modestly conducted. With such airway facilities the South American continent is not too far away from New Zealand and Australia. Future exploration will be conditioned by flight, for it is fairly safe to predict that the near future will produce developments in the conquest of the air far transcending any present achievement.

What vistas of work still remain to be done by parties in permanent occupation of a station in Banzare Land, in South Victoria Land (say in Wood Bay), in Edward VII Land, Graham Land, and even, meteorologically, at the South Pole itself!

Geographically, our knowledge is yet fragmentary. Vast unknown areas remain. New lands are to be found. Extensive coastal surveys are to be made, for less than 150° of longitude have so far been charted. The great transcontinental mountain ranges must be fully traced and examined. Some of the highest peaks, 15,000 feet high, and seen only at a distance, lie on the edge of the unknown. The Antarctic has its share of volcanoes, active, dormant, extinct and submarine. Many are unexplored, and all are to be studied; others may be found along the line of crustal weakness already known. Determination of the contour of the Ice Cap, which rises from about 3000 feet in the coastal regions to 10,000 feet at the Pole, is required. In some spots the plateau may be higher than that registered at the Pole—surely a matter of great interest to the Geographer, the Glaciologist, and, more particularly, the Meteorologist.

Associated with this is the determination of the thickness of the Ice Cap, its rate of movement and the nature of the underlying rocks.

Determination of the Antarctic Continental Shelf by systematic soundings is desirable; additional oceanic islands will probably be discovered.

Scientifically, the field of investigation is almost limitless in physics, biology, geology, and even in medicine, for Antarctica is a natural sanitorium, entirely germ-free, where the atmosphere is very dry and of immense benefit to those with tuberculosis. No colds can be contracted there, and no infectious diseases.

In meteorology a rich harvest of practical information lies ready to be garnered by the establishment of linked land bases properly selected. The polar regions hold the secrets of some of the cosmic problems such as those connected with earth magnetism, auroræ, and other exchanges of energy between the sun and the earth. Each phenomenon, large or small, must be examined in detail. What for the moment may appear purely scientific may have some bearing upon economic values sooner or later. Surprise is an essential element in Antarctic exploration. Even the phenomenal winds which sweep down as a steady torrent from the cold plateau to the sea may be harnessed in the future as a source of power.

Who will carry out all this splendid work to be done in Antarctica?

When I set out on a career of exploration conditions were very different to those existing to-day. There were no motorcars, no aeroplanes, and no wireless. Transport and communication with remote places on our globe was frequently difficult and slow. Therefore, young men who went exploring to the polar regions, or to the interior of Africa, South America, and Asia, had to be prepared to remain away from home and civilization for long periods. Out of sight out of mind. It was similar to some of our soldiers returning after more than four years from the Great War, to find most of the good jobs taken by those who had stopped at home. You had vanished like a lizard under the stones of forgetfulness.

To-day all that is changed. It is amazing how rapidly one can reach even the remote parts and whilst carrying out detailed exploration remain in touch by wireless with civilization. The Russian scientists when at the North Pole, and whilst drifting upon their ice floe for

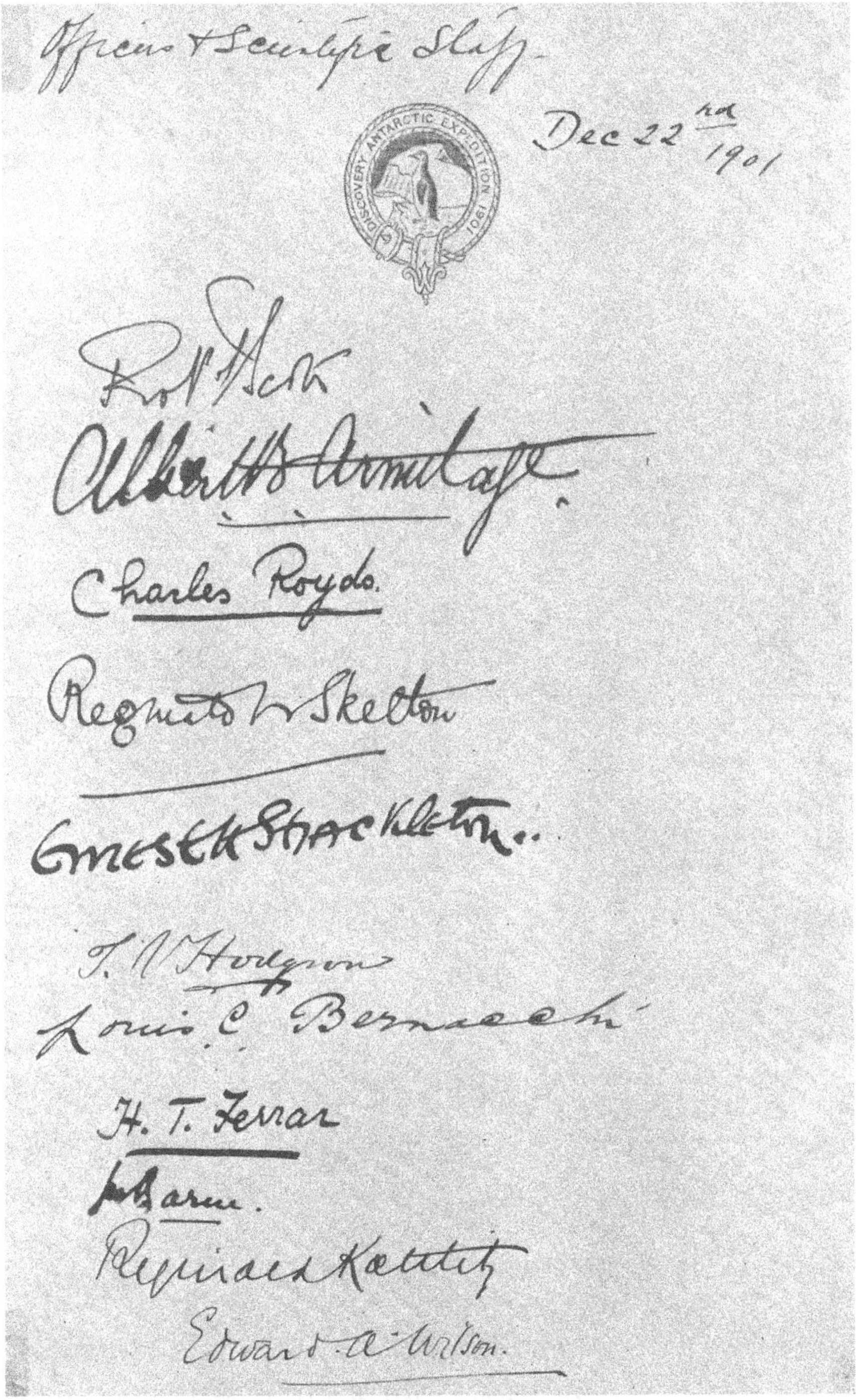
Officers & Scientific Staff.

Dec 22nd 1901

DISCOVERY ANTARCTIC EXPEDITION 1901

Robt. F. Scott

Albert B. Armitage.

Charles Royds.

Reginald W. Skelton

Ernest H. Shackleton..

T. V. Hodgson

Louis C. Bernacchi

H. T. Ferrar

M. Barne.

Reginald Koettlitz

Edward A. Wilson.

DISCOVERY IN WINTER QUARTERS

months, spoke to Moscow daily, and the weather conditions appeared each morning in the Weather Column of the London *Times*. Even talks between Russians in the Arctic and Admiral Byrd in the Antarctic took place in 1930 on a 42-metre wave. "My dear friend, we seem to have beaten the distance record for wireless communication. You are speaking with the base of Admiral Byrd's American expedition to the Antarctic." It was the polar night in Franz-Josef Land and the brilliant Antarctic summer at Little America.

The young explorers who will go out to-day and tomorrow will feel the joy of accomplishment just as keenly as explorers of the past. The work to be done will employ their vigour and initiative for years to come, and will call for the same qualities of enterprise and courage as in the past; but their energy will not be dissipated in difficult travel. They will be properly equipped with the necessary technical knowledge and modern appliances. Attached to serious organizations they will bring back with them facts, newly observed, and help gradually to fill in the picture of the earth and all its inhabitants, thereby getting a glimpse of the spirit of nature and feeling the touch of the Hand that weaves.

The same adventurous and resolute spirit as of old will be found.

Time, which unveils all things, will unveil—Antarctica.

Ten

Biographical Notes

These Biographical Notes refer only to members of Captain Scott's first expedition. It is impossible here to include the names of those who sailed in subsequent "Discovery" voyages at much later dates.

ROBERT FALCON SCOTT, R.N.—So much has been written in regard to Captain Scott, that a mere biographical note here appears not only superfluous and inadequate, but even impertinent. But the story of *Discovery* might be considered incomplete without some details of his career and of those who sailed with him on his first great expedition.

Scott was born in Devonshire on 6th June, 1868, the elder of two brothers—Con, as he was always known to his own family, destined for the navy, and Archibald, two years younger, for the army. There were also four sisters. The family was of Scots extraction, and had come from the Middle Marches of the Border, and consequently were frequently in the thick of fighting, and when the Jacobite risings came they were in them too. It is possible that a distant relation of Sir Walter Scott may have been the great-great-grand-uncle of Captain Scott (he bore an amazing likeness in his later years to Sir Walter Scott).

Two Scott brothers, irregularly descended from the house of Buccleuch, it is recorded, turned out to follow Prince Charlie. One brother was captured and hanged, the other escaped with his wife. A child was born to them in a fisherman's cottage at Leith, the port of Edinburgh, during the trouble of 1745. Subsequently the family lived a life of exile in France for many years, until, as a middle-aged man, the son born at Leith returned to Great Britain and settled in Devonshire, at Holbertson, as a school teacher and married. He had four sons and one daughter. Robert, the eldest son, was Captain Scott's grandfather. All four sons went into the navy. After twenty-one years' service Robert left the navy in 1826 and settled down in a house called "Outlands" at Stoke Damerel, near Devonport, where Robert Falcon was born in June, 1868.

Robert Scott had had five sons, three of whom served in the Indian army, one as a surgeon in the navy; the fifth, owing to his delicate physique, was the only civilian. John Edward (the explorer's father) married Miss Hannah Canning in 1862, and became the manager of the Hoegate Street Brewery at Plymouth, the property of his father and uncle. Financial trouble came to him later.

There were six children, four of whom were girls. Con took up the navy for his profession, and Archibald the army—unhappily he later contracted typhoid whilst on leave and died. There ended abruptly a most promising career, not only as a soldier, but in the administrative branch of the Colonial Service.

Sir James Barrie, in the introductory pages of Charles Thurley's *The Voyages of Captain Scott*, has given an interesting sketch of Scott's boyhood, and in Stephen Gwynn's *Captain Scott* there are more details of those early years. Briefly, he became a Cadet in the *Britannia* in 1881, and in due course became a Cadet-Captain, a difficult post to reach. In those days, as in later life, he was dreamy, untidy, quick-tempered, full of lights and shades, with alternate outbursts of strenuous work and complete slackness.

In 1883 he went to the *Boadicea* as a Midshipman, and subsequently served in various ships including the *Amphion*, stationed at Esquimault in British Columbia, where for three years he had many interesting adventures and had now become (1891) a full Lieutenant. In 1888 Scott had passed his examinations for Sub-Lieutenant with four first-class honours out of the five subjects required, and one second. He was now a young officer of great promise, quiet, intelligent, and with tact and patience in the handling of men. The next few years were spent in technical training at Portsmouth, and he was keenly engaged in the modern development of naval science, and thence on he advanced rapidly towards the brilliant Torpedo Officer he became, serving in various sea-going capital ships, *The Empress of India*, the *Jupiter*, the *Majestic*, flagship of the Channel Fleet. But he now had many anxieties. His father had died in 1897, leaving the family in very poor financial circumstances. His brother died in 1898, and the whole burden now fell on the surviving son, for there was practically nothing left of the family resources.

In 1899, when serving as First Lieutenant of the *Majestic*, Scott was on short leave in London, and chanced to meet Sir Clements Markham in Buckingham Palace Road and accompanied him home. He then learned for the first time that there was such a thing as a prospective Antarctic expedition. Two days later he wrote applying to command it. A year later he was officially appointed. But the appointment was far from being due to an accidental meeting, for Markham in his *Lands of Silence* writes: "I had selected the fittest commander in my own mind in 1887 when I was on board the *Active* in the West Indies, the guest of my cousin, Commodore Markham. . . . When we were at St. Kitts the Lieutenant got up a Service cutter race. The race tried several qualities. For a long time it was a close thing between two Midshipmen, Robert Falcon Scott and Hyde Parker. However, Scott won the race, and he dined with us. He was then eighteen, and I was much struck by his intelligence, information and the charm of his manner. My experience taught me that it would be years before an expedition would be ready, and I believed that Scott was the destined man to command it. At Vigo we were thrown together again, when my young friend was Torpedo Lieutenant of the *Empress of India*, and I was more than ever impressed by his evident vocation for such a command. When the time came for the selection, I consulted Captain (now Admiral Sir George) Egerton, an Arctic officer with a wide knowledge of men and much experience in the Service. He sent me several names, but Scott's was first, and he had excellent testimonials. As a Torpedo Lieutenant he had gone through a special course of training in Surveying, and he wrote the whole section on Mining Survey in the *Torpedo Manual*, and suggested all the instruments to be used. He had a thorough knowledge of the principles of Surveying and of surveying instruments as well as of Electricity and Magnetism. Seven of the ships in which he had sailed were masted and frequently under sail. Scott was now just the right age for a leader of a polar expedition and admirably adapted for such a responsible post from every point of view. He was recommended very strongly by Captain Egerton, and also by the First Lord and the First Sea Lord of the Admiralty. Yet there was long and tedious opposition from joint committees, special committees, sub-committees, and all the complicated apparatus which our junction with the Royal Society involved, harder to force a way through than the most impenetrable ice-pack. But we got through, and I had the pleasure of signing Scott's appointment on 9th January, 1900. On the 30th he was promoted to the rank of Commander, the numerous committees were gradually got rid of and Scott took command."

The story of Scott's voyages is fully told in his own records and those of his biographers, including his naval services during the period between his two expeditions.

References have been made to his character in various publications. There can be no harm, therefore, in recording one's own impressions, which more than three years under his command and some years of friendship in London afforded. My first impression on meeting him in 1901 was that of a fair, well-built man of medium height with true-blue eyes. Actually he was 5 ft. 9 in. in height, and weighed about 11 stone 6. He had a pleasant voice, a pleasant smile, and a crisp and charming manner. Lucky, you thought immediately, to sail under such a man with such a capable, kindly and understanding expression.

That was the first impression, and it remained with me throughout, but later one realized and appreciated more fully his sterling character and his special gifts.

Physically he was perfectly healthy and fit, always able, if inclined, to do more and travel farther than anyone else. On a sledge journey he was untiring, always on—on—although muscularly he was not as strong as many others.

Mentally he could do a lot of work, swiftly and clearly, but he could be lazy, too, at times, and slip into moods of silence and contemplation similar, no doubt, to those of his boyhood days mentioned by Barrie. These "brown studies" might be mistaken for the depression, moodiness and even ill-temper hinted at during his second expedition. He certainly could be irritable and impatient.

Either from disinclination or lack of means he had little taste for alcohol, and at special functions and dinners where he was expected to indulge, if only to a limited extent, it affected him quickly, making him very pleasantly and smilingly cheerful. He was very fond of smoking his pipe and of reading. Honest and truthful himself, he was inclined at first to take people at their own valuation, which led, sometimes, to bad judging of men. But when he found out a fraud he was quite ruthless in his reaction. One of his weaknesses was his strong likes and dislikes. He had no use for shifty, blustering and inept people, and his mind was clear of cant and snobbery. Humbugs, pretentious and pompous people annoyed him. Owing, perhaps, to the exigencies of his naval work and long sea voyages, he appeared to have only a slender knowledge of women. Their subtleties were perhaps beyond him. But he enjoyed their company if they were pretty, and more so if they also appeared to be intelligent. He was a great admirer of any woman who could do "a job of work" successfully. Hence his keen admiration for Pauline Chase, when she was famous as "Peter Pan"

He married Kathleen Bruce, the sculptress, in 1907.

It has been recorded that Scott, on his second voyage, was emotional, and was known to cry. This is difficult to believe in the sense it implies. There was little sign of such weakness in *Discovery*, and certainly the strong, noble letters he wrote within his tent before he died show no trace of such emotion. However, he was very sensitive and highly strung, could not bear the sight of blood, was full of tender sympathy for pain in animals and for the genuine troubles of his friends. No doubt in such circumstances he could "shed a tear of sympathy . . . " in the Masonic sense.

What, then, was his predominant trait? Personally, I should say his sense of right and justice. He had a terrible sense of justice. Truth and right and justice were his gods, and these did not come from any religious sense. They were something within himself. As to his religious outlook this, I have little doubt, underwent gradual expansion during the course of his two great voyages. He led a decent human life because he was a decent human being. Theological baits to right living were not required, and his mind was, I think, too analytical to accept complicated and roundabout theories of the creation, sin, redemption and third-party obligations in heaven. His was the type of mind that required direct proof. With his quick brain he could analyse statements and theories in a very embarrassing manner, and the scientists on board soon learned to row cautiously in connexion therewith, even as applied to their own specialities. Any weakness in the argument was quickly pounced upon. But Scott had a deep and reverent attitude towards nature and a most genuine love of science. He was interested in every branch of research carried on in *Discovery*, and frequently made original suggestions to the workers. He could have been a scientist or a most capable colonial administrator. In any case, he was on the road to being a high-minded scholar.

LIEUTENANT ALBERT B. ARMITAGE, R.N.R., was the Senior Lieutenant, navigator and second in command of *Discovery*. He was born in 1864 in the Perthshire Highlands, and was one of nine children, seven of whom grew up and served in the army, the navy, the medical service and in the Colonial Administrative Service. He elected to go to sea in the Merchant Service, and became a Cadet at the Thames Nautical Training College in H.M.S. *Worcester*. Having passed through his training with credit, and after serving some time as apprentice and mate in sailing ships, he was appointed to a position in the P.&O. Company, in which service he remained all his life. In 1894 he was granted leave of absence to join the Jackson-Harmsworth North Polar Expedition as second in command, and there he carried out the duties of astronomical, meteorological and magnetic observer. It was Jackson's winter quarters in Franz Josef Land that Nansen reached after he had left the *Fram* on his famous North Polar Expedition.

The expedition was absent for nearly four years, and on its return Armitage's service was not only gratefully recognized by his company, but was acknowledged by the Royal Geographical Society, which presented him with its Murchison Grant. After this, he returned to the P.&O. Company as first officer, until in January, 1901, he was again lent for polar work as navigator and second in command of *Discovery*. He was responsible for Ernest Shackleton's appointment as an executive officer of the expedition. Armitage was thirty-seven when he joined, one of the oldest on board, and one of the very few married men. His services under Captain Scott are well known. The value of his polar experience and his navigational work are particularly mentioned by Scott.

Cape Armitage, now so well know in McMurdo Sound, is named after him, and it was he who made the pioneer journey to the top of the Antarctic Ice Cap. He rejoined his company in 1905, and soon after was appointed to command.

When the War broke out in 1914, he was still in command of one of the company's passenger ships and was frequently in action with enemy submarines, being torpedoed and sunk in 1917. He was in command at different times of mail, food and troop ships.

In 1923-4 he became Commodore of the P.&O. Fleet and retired at the age limit in 1926, when he was appointed Resident Governor of the Royal Merchant Seaman's Orphanage. He is the author of various books dealing with his polar work and his experiences.

CHARLES W. R. ROYDS, R.N., born in February, 1876, was the First Lieutenant and had control of the men and the internal economy of the ship, as it is customary for an officer of his position to have in a man-of-war. He had passed into the Naval Service from the *Conway* in 1890, and had been promoted early for a feat of gallantry in the Baltic. He joined *Discovery* from H.M.S. *Crescent*, then serving as flagship on the North American station, and had an excellent record of service. He was a native of Leighurst, Rochdale, Lancashire, and came of a family rich in naval distinction. An uncle—Wyatt Rawson—had taken part in the 1875 Naval Arctic Expedition under Sir George Nares, and had actually sailed in a former *Discovery*. Royds was a man of fine physique, a hard and conscientious worker and a happy companion.

Some of his sledge journeys were very arduous, involving heavy loads to pull, extremely low temperatures, and shortage of food. Cape Royds, where Shackleton subsequently established his base, was named after him by Captain Scott.

On his return from Antarctica he served in Lord Charles Beresford's flagship the *Bulwark*, and was later transferred to the *King Edward VII*, flagship of Vice-Admiral Sir Berkely Milne, where he was promoted to Commander in 1909. Later he was chosen to be the Commander of the then new battleship *Hercules*, which became Admiral Jellicoe's flagship before the War. Soon after the outbreak of war he was promoted to Captain, and was soon in command of the battleship *Emperor of India*, and for his war services was created C.M.G., in 1919.

His next post was the command of the R.N. College at Osborne, and he was subsequently selected as the Director of Physical Training at the Admiralty. In October, 1923, he became Commodore of Devonport Barracks, he was promoted Rear-Admiral in 1926, and became a Vice-Admiral on his retirement.

In 1926 he was appointed Deputy Commissioner of Metropolitan Police under Lord Byng, and was knighted in 1929. Royds died in January, 1931, from a sudden heart attack at the Savoy Hotel during the rehearsal of a ball for a well-known charity.

REGINALD W. SKELTON, the Chief Engineer of *Discovery*, was serving in H.M.S. *Majestic* with Captain Scott. One of Scott's earliest acts on behalf of the expedition was to apply for his services. The selection, Scott writes, "was certainly a very fortunate one: from first to last of our voyage we never had serious difficulty with our machinery, or with anything concerning it. But Skelton's utility extended far beyond his primary duties. I shall have reason to tell of the many ways in which he assisted the scientific work of the expedition, whilst, thanks to his ability with the camera, in the course of his work as photographer-in-chief he produced the most excellent pictures that have ever been obtained by a polar expedition."

Skelton was born at Long Sutton in Lincolnshire in 1872, joined the Royal Naval Engineering College, Devonport, in 1887, and went to sea in 1892. He served in the flagship *Centurion*, China, in 1894, and saw much of the first Sino-Japanese War. From that time until his appointment to *Discovery* early in 1900 he served in various warships in many waters.

He married a New Zealand lady soon after his return from Antarctica.

His subsequent record in many ships and in the submarine service in particular is one of continuous advancement.

At the outbreak of war he was serving as Engineer-Captain in H.M.S. *Agincourt*, and took part in the battle of Jutland where he gained the D.S.O., and later was the engineer officer on the staff of Admiral Sir J. Green in North Russia, Archangel, 1918-9, and was made C.B. and C.B.E. After the War he served as Fleet-Engineer Officer, Mediterranean Station and the Atlantic Station, and promoted to Engineer Rear-Admiral.

Finally, he went to the Admiralty with the rank of Engineer Vice-Admiral, and in 1928 was promoted to the highest possible rank in his branch, viz. Engineer-in-Chief of the Fleet.

He was made a K.C.B. in 1931 and retired in 1932.

MICHAEL BARNE, born in 1877, was the Second Lieutenant of *Discovery*. He was Captain Scott's special choice, and came with him from H.M.S. *Majestic*. He was the younger son of Colonel and Lady Constance Barne of Sotterley in Suffolk, and a great-grandson of Admiral Sir George Seymour. He joined the navy (H.M.S. *Britannia*) in 1891, and saw service in the Mediterranean, North American Station, Channel Fleet and China Station before coming to *Discovery*. He retired in 1910 and married in 1911. He rejoined the navy at the outbreak of war, on board his old ship *Majestic*, and was with her when she was torpedoed and sunk in the Dardanelles in 1915, and subsequently commanded H.M.S. *Monitor* in 27 Dover Patrol and H.M.S. *Halcyon*, North Sea Patrol, and retired with the rank of Captain, R.N., and a D.S.O., in 1919.

ERNEST HENRY SHACKLETON was the Junior Executive Officer in *Discovery*, and became as famous as Captain Scott in Antarctic exploration. Details of his expeditions in the *Nimrod, Endurance* and *Quest* cannot be included here. His biographer, Dr. Hugh Robert Mill, wrote a splendid life of Sir Ernest Shackleton in 1923, soon after his death. Shackleton was born in County Kildare in 1874. The family can be traced back to the thirteenth century in the West Riding of Yorkshire. His immediate forbears were strict and uncompromising Quakers, and it was Abraham Shackleton, a teacher in Skipton, who in 1726 transferred to Ireland and opened a boarding school at Ballitore. Some famous men were educated there, including Edmund Burke. Richard Shackleton, who succeeded his father as headmaster, was three years Burke's senior, and a close and affectionate friendship sprang up between them during their lives. Henry Shackleton, the father of Ernest, was a descendant of this Richard, and turned to farming instead of teaching, at Kilkea in Kildare. From Kilkea the family went to Dublin, where the father took his medical degree, specializing in homœopathy, and came to Sydenham, near London, to practise. He was a retiring, kindly man with scholarly tastes, especially in poetry. From a preparatory school Ernest Shackleton was sent to Dulwich College for three years, where he left very little impression either on his masters or his school-mates. He was backward for his age, inclined to be listless, idle and inaccurate. However, he was quite good at school games. On leaving school the boy's mind turned to the sea, a life of freedom and adventure. At the age of sixteen, in the White Star uniform, he set out from Liverpool as an Apprentice in the full-rigged ship *Hoghton Tower*, a fine clipper of 1600 tons, on his first adventure.

Then followed years of sea life and adventures in various ships, and he took the Board of Trade examination for First Mate and later his Master's Certificate. He was back in England in 1898 and met Miss Emily Dorman, a lady of private means, and his future wife. It was Miss Dorman who introduced him to the poetry of Robert Browning.

In 1899 he secured an appointment with the Union Castle Line, and sailed in the *Tantallon Castle* as Fourth Officer, to be transferred later as Third Officer to the *Tintagel Castle*, carrying troops during the South African War from Southampton to the Cape. He was the life and soul of the ship, organizing all manner of things, getting up concerts and sports, stage-managing, and even editing a shipboard journal. Starting with the reputation of being a poetical sort of a chap, it is on record that on one occasion a rather pompous captain, wishing to score off the poet, said to him when on watch, "Is the glorious orb of day visible, Mr. Shackleton?" And instantly came the reply, "No, sir; the effulgence of King Sol is temporarily obscured by the nebulous condition of the intervening atmosphere." "Got him with his own tackle," commented Shackleton to his brother watch-keeper on the bridge. This quickness of repartee was characteristic of Shackleton and indeed a key to his character. His aptitude for satire, for bantering his companions, could be embarrassing and sometimes annoying. However, it was always done without malice. Shackleton was responsible for most of the nicknames on board *Discovery*, some of them given for reasons only known to himself.

It is interesting to note that, although Shackleton was always alert for any new interest, energetic, full of flashing new ideas (many of them impracticable), an omnivorous reader, an earnest student of poetry, an amateur astronomer, chiefly of the stars in a poetic sense, Antarctica to him did not exist. He evinced no interest in either the *Belgica* or the *Southern Cross* expeditions whose exploits were being recorded in the daily papers. However, he was hungry for adventure and fame, and when he heard that a National Antarctic Expedition was being organized, it presented to him a shorter cut to fame than just following the sea. With his usual impetuousness, he applied to go, at first unsuccessfully, but he kept hammering away, pulling all the strings available to him, and at last, in March, 1901, on his return to Southampton in the *Carisbrooke Castle*, his last voyage in the Mercantile Marine, he reaped the reward of his persistency and found he had been appointed junior officer of *Discovery*. This appointment was the first rung of his ladder to fame.

The story of his services in *Discovery* are well known. Scott writes: "His experience was useful to us in many ways, and as he was always brimful of enthusiasm and good fellowship, it was to the regret of all that he left us in 1903."

Dr. Mill, in his *Life of Sir Ernest Shackleton*, so full of appreciation of his character and his work, to which I am indebted, writes that this appointment was to Shackleton "an opportunity and nothing more. He would have tried to join just as eagerly a ship bound to seek buried treasure on the Spanish Main. He had no natural affinity for the polar regions, no genius for research; but an overmastering passion possessed him and raised his whole being on a wave of ambition which carried him to, and far beyond, the simple goal he had in view."

Just as he had been in his former ships, Shackleton was the life and soul of *Discovery*. His mind was alert, his good humour inexhaustible. Besides being in charge of the holds and of the stores, he carried out his ordinary duties as an executive officer. He was a fine, self-reliant seaman, fearless and dominant, with a stern regard for detail and discipline. He permitted no liberties from those under his command, and could be brutally truculent if such occasion arose. But he was singularly sympathetic and understanding, sentimental to the verge of tears when expressing his own feelings or spouting lines from his favourite poets. In his deep Irish voice he could wheedle and coax; successfully if he required something, which he generally did.

There were many amusing incidents in connexion with Shackleton, such as the Maori dances on deck that he organized amongst the officers on the way south to the pack; his arguments at mess during the winter, and his editing of the *South Polar Times*. On one occasion when taking prayers he read the Absolution accidentally, though not ordained. On another occasion he invented a new sledge consisting of two rum-barrels for wheels under a framework for the intended load. Its construction had been kept a profound secret until it appeared, uncouth and futile; a rum-cart at which his comrades scoffed unmercifully, and at which the skua gulls shrieked as it clumsily trundled along.

After his return to England he gave some lectures on his experiences, but as it was imperative to find a remunerative job, he accepted the position of sub-editor of the *Royal Magazine* under Sir Arthur Pearson; but the path to fortune through journalism was not his line, and he soon after found a vacancy in the secretaryship of the Royal Scottish Geographical Society. Although financially this appointment was no better than journalism, it offered him more opportunity, and he felt justified in marrying Miss Dorman. However, he remained only about eighteen months as Secretary and Treasurer of the Society, but on his resignation he had increased the membership by five hundred, and improved its finances.

He was now persuaded to stand for Parliament as Liberal-Unionist candidate for Dundee. He was an amusing candidate with no political knowledge whatsoever, and easily beaten by the Liberal and Labour candidates. Then his friend Mr. William Beardmore, afterwards Lord Invernairn, found him a secure job in his great engineering works at Parkhead, Glasgow, where he had the opportunity of meeting hard-headed, shrewd business men—a wholesome correction to his visionary outlook.

In the meantime, plans for renewed Antarctic exploration had been quietly maturing in his mind, and in 1906 he persuaded Beardmore to guarantee most of the expenses of a new expedition. The story of that great and most successful expedition which sailed in the *Nimrod* from New Zealand in 1908 is part of Antarctic history. The story is told by Shackleton in *The Heart of the Antarctic*. It placed him in the front rank as an explorer, he became immensely popular, was knighted, and received honours and decorations from nearly every country. Then followed a period of hard work writing up his records, lecturing all over the world, to pay off the liabilities in connexion with his expedition. Financially he was no better off than before.

He now interested himself in various business enterprises, some rather fantastic and all unprofitable, but the return of the survivors

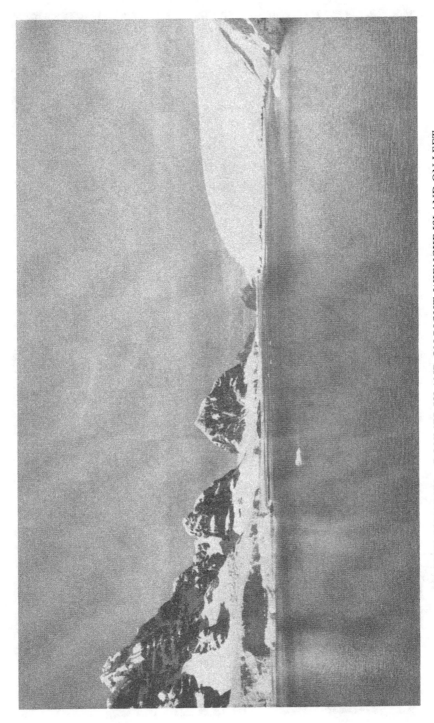

PELTIER CHANNEL—DOUMER ISLAND ON RIGHT, WIENCKE ISLAND ON LEFT

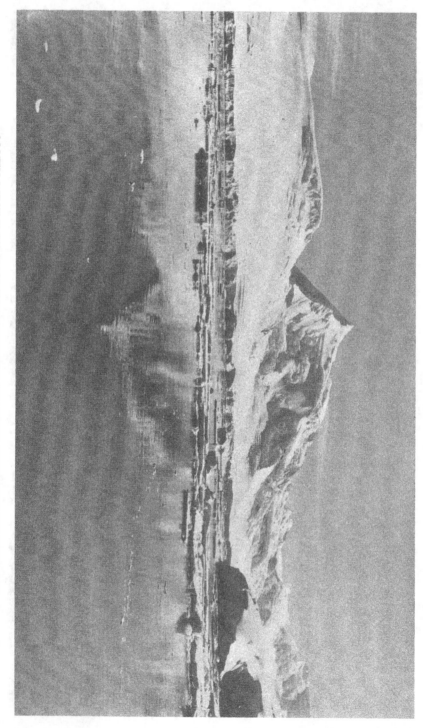

SOUTH-WEST ENTRANCE TO NEUMAYER CHANNEL, SHOWING MT. WILLIAM

of Scott's second expedition in 1913 again made him restless for the Antarctic. He now planned a Trans-Antarctic Expedition, from the Weddell to the Ross Sea, across the South Pole, and £50,000 would be required for its equipment—no easy task. However, Robert Donald, the editor of the *Daily Chronicle*, supported his plans and introduced him to Sir James Caird, the Dundee jute manufacturer, who was induced to give him a cheque for £24,000; the rest was found by many other private contributions, including a generous grant of £10,000 from the Government, and the keen support now of the Royal Geographical Society.

The *Endurance* sailed on 4th August, 1914, the date of the outbreak of war. Shackleton offered to abandon his expedition, but the King, who received him on that day, assured him that he might proceed.

The story of the *Endurance* lost in the ice in the Weddell Sea, of his drifting party on the ice-floes for six months, his famous boat journey from Elephant Island to South Georgia, and the ultimate rescue by him of all his people, has become a part of Antarctic history.

After rescuing his Ross Sea party, south of New Zealand, he returned to England in 1917 and was employed by the Government for a time doing propaganda work in South America, and later by the War Office in North Russia.

The story of Shackleton's last quest is also well known, how accidentally he met John Q. Rowett, an old Dulwich school-mate, who had made a fortune out of rum during the War, and who contributed a very handsome sum for a new expedition to the Antarctic. A small Norwegian sealer was purchased and renamed the *Quest*, and sailed from Plymouth in September, 1921. On 4th January, 1922, she anchored off Grytviken, the South Georgia whaling station, and Shackleton died suddenly that night in an attack of *angina pectoris* before medical aid could be given.

Shackleton's character was a queer combination of elements, difficult to understand. He was a buccaneer in some of his ways, dominating, truculent and challenging. He could be very unpleasant if he were attacked. Judged by the standards of ordinary people, at times he did things that appeared wrong and could make statements and tell stories that were true only in a poetic sense. Although sensitive and refined in his habits, he could carouse with the carousers, and was careless in his finances. But he knew his failings and never concealed his faults. He was essentially a fighter, afraid of nothing and of nobody, but, withal, he was human, overflowing with kindness and generosity, affectionate and loyal to all his friends.

Shackleton was determined to succeed and certainly did; but his restlessness, strivings, his overwhelming ambition, and particularly his long and arduous sledge journeys, his worries and privations with the *Endurance*, and the epic boat journey over 800 miles of boisterous ocean during the approaching winter months in a 22-ft. craft wore him out, and he died at the early age of forty-eight, a fascinating, strong personality and certainly a very great seaman explorer.

GEORGE FRANCIS ARTHUR MULOCK was born in 1882, passed into H.M.S. *Britannia* in 1895, and obtained seven months' Sea Time promotion as a Naval Cadet specializing in Chart Work.

On his promotion to Midshipman he was appointed to H.M.S. *Victorious*, in China, and two years later, on his promotion to Sub-Lieutenant, went to the surveying ship H.M.S. *Triton*, where he qualified in Marine Surveying.

In 1902 he was appointed to the National Antarctic relief ship *Morning*, and transferred to *Discovery* in the Antarctic, where he took up the duties of Surveyor and Cartographer. On the return of the expedition, he was lent by the Admiralty to the Royal Geographical Society to complete the survey work and compilation of the charts of the expedition. He was awarded the "Back Request" for 1906 by the Society for his work.

From 1907 to the outbreak of war he commanded various torpedo-boat destroyers, and the gunboat H.M.S. *Woodlark*, on the Upper Yangtze, China.

In 1914 he commanded H.M.S. *Yed* in the Dardanelles, and was commended for his conspicuous services in action. In 1915 he was Executive Officer and Beach Master at Cape Helles, Gallipoli; was in charge of "B" and "C" Beaches at Suvla Bay during the evacuation; Beach Master again at Cape Helles during the evacuation, there commended for service in action at both beaches, awarded the D.S.O. and promoted to Commander.

He subsequently served in command of gunboats in Mesopotamia, and retired from the navy at his own request in 1920 to join the Asiatic Petroleum Co. (North China), Ltd., as Marine Superintendent at Shanghai. He was promoted to Captain (Retired List) R.N. in 1927, and retired from the Asiatic Petroleum Co. in 1935.

EDWARD ADRIAN WILSON, the second Doctor, Zoologist and Artist in *Discovery*, is one of the best-known personalities associated with Captain Scott's expeditions. The story of his life has been written by George Seaver in *Edward Wilson of the Antarctic*, and the introduction to it by Cherry-Garrard, who was with Scott in the *Terra Nova*, is a beautifully written synopsis of his character. There are endless references, too, in Scott's books dealing with both voyages. In Scott's words, he "stands very high in the scale of human beings. I believe he really is the finest character I ever met—the closer one gets to him the more there is to admire. Every quality is solid and dependable."

Wilson was Chief of the Scientific Staff and Zoologist in Scott's last expedition, and died with him out on the Great Ice Barrier on that tragic journey from the Pole which has become a national epic. Like Scott, his interest in Antarctica was chiefly scientific; he belongs to the group of pioneers, and it was the completion and extension of his former work that took him to the Antarctic a second time. Also his devotion to and his high faith in Scott.

Wilson was born at Cheltenham in 1872, the second son of Doctor Edward Thomas Wilson (and Mary, *née* Whishaw, his wife). Like Shackleton, he could on his father's side "look back to a long line of Quaker ancestors". He had the Quaker characteristics of industry and modesty, and like his family motto, *Res non Verba*, was much stronger in deeds than words, although, quite early in childhood, he could write most interesting descriptions of his country rambles. He had a passion for making nature collections, such as flowers and shells and butterflies, and, under his mother's tuition, learned to draw all manner of things as early as seven years old, without having to resort to "copying". At the age of nine he had made up his mind to be a naturalist, and had taken first lessons in taxidermy. After some time at Wilkinson's Preparatory School at Clifton, where he was made to work and not to look about, but where, nevertheless, he kept a regular menagerie, he entered (1886) Cheltenham College as a day boy, having failed previously for a scholarship at Charterhouse. Wilkinson's was a wonderfully high-toned school, where he never heard a dirty word or a doubtful tale. As a result, when later he inevitably encountered vulgarity, he turned away with disgust from impure talk and impurities in every shape. At that time he was a thin schoolboy, with dark red hair, bright blue eyes and a half-amused expression.

He was poor in mathematics, a defect from which he always suffered, was average in classics, but in science he obtained Honours in the Oxford and Cambridge Board Examinations. He won the school prize for drawing four years in succession.

As early as 1889 he commenced to keep a journal, a practice he kept to the end of his life. In *Discovery* before "turning in" he wrote pages in his large specially designed diary without lines, and generally illustrated with his delicate and very accurate pencil sketches. But even in those early schooldays his diaries included detailed notes on birds and insects, zoology and botany and miscellaneous. Even temperatures and winds were tabulated. In this respect his notes were similar to the books of the early naturalists—Darwin's *Voyage of the Beagle*, and Wallace's *Travels on the Amazon*, which already he had read. Wilson entered Caius College, Cambridge, in 1891 as an Exhibitioner.

He was four years at college, took his B.A. degree, and passed with First Class Honours in the Natural Science Tripos, Part I. At the end of May, 1894, he had successfully passed the first part of his M.B. examination, but he failed in the second M.B. examination, and in Part II of the Natural Science Tripos—a great disappointment to him.

Wilson's life at college is fully told by George Seaver: his high principles and strong moral sense were an influence for good in a college which, at that time, had a reputation for being turbulent and quarrelsome. However, he was "always in the midst of whatever fun and jollity that might be going, noisy among the noisiest". He took up rowing with great zest, and rowed in the College boat and carried off the university prize for diving.

Although he gave strict obedience to high principles at college, he had "a curious indifference to academic rules and regulations" which, on one occasion, led him into trouble. There was a large and well-known trout in the mill-race of a certain pool that nobody could catch. Wilson slipped out of college, caught the trout, and presented it to the Master, Dr. Ferrers, who was delighted with the gift, but discovered that it had been caught at three o'clock in the morning, and Wilson had no leave. The Master was a strict disciplinarian, and sent him down for the last few days of the term.

The end of 1895 found Wilson in London as a student at St. George's Hospital, living at first in Paddington in a single room (8s. a week and quite comfortable), and later in Battersea. He was deeply interested in the slum life of Battersea, and found it difficult to resist appeals for help. He lived a most frugal life on meagre fare, denying himself every luxury, excepting tobacco. Whatever money he had was immediately spent, and at times he was driven to put his watch and chain "in durance vile". But although his clothes and books were too often old and worn, they were always scrupulously clean and neat. In the Antarctic he was conspicuous for his neatness and tidiness; "tidiness", he said, "is all one with general restraint, patience and godliness". He was precise, delicate and deft in everything he touched.

He lived at too high pressure in London, undertaking in addition to his strenuous hospital work long hours in the slums, children's services, and Bible teaching. He also continued his art, frequently visiting and working at the Zoo and the Natural History Museum, to draw and study birds; he visited the National Gallery, where he laid the foundation of his own very special skill, being "smitten to distraction with Turner's drawings". He even illustrated a medical book on *The Diseases of the Liver*, and part illustrated a book on fishing-flies. It was about this time that he met Miss Souper in London, whom he married four years later, just before *Discovery* sailed. He had made up his mind to remain a bachelor, but after the meeting he wrote, "perhaps I will write a paper on Marriage some day, with all the symptoms and signs of acute love". It was a beautiful and perfect union which brought him great happiness.

During vacation he had occasionally gone abroad, particularly to France. He was enchanted with some of the cathedrals he visited, and in love with the South. But notwithstanding these short holidays his health commenced to fail. The extensive hospital and mission work, combined with his many other activities, were beyond his strength;

he looked delicate and worn, having crammed two years' reading into fifteen months. Finally, he developed a temperature, pains and giddiness, and, on examination, it was found he was suffering from pulmonary tuberculosis, and was ordered to Davos. But before going he had an invitation from friends to spend some months in the north of Norway, where he was very happy rambling, bird-nesting and sketching. However, the mischief in his lungs was only checked, and he had to go to Davos in October as previously arranged. There he lost weight, grew very frail and depressed, but gradually his lungs responded to the treatment, and in May he was back home.

But Davos had left its mark upon him. It laid the foundations of his mysticism and, perhaps, intensified his deep religious outlook. Wilson's religion was to him something divine. His faith was complete, and was the very substance of his life. He was a believer in the strictest sense of the word, and like St. Francis of Assisi, whom he so greatly admired, he certainly carried out in his daily life the principles of Christ. Nevertheless, he was extremely reticent about his religious convictions and never in his *Discovery* days did be confide them to his messmates, nor endeavour to influence them. In his own words, as long as he stuck to nature and the New Testament, he grew happier every day.

In June, 1900, he received his M.B. degree at the time when the *Discovery* expedition was being organized, and it was Dr. Philip Sclater, then the president of the Zoological Society, and on the expedition Committee to make appointments, who first suggested to him that he was a suitable person for the post of junior surgeon and zoologist. This turned his thoughts in a totally different direction, but he was still far from fit, and suffering, too, from blood poisoning and an abscess in the axilla due to a pricked finger in a *post mortem*. He was, therefore, very doubtful about his suitability. His uncle, Sir Charles Wilson, interested himself, and after an interview Scott definitely offered him the appointment provided his health improved.

To fit himself for his Antarctic duties he took lessons in taxidermy at the Zoo, and worked on the *Southern Cross* collections at the Natural History Museum, which had arrived some months before. It was then that I first met him. He was inclined to be tall, very lean and frail-looking, and a little stooping. He had close-cut auburn hair, inclined to wave, blue eyes, was slightly freckled, and had long slender freckled hands. His voice was quiet, rather lowpitched, and he had a rather whimsical smile, sometimes inclined to be a little cynical. I had occasion to see him many times before the sailing of the ship in connexion with the collections, and quickly learned to admire his courteous and most considerate manner. In *Discovery* Wilson had not the senior position that he later occupied in *Terra Nova*. He was round about our own age and to us he was just "Billy Wilson", admired and beloved for himself. In *Terra Nova* he was a senior officer older than most members in the wardroom, with much Antarctic experience behind him. Although in *Discovery* there never was any occasion to act as a Peacemaker, it was amazing how frequently he was consulted on all kinds of matters—any excuse to "loaf" in Billy's cabin talking to him although he might not reply. He was a good listener, comforting to talk to and restful. His sympathetic, attentive attitude and amused smile were sufficient reward. His energy was untiring, and he was always willing to do anything for one provided he was approached in a kind and courteous manner. Rudeness he would not tolerate. Then his fundamentally quick temper temporarily asserted itself, but was quickly controlled. His long, thin, firmly closed mouth gave him then an expression of hardness. I never knew him admit to fatigue and indisposition.

The story of his fine work in *Discovery*, zoological and as an artist, has been told in the *Discovery* records. The period between the two Scott expeditions was one of tireless activity for him. He gave many lectures on various technical subjects, but, like Scott, he was a shy and nervous public speaker. He visited Ireland, sketching birds and studying the architecture of the abbeys and castles and making illustrations for a publication of British Mammals. In 1905 a disastrous grouse disease swept the British Isles, and a Grouse Disease Inquiry was established. Wilson was appointed field observer, physiologist and anatomist in connexion with it, and for five years he was an indefatigable worker. The output of his work was immense notwithstanding the loss of his notes, covering two years, by the theft of his suitcase. His work on grouse prevented him joining Shackleton's *Nimrod* expedition, which he was anxious to do. Shackleton made every effort to get him to give up his job, but in 1909 the Grouse Disease Inquiry was practically concluded, and he was free to accept Scott's invitation to join him as chief of the scientific staff of the *Terra Nova* expedition. He sailed the following year.

REGINALD KOETTLITZ was the senior Doctor. He was also senior in age, being forty when he joined. His father, a minister of the Reformed Lutheran Church, had married an English lady and settled at Dover in the 'sixties. Educated at Dover College, he had passed into and qualified at Guy's Hospital. After remaining quietly in a country practice for eight years, he impulsively volunteered his services as doctor to the Jackson-Harmsworth Expedition. His experiences in the Arctic made him a wanderer for some years after his return, and he accompanied expeditions to Brazil, Abyssinia and Somaliland. These experiences were a factor in his favour on his application to join *Discovery*, where he carried out practically all the duties required of a doctor, and also the services of a botanist, limited in its scope, it is true, because of the very limited nature of the vegetation. He also collected various forms of marine plant life known as *phyto-plankton*. He had a delightful personality, was kind-hearted, very tolerant, and, withal, he was a scholar—a popular member of the expedition in the ward room and on the mess-deck.

After the expedition he went out to the Transvaal, where he practised for a number of years amongst the Boers. He and his wife contracted typhoid and died at Port Elizabeth in 1916, within two days of each other.

THOMAS V. HODGSON, the Biologist, was a native of Birmingham, and devoted many years to the study of biological science. He was thirty-seven years of age when he joined *Discovery*, and was closely identified with the Plymouth Biological Laboratory. Later he became the curator of the Plymouth Museum, of which he may be said to have been the creator. On the return of the expedition he became the head of the Biological Laboratory, and for a long time was occupied in helping to prepare his extensive biological work for publication. He died a few years ago.

HARTLEY TRAVERS FERRAR was born in Dublin in 1879, but

spent his early boyhood in South Africa, where he lived a very free and adventurous life with his brothers. He returned at the age of fourteen with one of his brothers to England, and went to Oundle School, and was there for four years under Mr. Sanderson. His future was very much influenced by the standards and ideals learnt from this great headmaster. He gained a sizarship (1898-1901) at Sidney Sussex College, Cambridge, and his B.A. with honours in National Science Tripos, 1901. He also did well in sport, and got his trial cap for rowing, and was a keen worker and an enthusiast in all sport, both at school and college. It was after rowing a race at Henley that he received the news of his appointment as Geologist to *Discovery*.

On his return from the Antarctic in 1904, and after writing the geological report on his work in the south, Ferrar was appointed to the Geological Survey in Egypt. From 1905-14 he did much valuable work mapping parts of the Eastern desert and going for long treks with camels and camel-men for two or three months at a time. He subsequently worked on the sub-soil of Upper Egypt, and on the effect of water on the cultivation of cotton, and wrote reports and pamphlets on these subjects and others in the Cairo scientific and other journals. He married a New Zealand lady in 1909.

He saw active service in Palestine during the War, and was afterwards appointed to the New Zealand Geological Survey Department. From 1919 till the time of his death in 1932, he gave unstintingly of his knowledge and labour—first of all in North Auckland, where his camp was known as one of the best-run and hardest working ones in New Zealand, and his men were all keen students. Then he did an excellent soil survey of irrigation areas in Central Otago, and wrote extensively about them, for which he was rewarded with his Doctorate of Science.

He was always deeply interested in all scientific matters, and kept in close touch with work done in the Antarctic; was a prominent member of, and lecturer at, the Philosophical Institute of Wellington, and was present at and reported at length on one of New Zealand's big earthquakes, doing some investigations for the Department. He died suddenly, after a slight operation, when he seemed to be physically and mentally in the prime of his life.

LOUIS CHARLES BERNACCHI, elder son of A. G. D. Bernacchi, J.P., late owner of Maria Island, Tasmania. As the name implies, it is of Northern Italian origin and well known in Lombardy. The grandfather was a landowner in the vicinity of Como, at the foot of the Alps, and was largely interested in the raw silk industry from which my father benefited.

Ill-health took my father on an ocean voyage to Tasmania as a young man, where he decided to remain and sell out his silk interests in England.

By a special Act of Parliament he acquired Maria Island (nearly 60,000 acres) from the Tasmanian Government on condition that he spent £10,000 in the first five years, and a similar sum in the following five years, in developing the natural resources of the island. He was a brilliant scholar, deeply interested in scientific subjects, spoke five languages fluently, and had been educated chiefly at Heidelberg University.

Maria Island, discovered by Tasman in 1642, is striking and picturesque in appearance. A lofty mountain range traverses it from north to south. Beautiful sandy beaches, creeks, woods and lagoons with game and wild fowl, are to be found on its sheltered west coast, whilst on the eastern shores the great seas of the "Roaring Forties", unbroken by any intervening obstacle, between Tasmania and the Antarctic, break violently against its perpendicular granite walls. As a boy, amidst those wild but enchanting surroundings, I learnt to ride, to shoot, to manage, single-handed, a 22-ft. whale-boat, and to "rough it" in many outdoor ways, until the time came for Public School.

Three years at Public School in Hobart was followed by some years at the Melbourne Observatory (a branch of the University) qualifying to become an Astronomer, Meteorologist, and Magnetologist. It was from the Observatory that I volunteered, as Physicist, to join the *Southern Cross* Expedition to Antarctica, to be followed by Captain Scott's Expedition in *Discovery*, covering, in all, over five years of Antarctic research.

The end of the National Antarctic Expedition in *Discovery* found little recognition for the scientists and no employment in England for an Australian physicist.

Some years of private exploration followed—in the primeval forests of Tropical Peru to the banks of the Inambari in the upper Amazon Basin; in Namaqualand and German South West Africa, when the Hereroes and Fighting Hottentots were at war with Germany. Visits were made to Malaya, Java and Central Borneo in connexion with the then young and growing rubber plantation industry.

In 1910, a period of political activity in England, I contested two parliamentary elections on behalf of the Liberal Party—the Widnes Division in Lancashire, and Chatham Borough in Kent.

At the outbreak of war I was granted a commission in the Royal Naval Volunteer Reserve and given command of Auxiliary Patrol ships in the Narrow Seas, the Orkney Islands, and in the Mediterranean, where, for a time, minesweeping in the Bitter Lakes of the Suez Canal was carried out.

On Admiral Jellicoe's appointment to the Admiralty at the end of 1916 I was transferred to the Naval Staff there (Anti-submarine Division), and organized all the British Naval bases for hydrophone and other patrol anti-submarine listening and electrical gear. Attached to the American destroyers for a short period in connexion with anti-submarine gear and awarded the United States Navy Cross, the highest American Naval decoration, and made a Military O.B.E. at the end of the War. On demobilization returned to rubber plantation interests —and took an active part in various scientific organizations—such as the British Science Guild and others.

Member of the Council of the Royal Geographical Society (1929-32), Member of Committee of The International Polar Year and of the British Association for the Advancement of Science.

FRED E. DAILEY, our Naval Warrant Officer carpenter, was accepted to join the *Discovery* expedition quite early in its history. He had a fine record, having been apprenticed to shipbuilding in H.M. Dockyard, Devonport, and transferred to the Royal Navy after seven years of practical and theoretical shipbuilding. He had served a number of years on the China Station and in Home Waters, and was sent to Dundee during the building of *Discovery*, and later to the East India Docks whilst fitting out.

He was held in high esteem by Scott, who writes of his zealous care, his "eye" for defects, and his determination that his particular work should be beyond reproach. The small Dailey Islands in McMurdo Sound are named after him.

On his return he again served with Scott in H.M.S. *Bulwark*, and was thence appointed to the battle cruiser H.M.S. *Lion*, building at Devonport. The outbreak of war found him still in the *Lion* under Admiral Beatty, and he was present at the battles of Heligoland Bight, Dogger Bank and Jutland, and was mentioned in dispatches, received the Distinguished Service Cross, and promoted to Lieutenant. Later he was in charge of destroyer repairs at the naval base, Port Edgar, afterwards returning to Devonport as Barrack Master of R.N. Barracks. On retirement he was promoted to Lieutenant-Commander.

PETTY OFFICER JACOB CROSS was the senior Petty Officer in *Discovery*; born near Clacton-on-Sea in 1876. His twin brother had been named Esau. After working as a small boy in the fields for 1s. 6d. per week (half-day), he joined the navy in 1891 on board H.M.S. *Hotspur* at Harwich. He served in the *Amphion* in the Mediterranean, the year of the *Camperdown* and *Victoria* disaster, and various ships after that. In 1901, when serving in H.M.S. *Jupiter*, he volunteered for the *Discovery* expedition, and was selected. Although young at the time, he was already a first-class petty officer, an acting captain of a gun crew, and a diver. He was attached to Dr. Wilson, as a taxidermist. His work was of great value in making the collection of Antarctic animal life.

After the expedition he served in various ships, was on the staff of Chatham Detention Quarters during the War, and in Government employment for a number of years until retirement, when he became one of the best-known breeders of high-class Sealyham terriers in Kent.

It is impracticable in these brief biographical notes to tell the story of all the Warrant Officers, Petty Officers and Seamen who sailed in *Discovery*. Some careers are difficult, if not impossible, to trace. In the story of his first voyage Scott writes with admiration of the work done by *Thomas Feather*, our boatswain, "he proved his excellence, for I do not remember a single complaint or breakdown that could have been obviated by more careful preparation". Of Warrant Officer

Delibridge, too, the Chief Engineer's right-hand man, he writes with warm approval; and of *C. R. Ford*, the ship's steward, a very young man, "he soon mastered every detail of our stores and kept his books with such accuracy that I could rely implicitly on his statements". Ford was a valuable contributor to our *South Polar Times*.

The story of *Edgar Evans, P.O., R.N.*, is too well known to need repetition. He died on Scott's last expedition after reaching the South Pole. *Frank Wild* subsequently became famous in his association with Shackleton's expedition, and with Mawson. He was in the *Nimrod* in 1907-9, and was with Shackleton when they reached to within ninety geographical miles of the South Pole. He was with Mawson in Queen Mary Land, 1911-3, in Shackleton's *Endurance*, 1914-6, and left in command on Elephant Island whilst Shackleton made his famous boat journey to South Georgia. He was second in command of the *Quest* expedition when Shackleton died. On his return he was made a C.B.E., and received the Patron's Medal of the Royal Geographical Society in 1924.

Ernest E. Joyce, too, became well known under Shackleton, and especially for his charge of the depôt-laying expedition from McMurdo Sound to the Beardmore Glacier in connexion with Shackleton's transcontinental expedition, which failed through the loss of the *Endurance* by crushing in the Weddell Sea. But Joyce's depôts still remained stretched out across the Barrier for three hundred miles. Joyce has, perhaps, more experience of Antarctic sledging than anyone else. He has covered nearly two thousand miles, and won the Albert Medal for his splendid rescue work on his last sledge journey.

Tom Crean, too, was with Shackleton in the *Endurance*, and, together with *Lashly* and *Williamson*, with Scott on his last expedition. Crean and Lashly won the Albert Medal on this occasion for saving the life of Commander Evans. Petty Officer Thomas Williamson was with the party that found Scott's last camp and the bodies of those who died there with him. Seaman *George B. Croucher* became an officer in the R.N.R., and died during the War whilst in command of a naval trawler.

CAPTAIN WILLIAM COLBECK, R.N.R., who died in 1930 of cardiac trouble, was one of the pioneers of Antarctic exploration. He was born in Hull in 1871, educated at Hull Grammar School, and went to sea as an apprentice at the age of fifteen. He took his Master's Extra Certificate in 1897. In 1898 C. E. Borchgrevink succeeded in persuading Sir George Newnes, the well-known publisher, to purchase and refit a Norwegian whaler, renamed the *Southern Cross*, and to bear the whole expense (£40,000) of an expedition to the Antarctic Seas. Colbeck, who was Chief Officer of the *Montibello* (Wilson Line) at the time, volunteered for service with the expedition. After going through a course of Magnetism at Kew Observatory under Dr. Charles Chree, F.R.S., he joined the *Southern Cross* as Navigator, Cartographer, and Assistant to the Magnetic and Meteorological Observer.

He proved to be an accurate and an intelligent observer, and during the forty-five days that the *Southern Cross* was caught in the Antarctic pack-ice he acquired considerable experience of ice-navigation.

He was one of the small party of ten to spend the first winter ever passed by human beings on the Antarctic continent, viz, at Cape Adare, in Lat. 71° 18′ S.—a winter which proved to be a very severe experience. Fierce blizzards of altogether unexpected fury were experienced. On the return of the *Southern Cross* in 1899 she proceeded south towards McMurdo Sound and steamed close to nearly the whole length of the Great Ice Barrier, which enabled Colbeck to make a fairly accurate chart of the Barrier position at that time, and to show that the whole of this enormous wall of ice, 500 miles in length, had receded an average of thirty miles since its discovery by Captain James Clark Ross in 1842. In 1902 Colbeck was appointed by the Royal Geographical Society to command the relief ship *Morning* in connexion with *Discovery*.

About the author

Louis Bernacchi, son of an Italian father and Belgian mother, was born in Belgium in 1876 and brought up on Maria Island, off the coast of Tasmania, and is regarded as the first Australian Antarctic explorer.

He first visited Antarctica as the Physicist and Photographer for Carsten Borchgrevink's *Southern Cross* Antarctic Expedition of 1898 to 1900. On his return he published an account of the expedition, *To the South Polar Region*, in 1901. In 1998 another book was published, based on Bernacchi's diaries of this expedition, *That First Antarctic Winter*, written and edited by his granddaughter, Janet Crawford.

Bernacchi was appointed as Physicist to the National Antarctic Expedition of 1901 to 1904, led by Captain Scott.

He later settled in London, becoming a lieutenant commander in the Royal Naval Volunteer Reserve during the First World War. His name became well known in naval circles for his work on anti-submarine devices. France made him Chevalier d'Honor for his polar work and in Britain he received the Polar medal. He was a Member of the Council of the Royal Geographical Society and died in 1942.